ADVANCED PLACEMENT ENGLISH

Advanced Placement English

Theory, Politics, and Pedagogy

EDITED BY

GARY A. OLSON
ELIZABETH METZGER
EVELYN ASHTON-JONES

BOYNTON/COOK PUBLISHERS
HEINEMANN
PORTSMOUTH, NH

Boynton/Cook Publishers
A Division of
Heinemann Educational Books, Inc.
70 Court Street, Portsmouth, NH 03801
Offices and agents throughout the world

The following have generously given permission to use quotations from copyrighted works:

Pages 183–191: AP questions selected from *Advanced Placement Examinations*, 1988. Reprinted by permission of Educational Testing Service. Permission to reprint AP material does not constitute review or endorsement by Educational Testing Service or the College Board of this publication as a whole or of any other testing information it may contain.

Page 188: "Choose Something Like a Star." Copyright © 1949, © 1969 by Holt, Rinehart and Winston. Reprinted from *The Poetry of Robert Frost* edited by Edward Connery Lathem, by permission of Henry Holt and Company, Inc.

Pages 188–191: "Reunion" by John Cheever. Copyright © 1962 by John Cheever. Reprinted from *The Stories of John Cheever*, by permission of Alfred A. Knopf, Inc.

Pages 193–196: Rubrics for the 1987 Literature and Composition Essay Topics, Scoring Guide. Reprinted by Permission of Educational Testing Service.

Library of Congress Cataloging-in-Publication Data
Advanced placement English : theory, politics, and pedagogy / edited
  by Gary A. Olson, Elizabeth Metzger, Evelyn Ashton-Jones.
     p.   cm.
  Bibliography: p.
  ISBN 0-86709-246-7
  1. English philology—Study and teaching (Higher)—United States.
  2. English philology—Study and teaching (Secondary)—United States.
  3. Advanced placement programs (Education) I. Olson, Gary A.,
  1954– . II. Metzger, Elizabeth, 1947– . III. Ashton-Jones,
  Evelyn, 1953–
  PE68.U5A36   1989
  420'.7'273—dc20   89-31480
                                                                     CIP

Designed by Vic Schwarz.
Printed in the United States of America.
92 91 90 89   9 8 7 6 5 4 3 2 1

Contents

Preface

The College Board's Advanced Placement program has significantly influenced English education for over three decades. Despite this influence, however, no comprehensive scholarly examination of the program has yet been published. Except for an occasional journal article, most published accounts of the Advanced Placement program have been descriptive or anecdotal, many of them appearing in College Board-sponsored publications. Yet, AP teachers and the professors who teach them *must* have access to current information about the theory and practice of Advanced Placement English. *Advanced Placement English: Theory, Politics, and Pedagogy* attempts to satisfy this obvious need by providing essays on pertinent issues, written by nationally recognized experts in composition, Advanced Placement, and related fields.

While *Advanced Placement English: Theory, Politics, and Pedagogy* is in part a guide to AP administration and instruction, it is more than a discussion of program and classroom management procedures. Nearly half of the chapters are devoted to examining the issues and concerns that have created controversy in the field. These chapters address questions that have occasionally led to bitter debate. Is the program truly effective? Do the examinations adequately measure student competence? Are the examinations biased? Should AP teachers be evaluated according to the number of their students who pass the examination? Do universities vie for increased enrollment by lowering the examination scores for which they award college credit? Do universities make valid distinctions between the two AP English courses? These and similar issues are presented for consideration.

Advanced Placement English: Theory, Politics, and Pedagogy is divided into three sections. Part I, The Theory and Politics of AP, begins with David Foster's examination of the AP English program in light of current composition and literary theory. In Chapter 2, Karen Spear and Gretchen Flesher explore what research into cognitive development can tell us about students in AP English. James Vopat analyzes in the third chapter several political concerns relevant to AP English. In Chapter 4, Sylvia Holladay summarizes the professional literature on testing in English, describes AP examination procedures, and identifies problems inherent in the AP testing process.

Part II, The AP English Programs, begins with Diane Kanzler's primer for establishing and maintaining an AP English program. In Chapter 6, Jan Guffin describes ways to organize and teach the Literature and Composition course. In Chapter 7, Gary Olson and Elizabeth Metzger describe the Language and Composition course, demonstrating how it should mirror the typical freshman English course. R. W. Reising and Benjamin Stewart outline, in Chapter 8, several methods of evaluation that AP teachers can use to respond to student papers effectively and efficiently. In the final chapter in Part II, John Iorio argues that AP teachers must avoid teaching for the test and must instead teach a true college-level course that focuses on critical analytical skills in reading and writing.

Part III, Alternative Advanced Placement Programs, presents two successful alternatives to the College Board's program. In Chapter 10, Marilyn Sternglass and Thomas Vander Ven describe and evaluate the Advance College Project, a program sponsored by Indiana University. In the final chapter, Bette Gaines and Rosanna Grassi discuss Project Advance, a prototypical independent advanced placement program.

The appendixes contain a list of publications available from College Board, as well as sample AP examination topics and rubrics. These materials are followed by a selected bibliography of books, articles, and other publications relevant to advanced placement.

This text is the first critical look at the AP English program—one we hope will begin a dialogue about the theory and pedagogy of AP. In fact, the primary objective of this text is to establish connections and lines of communication between university and high school English teachers. AP English is a natural link between English teachers from both levels, and this text provides a forum for better communication between both groups—a forum too long absent from the field. It is our hope that university professors and English teachers will, through trust and cooperation, enhance the environment in which student excellence is encouraged and rewarded.

Gary A. Olson
Elizabeth Metzger
Evelyn Ashton-Jones

PART I

The Theory and Politics of AP

1

The Theory of AP English
A Critique

DAVID FOSTER

Drake University

Foster examines the AP English program in light of current composition and literary theory. He juxtaposes the theoretical assumptions of both English programs with those of the field in general. The author proposes changes in the AP program based on the most recent theory and research.

Thirty years ago, in a time green with possibility, faculty from some elite, highly visible prep schools and colleges decided that giving high school students college-level work was an idea whose time had come. Behind their decision lay two desires: to give better high school students more challenging work and to channel the best of the increasing number of college-bound students into their schools. In the bland prose of a Harvard report, the proprietary intent of the Advanced Placement idea, with respect to the best secondary students, is clear: "What is needed is a set of achievement examinations in the major subjects taught in secondary schools which would enable the colleges supporting these examinations to give an entering student advanced placement" (Krieder 7). If only students taking college preparatory courses could take some examinations for college credit, went this reasoning, the colleges subscribing to the results could claim the best of the matriculating students.

And, of course, establishing special examinations necessitated some way of readying students for them: Advanced Placement required Advanced Preparation. Through the back door, as it were, the cagey pioneers of Advanced Placement gained entry into high school curricula. To ensure that students' "intellectual momentum and curiosity" would not "languish" in the transition from high school to college, says one historian of the program, the developers of AP linked placement with preparation in "subject matter traditionally studied in the first college years" (Krieder 8). The "course syllabus" became "a standard for achievement, a basis for testing, and a reference for colleges" (Krieder 8). Ambitious high school seniors could simultaneously become college freshmen, studying subject matter at a level that allowed them to begin at more advanced levels when they actually arrived at college.

The kernel of the Advanced Placement idea, therefore, was a set of examinations preceded by a study program whose outlines reflected what colleges wanted. No particular guiding ideal or principle seems to have animated the AP planners. Their concern with "intellectual momentum" may reflect sympathy with the anti-progressivist school, which identified "a lack of intellectual rigor and historical perspective" as the besetting sin of post-World War II education (Applebee 185). But in the glow of the practical advantages of AP, its complex assumptions and unarticulated premises seem not to have been much debated. It seems to have been taken for granted then (as it apparently still is) that, in the words of a recent AP pamphlet, "many young people can, with profit and delight, complete college-level studies in their secondary schools" (*Advanced Placement Course Description—English* i). But for whose delight, and whose profit?

Beyond doubt, Advanced Placement benefits both high schools and colleges. Many high school teachers find both the students and the course work of AP classes more challenging than those found in conventional required courses. Although Advanced Placement is most common in schools with a large segment of college-track students, it is given an honored position in most school curricula, attracting the best-motivated students and—usually—the best-prepared senior teachers. High school administrators also find AP attractive since it can increase the visibility of college-bound students and thus enhance the school's prestige with respect to other schools in the area. Finally, most colleges and universities are eager to acquire students who have been exposed to ostensibly college-level material. Not that institutions welcome the prospect of giving away credits in advance; tuition is lost that way. As a trade-off, most institutions hope that advanced students will take more upper-level courses, reducing loads in introductory courses and swelling the upper-level classes the faculty prefer to teach.

Needless to say, Advanced Placement has become a source of profit for the Educational Testing Service (ETS). Not surprisingly, the group of elite institutions proposing AP in the mid-1950s turned to an official body already versed in entrance examinations—the College Entrance Examination Board (CEEB)—and to their professional executors, the then young Educational Testing Service, for the development of the AP examinations. Now, thirty years later, no test program within ETS seems to gain more direct cooperation from American high schools and colleges and their faculties than AP. Many of the AP exams require essay writing, art work, and other kinds of student performances not reducible to machine grading. Faculty are pressed willingly into service for reading student essays, judging art work, and evaluating foreign-language oral responses, laboring in the early summer like so many Bob Cratchits in unremitting toil, reading exam after exam until the work is done. Thus, while AP is not one of ETS's financial cornucopias, it does profit and delight them: it puts an ETS program directly into high school curricula and college catalogs, it enlists the eager cooperation of secondary and college faculties, and it maintains a visibility within the academic community crucial to ETS's continued flourishing.

Advanced Placement is good for academic institutions and a testing business. But is it good for students? Does Advanced Placement English really benefit the high school students encouraged by schools, colleges, and ETS to take it? An informed discussion of this central question involves a cluster of issues heretofore largely unexamined: the meaning of the term "college-level," the assumptions about student motivations and intellectual readiness buried in the idea of Advanced Placement, and the implications of the AP structure itself—a year's study followed by a standardized examination. Because the first two issues will be considered at length elsewhere in this volume, I wish only to review them before considering the AP structure itself.

Can AP English courses be integrated successfully into a high school curriculum? Is it possible to allocate responsibility for planning and teaching an AP course appropriately between two fundamentally different levels of educational institutions? Is it possible in the design and evaluation of the examination to apportion responsibility properly between these two constituencies? What is the effect upon the examination graders and their reading efforts of ETS's efforts to standardize evaluative responses in order to fit AP's claim of reliability in the essay-reading? The politics, sociology, and economics of AP English are dealt with extensively in James Vopat's chapter in this volume.

Beneath the AP concept is a group of assumptions about high school students' readiness to learn from college-level course work. Are there specific intellectual and/or emotional abilities necessary for success in AP English? To what extent will students' cognitive strategies, successful in conventional senior-high literature and writing courses, prove useful in AP courses? What essential differences between high school and college classroom environments must the secondary teacher be aware of? Between high school and college student-teacher relationships? In their chapter on cognitive development for the AP English student, Karen Spear and Gretchen Flesher examine these important issues.

The Writing Process and the Language and Composition Course

AP English began as a tail that grew a body: an examination was envisioned that required preparing a course. This pattern remains unchanged today. AP planners spend most of their time preparing and evaluating the exams. AP teachers are given extensive guidance material in the form of sample assignments, course outlines, and sample final test questions. Yet, although they are free to organize their own courses, only by incorporating many of the exam-oriented strategies can AP teachers give their students the best possible preparation for the exam. Indeed the limits of this standardized final exam, over which teachers have no control, constrain the entire AP learning experience. The course and the standardized exam together form the essential AP pattern.

If AP English can be said to have a theory, then, it is to be found in the assumptions about literature and writing inherent in this pattern. Two major assumptions pervade the advisory material (teaching strategies, sample assignments, course outlines, and sample test questions) that is available to all AP English teachers and from which some informing principles of AP English may be inferred. The first is that *the written product—the text itself—is the course focus, not the composing process that generates text nor the reading process that re-creates it.* The second is that *"meaning" in discourse (prose or poetry, fiction or nonfiction) is the sum of textual elements that are best studied piece by piece to discover how the parts fit together to make the whole.* Both assumptions reflect a faith in textual autonomy and objectivity, characteristics of the New Criticism. Even though they have increasingly been called into question by subjective composing and critical theory, such assumptions still command the loyalty of many high school and college teachers. With these assumptions in mind, let's consider the product orientation of the Language and Composition course.

AP Language and Composition offers writing assignments of different magnitudes and duration, accompanied by literary and popular readings. The exam features three types of questions: multiple-choice sentence manipulation, multiple-choice reading comprehension, and three 30- to 45-minute essay responses to lengthy questions. Let's examine this course-exam connection in terms of what writing teachers have learned about the composing process, the core of contemporary writing pedagogy.

Fifteen years ago Donald Murray called attention to the process-product distinction, urging teachers to recognize that "when we teach composition we are not teaching a product, we are teaching a process" (79). He asserted that for too long teachers had responded to students' writing as they had been trained to respond to literature. Murray argued that the habit of seeing students' writing as finished products was damaging to young and inexperienced writers. In the years since that article appeared, the meaning of the term "writing process" has been continuously refined and elaborated by researchers drawing on the insights of psycholinguistics, cognitive and behaviorist psychology, and rhetorical theory.

Modern theorists like Piaget, Vygotsky, and Bruner have postulated language's power to objectify and categorize experience, making learning possible. They and others have argued that as a mode of learning writing is uniquely personal and holistic, enabling the user to make connections among pieces of data and experience, formulate hypotheses and syntheses, and create "self-provided feedback" (Emig). But the developing and clarifying power of writing does not come easy; first efforts to compose often end in what Linda Flower calls "writer-based prose," characterized by episodic and narrative structures that lack the connectedness that permits conceptualization and synthesis. Converting writer-based prose into discourse that coheres for the reader requires full exploitation of the revision process. Moreover, composing is not simply a linear process of prewriting-writing-rewriting. Rather, it is continuous and recursive. The process turns the text back upon itself as the writer's articulated meanings grow, change, and accumulate.

Many college writing textbooks now emphasize the recursiveness of composing and the incompleteness of any given text: revision is inventing, urges one textbook, because "to see again is to see something new, and that is a process of discovery" (Gere 261). Robert Connors suggests that today's new writing teachers, having themselves studied theoretical and empirical research on writing, seek texts that will help "students learn the processes of writing" (192). Revision is the heart of the composing process; it demands time and psychological distance between writer and text.

Research has demonstrated what happens when inexperienced student writers do not understand what revision means. Generalizing from student writing samples, researchers like Linda Flower, Lester Faigley and Stephen Witte, and Nancy Sommers have established that the major difference between skilled and unskilled writers is the latter's tendency to limit revision to changing words and sentences and editing mechanical errors. Faigley and Witte conclude that "inexperienced writers' changes were overwhelmingly Surface Changes"—changes in spelling, punctuation, usage, diction, and syntax that neither add nor delete meaning (407). Among the freshman writers she studied, Sommers identifies an "inability to 'see' revision as a process," which results in their making "lexical changes but not semantic changes" when they perform what they understand to be revision (382). Because they avoid the text-reshaping of genuine revision, student writers fail to realize its chief benefit: the discovery of meaning.

Given the central importance of the writing process in college-level composition pedagogy today, it is reasonable to expect this process to play a major role in AP English courses and examinations. In an introduction to the Language and Composition course, one sentence apparently encourages the study of process: "The course will include . . . the process of writing—from the discovery of the topic to the preliminary drafts to the final edited draft" *(Advanced Placement Course* 4). But in the next paragraph, the emphasis shifts to the written product and its parts. AP teachers are urged to study "the structures of sentences, paragraphs and larger discursive patterns," including diction, syntax, discourse modes and aims, and "rhetorical strategies" such as the Aristotelian logical, emotional, and ethical appeals (5). And, as we shall see, the Language and Composition exam matches this emphasis with its own focus on sentence manipulation and stylistic analysis.

An uneasy tension between product and process runs throughout the College Board's *Teacher's Guide to Advanced Placement Courses in English Language and Composition* (Gadda et al.), which offers detailed advice to AP teachers about course outlines and teaching strategies. "Although the course . . . should include [such skills as] the planning, writing, and revising of sustained essays . . . the present AP examination, three hours long, can test only a sample of those skills," the *Guide* confesses (1). While the multiple-choice section of the exam tests reading analysis and "manipulation of syntax," it continues, "the free-response section . . . provides a direct measure of the student's compositional skills" (2). But what sort of "compositional skills" are meant here? Not the skills that, a few pages later, the AP teacher is urged to nurture: students "should be comfortable turning out successive drafts of a piece of writing, studying what they have done, seeking criticism and suggestions, then making improvements" (5–6). These are precisely the recursive elements of the composing process that the *Guide's* authors have already implied cannot be adequately measured by an impromptu essay. Apparently, the authors' awareness of the importance of process in writing takes a back seat to their recognition of the demands of the exam format.

Another indication of inadequate process emphasis in AP English materials may be found in the *Guide's* sample course outlines from several high schools and universities, chosen apparently as models of AP effectiveness. Of the seven lengthy outlines, only two—one high school, one university—give serious attention to teaching composing. "One of the main goals of the course," says the university course outline, "is that you learn to revise and reword your own writing" (120). A high school outline devotes considerable space to phases of the writing process. It gives students extensive suggestions for prewriting and rewriting and shows a refreshing awareness of the difference between revising and editing. The other five course outlines show little interest in, or understanding of, the writing process. One outline offers an over-simplified version of the recursiveness of writing: "Proofreading and revision should take place after the completion of each assigned paper" (77). Another reduces revision to fixing: "Occasionally, a student will be *required* [original italics] to re-write [sic] a paper in order to correct conspicuous errors" (91).

Thus, despite its occasional attention to the whole writing process, the *Teacher's Guide* makes it clear that aspects of the text—words, sentences, paragraphs, modes and patterns, style and tone—will get the most emphasis in the Language and Composition course. The reason is clear enough: these elements of discourse are the most amenable to testing, and the AP course must train students for the AP exam. In a tacit admission of its real priorities, the *Guide* asserts that rapid composing is crucial: "sometimes a first draft must suffice, as is usually the case in examinations," and quick composing becomes a virtue when students need to "write a well-organized essay in a short period of time" (6). Quick composing is what they will be tested on and therefore what the course tends to teach them.

Of the three types of questions on the exam, the multiple-choice sentence manipulations—requiring students to choose the approved rephrasing of given sentence parts—raise the most serious questions of pedagogical justification. The multiple-choice text interpretations require students to choose the official "best" interpretation of the style or tone of words, sentences, and sometimes larger chunks of text. The third type features 30- to 45-minute essays, and the directions themselves may run several hundred words.

The sentence manipulations in the Language and Composition examination require students to be able to rearrange sentences using different idioms, usages, and syntactic structures. Some manipulations improve the original, as in this sample from the *Advanced Placement Course Description: English* (13):

> Fast-growing trees are an efficient and economical means of converting sunlight into fuel, and they are not a blight on the landscape.
> Begin with *Fast-growing trees convert.*
> A. without blighting
> B. so as not to blight
> C. but not as a blight
> D. but without a blight
> E. not, however, blighting

"A" is the approved choice. It requires students to form a somewhat tighter sentence in order to arrive at the correct answer: "Fast-growing trees convert sunlight into fuel efficiently and economically without blighting the landscape." Unfortunately, not all such manipulations are equally justifiable; another sample sentence requires students to make the following alteration to arrive at the right answer:

> England's system of turnpikes and canals, begun in the eighteenth century, was expanded during the first thirty years of the nineteenth. (Begin with *During* and change *England's system* to *England expanded*) (*Advanced Placement Course* 9).

The expected revision is:

> During the first thirty years of the nineteenth century, England
> expanded its system of turnpikes and canals begun in the eigh-
> teenth century.

Given this isolated sentence, there is no evident need or justification for
such a revision; nothing is corrected or improved. Were this sentence quoted
within a larger passage, some reason for putting the "thirty years" phrase
in the lead might be evident, but without a context, the change is pointless.
Even more mystifying is the manipulation required to answer the following
question correctly:

> Thorough critics review books only after they have read eve-
> rything else written by the author. (Begin with *To be a thorough
> critic* and include *you must read*) (*Advanced Placement Course*
> 9).

The expected revision is something like:

> To be a thorough critic [of a book?] you must read everything
> else written by the author.

These manipulations encourage exactly that kind of revising behavior identified with inexperienced freshman writers—the tendency to rearrange
words and sentence bits. Such questions, requiring students to edit small
pieces of discourse, discourage that readiness for holistic revision that is at
the heart of current writing pedagogy. And when the required changes
appear as pointless as those in the last example, student test-takers will read
the message clearly: college writing must be a matter of fixing mechanics,
words, and sentences—that is, getting your sentences just so, in order to
conform to arbitrary expectations. Nor are these miscues merely test-makers'
isolated errors; they are the systematic results of the particle approach to
language testing.

   In their own way, the AP Language and Composition essay questions
also subvert the importance of process. Here is an example from the *Advanced Placement Course Description: English* (29):

> (Suggested time—45 minutes)
> Every society must expect of its members a certain degree of
> conformity. But from time to time, and for a variety of reasons,
> individuals have dissented from the established social norm, and
> have come into conflict with society. Some of these rebels society
> has tolerated, but not infrequently to its belated regret; some of
> them it has punished, even with death, but often such action has

later seemed a mistake, and society has then exonerated the rebel, accepting his new light. . . . How can society deal intelligently with those individuals who in any important respect disagree with it and challenge it?

Construct a carefully reasoned argument that proposes an answer to the final sentence in this paragraph. You may wish to structure your argument around examples from your experience or your reading.

Consider the prewriting necessary for a response to this task. First students must cut through the vague circumlocutions ("established social norm") and the ponderous Latinisms ("exonerated") to realize the individual versus society theme of the passage. Urged to make a reasoned argument, the student writer will probably construct an outline categorizing what he or she perceives to be the main types of rebellion against society, with appropriate examples jotted down for each. A major interpretive problem must be addressed: what does "established social norm" mean? An ethical rule? A law? A social guideline (don't slurp your soup)? If all of the above, what examples are appropriate? Literary? Real?

These prewriting notes took me ten minutes to compose. Now I have barely half an hour to write the essay, and I have to use a pencil, not the word processor I usually write on. With so little writing time, I must follow the pattern my outline dictates and be careful to develop only enough examples to please the readers without deviating from my chosen organization. If I go on a tangent, I'm lost because I don't have time to explore it and to refocus or reshape my argument. My first thoughts freeze my thinking into a pattern I dare not abandon. I cannot revise. All that I have learned about composing evaporates as I watch the clock on the wall mark the waning minutes.

Another sample topic from the *Advanced Placement Course Description* is far longer and more complex, running nearly 400 words as it unfolds an extended definition of the Spanish *querencia,* which concludes with a flight of prose: "But the engagement from which all these larger attachments flow is a personal, specific affection for one's own place . . . the finite, almost sensual feeling for some little corner of the world . . . " (27). The student is asked to use "some of the ideas in the passage" in the course of identifying his or her own place and its meaning. Allowed writing time is 40 minutes. It took me several minutes to read it through once and try to understand such phrases as "fed by instinctual experience" and "insignificant by any abstract standard." There seems no reason why the simple thematic core of this passage—"Describe your favorite place to be and what it means to you"— could not serve perfectly well as a writing stimulus, without requiring such extensive information processing by the writer.

Indeed, what constitutes the well formed writing assignment has long been an issue in writing pedagogy. One school holds that extended topics are best because they provide the fullest semantic and rhetorical contexts. Some research, however, suggests that in timed writing situations extended topics result in the least well developed responses. In one study, students (not freshmen but more experienced undergraduates) coping with topics with a "high information load" took too much time sorting through and repeating the information, leaving too little time for composing (Brossell 172). They responded most fully to tasks averaging about 25 words in length; two of the sample essays in the *Advanced Placement Course Description* are over 400 words, while the other two range from 75 to 150 words.

To all of this, believers in the AP program will say, "So what?" For after all, irrefutable statistics from a controlled experiment show that AP students (second-semester, high school seniors) scored better than college students on a typical AP essay question consisting of passages totaling nearly 1,000 words from which they had to analyze "diction and choice of details" (Modu and Wimmers 616). From this study we learn what Advanced Placement educators have long known: good students can be trained to perform well in virtually any kind of writing situation, given enough rehearsal. Exercises in diction, sentence, and paragraph analysis abound in the course manual, as do longer writing tasks like summarizing, experimenting with viewpoint and style, and analyzing mode and structure. With year-long preparation in such work, good students can be expected to do it well.

From the psychometrician's viewpoint, then, the results of the AP standardized exam are heartwarmingly valid, for they show a positive correlation between AP students' training and their test achievements. Of course, the study just described suggests the delightfully circular logic of the testing ethos: design a test featuring certain tasks, then design a course around those tasks, then test those finishing the course (see Modu and Wimmers). If students are carefully selected for the course and adequately prepared for the tasks, they will do well on the test. Test results will show that, indeed, AP students have learned well how to manipulate sentences; answer multiple-choice, text analysis questions; and compose mini-essays quickly in response to complex prompts. Not surprisingly, they will do these things better than students who have not taken an AP course.

So the question comes to this: Is the AP emphasis upon sentence manipulation and time-forced composing of value? Are these the skills that most appropriately serve college students in the various writing situations they will face? The answer, of course, is both yes and no. Plainly, accurate editing and quick impromptu composing are useful academic skills, invaluable at essay-exam time and likely to produce a pleasingly correct text. Indeed, "correctness" is seen by many college teachers as the cardinal virtue of academic writing; the continued popularity of the error-anatomizing handbooks makes this clear. And unarguably valuable to all college students are the skills needed to organize and communicate information and judgments quickly on an essay test.

But just as clearly, AP courses taught primarily to help students learn to write in the exam formats will cheat them out of all the benefits of the writing process. To the extent that AP instructors use the recommended exercises and teach to the test, emphasizing sentence manipulation, timed writing tasks, and discourse analyses, they will not help students learn the demands of process or experience writing as a means of personal exploration. Of course, AP teachers are free to give full play to the composing process in the selection and pacing of their assignments; those knowledgeable in current writing pedagogy will do so despite the lack of attention to it in the AP guides. Moreover, veteran AP teachers know that many AP students decline to take the test precisely because they find the exam irrelevant to what they have actually learned in the course. It is unfortunate that the full AP pattern militates against the knowledge with which writing may empower students.

Critical Theory and the Literature and Composition Course

Just as the Language and Composition course and exam center on the study of the written product and the manipulation of text bits, so the Literature and Composition course and exam focus on the objective determinacy and intrinsic significance of the literary text. Such assumptions have their roots in the New Criticism, Brooks and Warren's textbooks, and the textual exegeses that emerged as the dominant critical approach of the mid-twentieth century. Though this tradition now competes with reader-response, deconstructionist, phenomenological, and other newer critical methods, textual objectivism remains a major force in literary pedagogy, giving high school and college literature courses a vocabulary and a methodology that encourages close readings of language, structure, and symbol. Indeed, with its confidence in the autonomy of texts, New Critical objectivism has left an impressive legacy of specific textual analyses.

Generations of high school and college teachers of literature have been trained to carry on this enterprise. It is not surprising, then, that the strategies, assignments, and exam questions of the Literature and Composition course are thoroughly text-centered. Before exploring the significance of this approach, it may be helpful to summarize those objectivist premises prevalent in the AP Literature and Composition material:

a. The text exists objectively and determinately.
b. Its meaning is distinct from the writer's intention or the reader's personal reaction.
c. Its meaning emerges from the coherence of textual elements and their relationship to context.
d. The business of literary study is to scrutinize textual elements to see how they form a coherent whole and to relate this whole to contextual aspects of the work.

These articles of faith underlie the strategies and assignments in the rec-ommended course outlines, as well as the questions on the standardized final exam.

In the learning objectives spelled out early in the *Teacher's Guide to Advanced Placement Courses in English Literature and Composition,* ample evidence of these assumptions may be found. They are manifest, for example, in the suggestion that students should "read critically, asking pertinent ques-tions about what they have read" (Corey et al. 5). "Pertinence" appears normative here: questions had better be related directly to the text and not to some vagrant, personal reaction. Reading "critically" and "analytically, seeing relationships between form and content" (an injunction which, iron-ically, defies the New Criticism's favorite axiom about the identity of meaning and form), examining "how language contributes both literally and figura-tively to the meaning of a work," describing the work's "stylistic features, evaluating them in light of the theme"—all argue for scrutinizing textual parts and their relationship to the whole as the student's primary method of literary study (6).

The conservative text-centeredness of AP literary study is also docu-mented in the "Sample Courses of Study" section of the *Teacher's Guide,* consisting of outlines submitted by experienced AP teachers and variously organized by theme, period, or genre. Within each unit, as one outline puts it, "each work is analyzed according to all the themes and literary elements it contains" (Corey et al. 10). In another course, fiction is analyzed in terms of "characterization," "a major idea," "symbolism and irony," and "point of view." In the same course, poetry is broken down into its textual aspects: "imagery, metaphor, personification, metonymy, symbolism, allegory, par-adox . . . irony" (22–3). In the same course, written work consists of "one poetry explication a week" and "one analytical theme a week on imagery, theme, or tone" (23).

Sample exercises from these outlines require intensive textual analysis. One assignment reads, "all the significant elements that should be analyzed in any work of literature" include "meaning, point of view, imagery, at-mosphere, mood, symbolism, metaphor, tone, style or language, structure." And students must learn how "each of the important literary elements con-tributes to the meaning of the novel" (Corey et al. 44). In a sample treatment of a poem (Elizabeth Bishop's "The Fish"), "a variety of multiple-choice questions, some dealing with the poem's meaning, others with the poet's craft," are envisioned as the best way to engage students in a close reading (50). Here is an example, apparently intended both to teach the poem and to rehearse students for the final exam (53):

The language used to describe the fish suggests that it is both

 A. beautiful and graceful
 B. sickly and submissive

C. aggressive and unyielding

D. ugly and awe-inspiring

E. wary and reckless

Given the vivid, grotesquely detailed visualizations of the fish rendered in the poem, students should have no trouble choosing "D" as the appropriate wording. But consider the effect upon the student test-takers of the sort of question that formulates language for the students: it suggests that there is one particular analytic phrase best suited to this specific text. It suggests that unlocking the door of meaning requires finding the right linguistic key. The students' own language isn't wanted; their recognition of a preformulated response is the action required. Such questions carry traditional objectivist premises to a pedagogical extreme; they suggest that students must crack a specific interpretive code for this poem. They also confirm that textual meaning is autonomous and discoverable only within a very specific language set. Meaning is there for those who get the words right.

It is this rigid interpretive process that is the biggest pedagogical failure of the AP exam. It implies a textural authoritativeness indefensible in the context of recent literary theory. The AP exam's prefabricated approach to literary analysis—interpretation by multiple choice—carries with it two major difficulties. One is the dilemma it poses for students responding to lexically precise questions about frequently ambiguous literary language. Too often, the spurious analytical exactness implied by the question is betrayed by the text's rich multiplicity. Students are forced to choose among words or phrases none of which, or sometimes more than one of which, will accurately fit the occasion. Another problem is the exam's exclusive focus on the text, leaving individual readers' responses wholly out of account. Objectivist attitudes toward literary texts justify such a focus, of course. But the recognition gained by the recent variety of reader oriented criticism makes supposedly precise interpretations of supposedly fixed texts a questionable enterprise. Yet the multiple-choice sections of the AP literature exam focus almost exclusively on such interpretations.

For example, the text of George Herbert's "The Collar" is the focus of 19 multiple-choice interpretative questions in the *Advanced Placement Course Description*, the majority of which students trained in multiple-choice strategy could probably find the credited answer for. Consider the following (35):

The tone of the speaker's questions in lines 3–16 is primarily one of

A. enthusiasm

B. timidity

C. haughtiness

D. inquisitiveness

E. bitterness

As a label for the speaker's protestations, the credited answer—"bitter-ness"—is certainly the best choice among the five. Whether the speaker's tone might be even better characterized by a different term is not open to the test-taker to decide. A particularly experienced or language-sensitive student, however, who does not like any of the choices, might wonder whether "bitter" implies too negative an emotional state in the poem's beginning, since the poem later moves from rebellious affirmation, to humble acquiescence, to a rather subdued ending. This exam question requires the kind of interpretive debate that allows each reader linguistic freedom to participate fully and that communicates the exciting complexity and variety of poetic response. But what is a student likely to learn from answering this question? Bound by another's term, the sensitive test-taker may note a moment of irritated disagreement before finding the credited "best" choice and moving to the next question. The student will gain nothing by thinking beyond the obvious choice presented.

Some of the questions require students to choose the "right" answer from among options more than one of which is convincingly appropriate. Here is another question from the same group on "The Collar" (34):

The speaker's statements within the quotation marks (lines 1–32) are addressed to
   A. an aging friend
   B. his parent
   C. his loved one
   D. the Lord
   E. himself

The credited choice is "himself," an accurate enough term in itself since the poem dramatizes the speaker sitting alone at a table, crying rebelliously against the strictures of his faith. He is certainly talking to himself, but is *he* his *only* hearer? The poem's last lines suggest the presence of another listener as well:

But as I raved and grew more fierce and wild
   At every word,
Methought I heard one calling, "Child!"
   And I replied, "My Lord."

"The Lord" (choice D) is also present during the speaker's discourse ("as I raved"), and interrupts in mid-diatribe to respond to the speaker, a communicative act made necessary because "the Lord," witnessing—hearing—the speaker's rebellion, finds it necessary to call him to heel. The poem's whole thrust is toward making its readers feel the astonishing and unpredictable power of God over the human spirit; "the Lord" is an elemental part of the poem's rhetorical situation. Forced to choose arbitrarily between equally plausible options, sensible students will feel, not that they are being asked to respond reasonably, but that they are participating in a grim guessing game with unknown interlocutors who alone possess the key to the poem's "real meaning." Like other AP test-takers, students will have experienced the pedagogical fallout from the rigid, often arbitrary, textual objectivism inherent in the multiple-choice approach to literature.

Though they do not arbitrarily constrain students' choices like the multiple-choice questions, the essay questions in the Literature and Composition exam reflect a similar text centeredness, and something else as well: within 30 to 45 minutes, the necessity for an impromptu analysis based on a rapid first response to a literary text. Some questions require straightforward thematic interpretation, such as the 30-minute question asking students to "write an essay discussing the difference between the conceptions of 'law' in lines 1–34 and those in lines 35–60" with respect to Auden's "Law Like Love." Couched in modern idiom and concise Audenesque statement, this poem is reasonably accessible to students geared for the effort by a year's worth of timed practice analyses.

Quite different is the sample 45-minute question (based on a passage of Samuel Johnson's particularly heavy-handed irony directed at Soame Jenyns) that requires students to "analyze Johnson's treatment of the argument and his attitude toward the author, Soame Jenyns." The extended ridicule of Jenyns' "flounder[ing] absurdity" mocks literary pretense in inflated, Latinate diction; understanding its drift requires students' ability to penetrate Augustan tonalities and structures. The period-specific style of Johnson's abuse poses difficulties in understanding and responding much beyond those of Auden's poem. The context of Johnson's work draws on the eighteenth-century dispute over the authorial principle featuring the rhetorically spectacular rival bashing exemplified in, for example, *The Dunciad*. For students not familiar with this literary ethos, the text itself is unlikely to suggest anything more than Johnson's personal contempt for another writer. Responding to text out of context is particularly reductive to an understanding of Johnson's rhetoric. Yet impromptu analyses of unfamiliar passages are advised for AP courses as practice for the exam itself, which presents literature as a set of opportunities to display analytic acuteness upon isolated texts. And because the exam may present passages from any literary period, nationality or movement, the test-taker's readiness to read and respond to a text within its context will depend entirely on a chance fit between course reading and exam.[1]

The pedagogical consequences of the text-centered approach, suggests Robert Probst, include requiring students to understand a text as that which "is best interpreted by the more experienced critic, represented in the classroom by the teacher." Students must be aware that their "task is to accept the meaning given, learn the information, and absorb the judgments of the critical establishment" (61). In the course of giving advice to potential AP teachers, the *Teacher's Guide* shows how thoroughly the AP planners internalize the authoritarian approach: although it is hard for teachers to stay in control of the demands of an AP course, they must nevertheless "evaluate students' work in an expeditious manner, return it to them, and discuss it adequately. . . . Good planning encourages the students' efforts and enhances the teachers' authority" (Corey et al. 9). Without authority, this reasoning suggests, teachers cannot persuade students to accept their interpretation of the text; lacking such acceptance, students will be unable to make meanings from the text.

Certainly, with their emphasis upon the structural and stylistic elements of literature, objectivist approaches remain important in the teaching of literature. It is impossible to imagine helping students understand how literature may have meaning for them without using the techniques and vocabulary of textual analysis. However, on the evidence of their advisory materials, the AP planners have not yet recognized the impact upon pedagogy—and thus upon the course-plus-exam pattern—of current, more subjective critical approaches. For a great shift in literary criticism has been gathering momentum in the last decade or so. Reader-response and deconstructionist approaches, for example, have altered the way in which many teachers talk about literary texts. While the current AP exams focus on meaning, structure, and style, course discussions conducted by recently prepared teachers increasingly emphasize the process of responding to the text.

What George Levine terms a "radical subjectivity" underlies the new critical approaches (158). Of these, reader-response theory has the most immediate pedagogical implications. Its primary effect is to call into question the objective determinacy of the text. Stanley Fish, a persuasive advocate of this theory, asks what a literary work "does" and opens the discussion with "an analysis of the developing responses of the reader in relation to the words" (*Self-Consuming Artifacts* 387–388). For Fish, meaning does not inhere in the structure of words; a text does not "mean" until it signifies something for a reader. He rejects such formalist mainstays as the notion of textual autonomy and Wimsatt's "fallacies" of intention and affect. The emotional content of textual response, that which Wimsatt rejected as too unstable to be allowed into an interpretive act, is part of what the reader brings to the act of signification. One reader-response theorist, David Bleich, identifies the reader's own perceptions and emotions as primary sources of meaning-making, while others like Fish himself find the reader's understanding guided by "interpretive communities" out of which individual responses are shaped.

In reader-response theory, the text is not simply whatever the reader makes it out to be. Rather, it emerges "as the consequence of our interpretive activities," as Fish puts it (*Is There a Text* 13). The meaning of a text is always relational. What a work means is not a product of its own elements and structure but a function of the reader's interaction with those things. Traditional literary terms—plot, symbol, stanza, metaphor—remain part of reader-response discussion, but instead of being seen as meaning, something which it is the reader's task to find out or interpret, text elements are treated as effect-producing stimuli. Interpreting a literary text is an act of creation, during which something new is brought into being specific to each reader's encounter. For Fish, to interpret the text is to constitute it, and a "text" emerges for each such act. Robert de Beaugrande postulates another definition of interpretation: it is bringing to life a text, by creating a "world" in response to that text, "constituting a world as a response to a given text" (537).

The focus of reader-response criticism is upon the reader's processing the text into life and meaning. From this comes a pedagogical focus upon what readers bring to reading and how the act of reading creates meaning. David Bleich's early text (1975), with the descriptive title *Readings and Feelings*, suggests many uses for students' personal responses to literature, from describing individual feelings to comparing responses within a group. Another teacher describes how she helps students " 'compose' their under-standings of texts" by writing and rewriting their interpretations "in personal terms" until other readers can understand just how the writer perceives the text (Flynn 342). A third emphasizes "response statements" focusing both on contextual materials and on purely personal responses. These are clarified as the students systematically deal with such questions as "What is the predominant effect of the text on you?"; "Why do you think the text had that effect?"; and "What does your response tell you about yourself?" (McCormick 838). These pedagogical applications help students focus on the forms and processes that shape their responses to texts.

The absence of concern for the reader's role in interpretation marks the biggest departure of the AP pattern from current literary theory. Amid the exhortations to textual analysis, there are occasional recognitions of students' personal investment in meaning: students should "think reflectively about what they have read and discussed and apply their findings to their own lives" (Corey et al. 6). This appears to invoke a more subjective ped-agogical approach; yet nearly all the recommended strategies in the *Guide* affirm the strong text orientation of AP literary study. Discernible in these occasional lapses into subjectivity is some recognition of relational, reader-oriented attitudes to literature. Developing them into a workable pedagogy, however, requires choices the AP planners have apparently not yet considered making. But the time is right for them.

Proposed Changes

The primacy of product over process and text over response is well entrenched in AP English partly because it is dictated by the course-plus-exam pattern, and partly because many high school and college teachers still find it their most comfortable pedagogical approach. One participant in a recent conference of high school and college teachers pointed out that "most of us had been trained as formalists, believing implicitly that if we could only master the proper reading skills we could unlock the content of any text" (Gruenberg 31). And this is precisely the notion embodied in the multiple-choice portion of the Literature and Composition exam: to teach students "skills" needed to understand "imagery," "irony," and "symbolism," so that they can read an unfamiliar poem by Richard Wilbur, for example, and in a few minutes answer ten questions about the implications of its animal imagery, its abstractions, and its "final vision" (*Advanced Placement Course* 44–46). We are all familiar with, and probably still attracted to, this pedagogical game of finding the meaning. As students, we found it exciting to announce some insight that drew an admiring compliment from the teacher; as teachers, we find satisfaction in telling classes of baffled students the "real meaning" of the hooded figure in "The Wasteland." But the subjective critics' reassessment of traditional attitudes suggests that the habit of treasure hunting for meaning can render the literary text "dead on the page rather than . . . living in the readers" (Gruenberg 31).

As part of the general pattern of Advanced Placement, the AP examinations must, like the AP courses they accompany, be justified by the quality of the learning experience they provide. We must ask, then, whether what the examinations teach is really what we want students to learn about writing and literature. Statistics don't help much in answering this question since all they really tell us is that good students, carefully trained to perform certain tasks, will do them well. It is rather a question of whether the tasks that the examination requires are appropriate to the ways we want students to learn about writing and literature. Do we want students to learn writing as a set of strategies for getting things just right or as a process of making meaning by first getting things wrong? Do we want students to respond to literature as a set of encoded meanings whose keys are precise analytical language, or to see it as "not a set of answers, but a process of seeking answers, knowing that there may . . . be none" (Gruenberg 31)?

The key to answering each of these questions lies in the word "process." For the great shift in writing pedagogy has been away from the written artifact and toward the meaning-making activity of the writer. Similarly, the subjective approaches to reading literature emphasize the reader's dynamic role in creating the *meaning* of a literary text. What has traditionally been termed "composition" is now actually "composing," while *text* and *meaning* cannot be spoken of apart from the act of *reading*. This doesn't mean that we can avoid dealing with the final drafts of our students' writings or avoid discussing the printed texts of the literature we teach. It does mean that we must decide whether the arguments for a dynamic process in composition and literature now command serious attention, and if they do, whether the principles of the AP examinations are compatible with such arguments. With their inherent resistance to the full writing process and their static view of the literary text, these exams are clearly out of touch with much of the best that is now being thought and said about writing and literature.

The constrictive effect of the exam format minimizes the process emphasis in the teaching materials, depriving students of that focus upon the writing process that is essential to writing growth. Rearranging sentence parts and writing quick mini-essays are not appropriate substitutes for sustained composing and revising. Entrenched in the standardized exam, however, they are the tail that wags the dog. Though many teachers of the Language and Composition course do emphasize the writing process, they are also obliged, in view of the exam, to exercise the students frequently in sentence manipulation and impromptu writing. Most instructors rightly feel that if they don't give students this practice, they aren't fulfilling their professional commitment to them. It isn't the AP teachers that need changing; it's the AP pattern itself. What can be done?

Two major changes in the pattern would introduce process into the AP pattern and shift its emphasis from particle to holistic composing:

1. Eliminate multiple-choice questions from both Language and Composition and Literature and Composition examinations.
2. Allow previously composed and revised essays to be submitted in partial fulfillment of the essay portion of each examination.

Deleting multiple-choice sections would eliminate that half of the exam easiest to grade but also the half that most seriously constricts students' opportunities to display their true mastery of composition and literary response. It would remove the arbitrary sentence manipulations of the Language and Composition exam and the too-frequent ambivalences inherent in the Literature and Composition multiple-choices. Replacing short-answer questions with written responses would eliminate the advantage to students skilled at picking the right multiple-choice options and vastly increase the value of students' abilities to focus, organize, and style their knowledge in convincing prose. And since "composition" is the term common to both course titles, an exam consisting entirely of compositions would more accurately measure what both courses traditionally claim to develop: students' abilities to shape their own discourse. The exams' validity would thus be enhanced, while their reliability would not be seriously affected because AP procedures for normalizing evaluations of the essays are already thoroughly developed.

Nothing of value to what should be the basic goal of the AP English exams—the accurate evaluation of students' writing abilities and perceptiveness about literature—would be lost by eliminating multiple-choice questions. Without them, the one best measure of knowledge and writing ability—their expression in sustained writing—would become the sole focus of the exams. Submitting planned and revised essays as one task for the

Literature and Composition exam would enable students to show in writing how "in the act of reading" they "bring conceptions, feelings, and attitudes, hold them up against the work, and confirm, modify, or refute them in the process" (Probst 62). Such an exam would offer students a final, major opportunity to demonstrate—and enjoy—reading and writing about literature as a dynamic, evolving process of discovering meaning. The same justification applies equally to the Language and Composition exam: essays on personal and general topics should also represent the dynamic, evolving process of finding meaning through writing.

Accepting revised essays in partial fulfillment of the exam would allow AP readers to evaluate writing representing students' command of the whole writing process. Such a change would not require teachers to cease exercising students in rapid composing tasks, since they are necessary to general academic success, because part of each AP exam would still consist of timed writings in response to specific prompts. But it would allow—indeed require—AP teachers to emphasize process in their courses since students would be aware that their ability to exploit the whole writing process, not just a truncated version of it, would eventually be evaluated. Essays composed and revised under the supervision of the AP teacher would permit students to write on topics directly related to their course materials, thus increasing students' chances of being able to relate text to context when analyzing literary works. They would, in short, allow students to demonstrate a range of skills and knowledge more closely approximating the actual content of the AP course than the present exams allow. Students would be more likely to perceive such an exam as an exciting opportunity rather than a high-stakes gamble required by the system.

The AP development committees are made up of active professionals in college and secondary English who believe in the good effects of the AP English program for all students. That it has benefited many students over the years is beyond question. But in the perspective afforded by current composition and literary theory, it is also clear that AP English needs to change its focus and structure if it is to realize its best potential in higher education in the United States.

Note

1. I was one of the hundreds of AP readers convened at Rider College, New Jersey, in the year in which the question about Johnson's satire on Soame Jenyns appeared on the exam. Some students' responses to these questions were, of course, quite sophisticated, as might be expected from the best students in the best schools. Many responses, however, revealed the writers desperately and unsuccessfully trying to make sense out of Johnson's ponderous irony, with sometimes sadly—and unintentionally—comic results. At an end-of-session gathering of all the readers, portions of some of these were read aloud to the group, occasioning gleeful amusement among the assembly.

Works Cited

Advanced Placement Course Description: English. N.p.: College Entrance Examination Board, 1986.

Applebee, Arthur N. *Tradition and Reform in the Teaching of English: A History*. Urbana: NCTE, 1974.

Bleich, David. *Readings and Feelings: An Introduction to Subjective Criticism*. Urbana: NCTE, 1975.

———. *Subjective Criticism*. Baltimore: Johns Hopkins UP, 1978.

Brossell, Gordon. "Rhetorical Specification in Essay Examination Topics." *College English* 45 (1983): 165–73.

Bruner, Jerome. *On Knowing*. Cambridge: Harvard UP, 1963.

———. *Toward a Theory of Instruction*. Cambridge: Harvard UP, 1966.

Connors, Robert J. "Textbooks and the Evolution of the Discipline." *College Composition and Communication* 37 (1986): 178–94.

Corey, Robert D., et al. *Teacher's Guide to Advanced Placement Courses in English Literature and Composition*. N.p.: College Entrance Examination Board, 1985.

de Beaugrande, Robert. "Writer, Reader, Critic: Comparing Critical Theories as Discourse." *College English* 46 (1984): 533–59.

Emig, Janet. "Writing as a Mode of Learning." *College Composition and Communication* 28 (1977): 122–28.

Faigley, Lester, and Stephen Witte. "Analyzing Revision." *College Composition and Communication* 32 (1981): 400–14.

Fish, Stanley. *Is There a Text in This Class?* Cambridge: Harvard UP, 1980.

———. *Self-Consuming Artifacts*. Berkeley: U of California P, 1972.

Flynn, Elizabeth. "Composing Responses to Literary Texts: A Process Approach." *College Composition and Communication* 34 (1983): 342–48.

Gadda, George, et al. *Teacher's Guide to Advanced Placement Courses in English Language and Composition*. N.p.: College Entrance Examination Board, 1985.

Gere, Anne Ruggles. *Writing and Learning*. New York: Macmillan, 1985.

Gruenberg, Alex. "Report from the Institute: Notes on the Teaching of Literature." *English Journal* 75.6 (1986): 30–32.

Krieder, Donald. "Credit by Examination in Historical Perspective." *Credit by Examination Comes of Age*. New York: College Entrance Examination Board, 1980. 3–15.

Levine, George. Rev. of *Literature against Itself: Literary Ideas in the Modern World*, by Gerald Graff, and *After the New Criticism*, by Frank Lentricchia. *College English* 43 (1981): 146–60.

McCormick, Kathleen. "Theory in the Reader: Bleich, Holland, and Beyond." *College English* 47 (1985): 836–50.

Modu, Christopher C., and Eric Wimmers. "The Validity of the Advanced Placement English Language and Composition Examination." *College English* 43 (1981): 609–20.

Murray, Donald. "Teach Writing as a Process not Product." *Rhetoric and Composition: A Sourcebook for Teachers and Writers*. Ed. Richard L. Graves. Portsmouth, NH: Boynton/Cook, 1984.

Piaget, Jean. *The Language and Thought of the Child*. Trans. Marjorie Warden. New York: Harcourt, 1926.

———. *Six Psychological Studies*. Trans. Anita Tenzer and David Elkind. New York: Random, 1967.

Probst, Robert E. "Three Relationships in the Teaching of Literature." *English Journal* 75.1 (1986): 60–67.

Sommers, Nancy. "Revision Strategies of Student Writers and Experienced Adult Writers." *College Composition and Communication* 31 (1980): 378–88.

Vygotsky, Lev. *Thought and Language*. 1934. Trans. Eugenia Hanfmann and Gertrude Vakar. Cambridge: MIT P, 1962.

2

Continuities in Cognitive Development *AP Students and College Writing*

KAREN SPEAR

University of South Florida—St. Petersburg

GRETCHEN FLESHER

Gustavus Adolphus College

The authors survey research on cognitive development and report on their research study that compares college students with and without experience in an AP program. The authors draw some important conclusions about cognitive development and its relation to language instruction and the Advanced Placement program.

The central contribution of developmental psychology is its depiction of knowledge not as a noun but as a verb, a dynamic and progressive process of knowing. In his seminal study, *Genetic Epistemology*, Jean Piaget defines knowledge as "a system of transformations that become progressively adequate" (15). Knowledge is the result of "continuous construction, since in each act of understanding, some degree of invention is involved; in development, the passage from one stage to the next is always characterized by the formation of new structures which did not exist before, either in the external world or in the subject's mind" (77).

Piaget's definition reflects the evolution of his own thinking after he began his investigations of learning and epistemology in the 1930s. Like the developmental psychologists who have succeeded him, Piaget gradually found that his initial identification of the nature and order of stages in thinking was not as adequate a way of describing cognitive development as was his later attention to the intellectual processes that trigger movement from one stage to another. William Perry, another developmentalist, likewise came to recognize the shortcomings of construing cognitive development as a linear journey from one intellectual benchmark to another. By 1981, he was describing cognitive growth as "recursive": "Perhaps the best model for growth is neither the straight line nor the circle, but a helix" (97). Like Piaget, Perry became increasingly interested in exploring the gaps between stages to understand the dynamics of transitions from less adequate to more adequate ways of knowing.

The evolution of knowledge about cognitive development closely parallels shifts in our understanding of composing—from the product-centered orientation of the traditional paradigm to explorations of writing as process. However, the relationship between development theory and composition theory has more in common than close parallelism. Given the central role of language to development theory, along with its emphasis on intellectual and ethical development within academic contexts, descriptions of student development have much to tell us about the how's and why's of writing development. The relationship of AP English to students' overall intellectual development is one area in which a look at the intersection of composition theory and development theory can help to inform decisions about the role of AP English. Such decisions include curriculum planning at both the secondary and college level, as well as policies governing placement in college writing courses—or waivers from them. Rather than making such decisions on faith or speculation alone, educators might profitably draw on development theory to facilitate an understanding of this special group of students. The following study is a beginning in that direction. But before we describe the study itself, some further theoretical background is essential.

Intellectual Development and Writing Development

A number of studies already point toward the value of development theory in understanding cognitive changes underlying students' growth in writing. Perry has heavily influenced Janice Hays's studies of "discursive maturity" in high school and college students. She concludes that "students experience great difficulty in negotiating the move from concrete and immediate to more abstract and universal writing, a difficulty suggesting that they may be struggling to achieve a new stage of cognitive development" (128), and she proposes a series of stages in writing development that correspond closely to Perry's stages of cognitive development. Similarly, Carl Bereiter observes in his study, "Development in Writing," that while "there is no natural order of writing development, in the sense of a fixed sequence that all writers must go through . . . it is at least meaningful to think of writing development in terms of discrete stages, each characterized by conscious focus on a particular aspect of writing" (89).

Other researchers have examined the unevenness that occurs regularly, both in cognitive development and in writing development. Joanne Kurfiss, matching students' capacity for paraphrase to several of Perry's developmental positions, finds considerable unevenness in different areas of an individual's development, and she concludes that "the areas in which the student is persistently engaged . . . are those most likely to advance first" (569). Freedman and Pringle find that as the intellectual complexity of writing activities increases, writing ability initially decreases to the point where writers find themselves unable to do in a new assignment what they had previously accomplished with ease. These studies, of course, are closely connected with the theoretical foundations of writing across the curriculum, based as it is on evidence that writing often deteriorates as students move not just from lower to higher orders of complexity but from one discipline to another. Finally, Greg Colomb's work has important implications for understanding the writing development of AP students in college. He concludes that much of what students learn about writing in one context is simply not transportable to another; it must be relearned according to the subtle rhetorical conventions that govern the new writing environment.

Development theory is also useful to help define what it means to develop as a writer, with respect both to qualities of writing and to qualities of mind. Perry sees students, in their progress toward intellectual maturity, moving toward a stage of "evolving commitments" in which one's commitments, though continually subject to change, "structure the relativistic world by providing focus in it and affirming the inseparable relation of the knower and the known" (97). The end of Lawrence Kohlberg's progression of stages in moral reasoning is quite similar to Perry's. Kohlberg proposes a final stage of post-conventional morality. In this stage, there is a clear effort to define moral values and principles which have validity and application apart from the authority of the groups or persons holding these principles and apart from the individuals' own identification with these groups. . . . Right is defined by the decision of conscience in accord with self-chosen ethical principles appealing to logical comprehensiveness, universality, and consistency. These principles are abstract and ethical . . . universal principles of justice, of the reciprocity and equality of human beings, and of respect for the dignity of human beings as individual persons. (Kohlberg and Turiel 415–16)

Such commitments, to use Perry's word again, are considered optimal because they provide for the greatest adequacy in a person's thought and expression. By adequacy, Piaget means (and Kohlberg and Perry would agree) thought that is nonegocentric—organized according to high-order abstractions, comprehensive in the thinker's ability to perceive connections across a broad range of experience, and self-reflective.

At least two turning points seem crucial for students to engage in higher-order thinking. First is students' ability to coordinate ideas and to do so in increasingly complex ways, such as perceiving and expressing relationships between relationships. Marlene Scardamalia argues that "much of the story of cognitive development may be construed as taking progressively more variables into account during single acts of judgment" (82). She finds that even children who have developed the linguistic capacity to utter coordinated sentences often fail to establish coordinations among ideas in their writing.

Second, along with the ability to coordinate ideas goes the students' capacity to recognize that this operation has, in fact, occurred. Perry finds that an emerging capacity for "meta-thinking"—the ability to compare "the assumptions and processes of different ways of thinking," to view ideas as metaphors, or expressions of multiple approaches to a problem—accompanies the journey out of purely multiplistic ways of thinking, in which any opinion is as valid as any other (85). Thinking meta-cognitively, students experience a shift from looking at the details of what they're learning ("the what") to looking at the patterns that organize it ("the way"). This shift, "a move toward a higher level of abstraction, frees the 'way' to become context, displacing the 'what' and relegating it to the status of a particular" (Perry 88). The capacity for recognizing one's own contextual thinking seems crucial in keeping the individual's eventual moral, ethical, and intellectual commitments from sinking into either unexamined dogmatism or indefensible multiplicity.

Michael Basseches's studies of adult development provide a glimpse of mature, adult reasoning beyond the college years. He suggests that there is a mode of thinking that extends beyond the final stages proposed by Perry and Kohlberg (and by critics of these stages). He calls this alternative "dialectical thinking," a fluid, integrative way of thinking in which "the process of creating order is seen as occurring through efforts to discover what is left out of existing ways of ordering the universe, and then to create new orderings which embrace and include what was previously excluded" (11). Basseches's characterization of the highest order of intellectual development as a *way* of thinking rather than as a specific stage reflects the ongoing shift from product to process that is central to composition and development theory. Perhaps more important, the concept of dialectical thinking as an optimal pattern of intellectual development may cast new light on recent criticisms of cultural, socio-economic, and sexual bias in the Perry and Kohlberg formulations.[1] Basseches would find these criticisms evidence of a larger dialectic, part of the process of finding more adequate explanations.

This theoretical summary, while general, yields a comprehensive view of the life span of cognitive development: the research of Piaget and others on childhood and early adolescence; the work of Perry, Kohlberg, and Turiel on late adolescence; and the studies of Basseches on adults.[2] It also provides a theoretical springboard for our study of the continuing cognitive development of college freshmen and sophomores. Further, it offers a framework for understanding the profiles below that reveal processes of reasoning that span most of this course of development.

The Study

Our study was conducted at a large, research-oriented commuter university. It includes 20 freshmen and sophomores arrayed in four categories: freshmen who did not take AP English; freshmen who took AP English and then elected to enroll in an honors freshman writing course; sophomores who took AP English and then the honors writing course; sophomores who took AP English but elected not to take the writing course.

Each student agreed to participate in a tape-recorded interview. The interviews ranged from 30 to 90 minutes. Our questions covered five areas: high school English preparation, both regular and AP; current understanding of the nature and function of writing; attitudes toward learning and understanding of higher education; ideal learning environment; and moral reasoning. Although a number of objective pencil-and-paper instruments are available for assessing cognitive and ethical development, we chose instead the method of in-depth interview established by Perry, Kohlberg, Basseches, and others. This approach seems best suited to provide insights into the themes of subjects' cognitive organization as they are manifested across a range of experiences and into subjects' degree of awareness about their own thinking.

Our objective was twofold: (1) to determine whether there are any striking developmental differences among these groups of students; and (2) to provide a sound rationale for either exempting AP students from college writing courses or placing them appropriately. In spite of the rigorous norming process behind the AP exam, we were concerned that claims about the equivalence of AP and college English instruction have not taken into account students' continuing intellectual development. The key issue for us was not simply finding the most efficient way for students to demonstrate competence and fulfill basic requirements but to see how the best students in the educational system might be challenged most fully. The interviews revealed dramatically cohesive profiles of each group of students, suggesting strong correlations between college writing experience, attitudes toward learning, and cognitive development. The profiles below describe these correlations as a prelude to our discussion of their implications for AP instruction in secondary school and writing instruction in college.

Profile 1: Regular Freshmen

We begin our profiles with a group of four regular college freshmen who serve as a control group against which to compare the AP students. These students are remarkably similar in their attitudes toward college, their views about writing, and their self-perceptions. Two of the four students, Shelly and Heather, took honors English in high school, while another, Courtney, took a college prep course that focused largely on grammar. The fourth student, Jim, followed a regular high school English program and delayed entering college for two years in order to complete a church mission. Despite the differences in their backgrounds, all four view college as a vastly more challenging experience than high school, even though both Courtney and Jim are carrying only two courses. Reflecting on their high school preparations, all agree that success in high school mainly requires "getting work in on time and being sure it's neat." As Jim puts it, "So long as you turn in work and it's neat, you get an 'A.' " None feel that high school challenged them intellectually, yet they believe now that they did not challenge themselves either.

College for these four entering freshmen seems to make wholly new intellectual demands. Although none can adequately describe the differences, Heather and Courtney comment on the degree of independent work their teachers expect. As Heather puts it, "There's more work to do just in my head." And Shelly, in the fifth week of her first term, is still somewhat overwhelmed at the pace of instruction, "because it really takes time to digest ideas." Perhaps because of the uniqueness of college, these students view themselves as outsiders rather than participants in their college experience. Courtney regards the university as "a place for really smart people," while Shelly expresses her chief goal as becoming a smarter person: "I don't want to be dumb!" College, then, is akin to a tanning salon or a hospital, places people go to have something done to them so they'll leave in better condition.

Writing

Their passive view of learning carries over to their view of writing and writing classes. They consider writing from strictly and narrowly utilitarian perspectives: one takes freshman composition to learn to write the kinds of papers that college professors expect. The course provides an added measure of protection to ensure success in college. The fact that freshman writing is required is explained as a humane gesture on the part of the university to help students succeed in their course work. All four students have some vague expectation that writing will also be important in their working lives, but they have difficulty characterizing writing as anything more than a response to a teacher's assignment. Both Jim and Shelly conclude that "people probably wouldn't take it if they didn't have to," and Shelly and Heather, successful writers in high school, are finding writing quite difficult in college and are wondering whether they ever *really* knew how to do it.

Like learning in general, determinations of quality in writing are imposed from the outside. All four students insist that good writing is "clear," "interesting," and "well-organized." Notably, all these are qualities having to do with the presentation of material, reflecting these students' beliefs that their writing class, again like the tanning salon, exists to help them dress up the appearance of their thoughts. How teachers determine these qualities, however, remains a mystery to them. Heather believes that teachers assign grades according to "what they enjoyed," while Courtney assumes that one of her friends receives poor grades on his work because "he doesn't want to change it to what the teacher likes." Shelly and Jim also see successful writing as the ability to please the teacher. Both describe good grades as a consequence of accurately discerning what the assignment really requires. Shelly finds it hard to know what a teacher expects in an "A" paper, but with the tremendous faith that characterizes all these students' attitudes toward writing and learning, she ventures, "With practice I'm sure my writing will keep getting better." Her faith echoes that of William Perry's dualistic students who were convinced that hard work, determination, and adherence to the rules would bring them success.

None of the students seem able to understand our suggestion that some ideas or topics might simply be more worthwhile to write about than others or that there might be internal considerations that governed questions of quality. Shelly and Courtney are beginning to understand that good writing has something to do with a writer's presence in the writing, but at this point they are able to conclude only, as Courtney put it, that "a paper is better if you put your feelings in it." All four are strictly multiplistic in their understanding of writing quality: "Some people might like some ideas and not others." The students seem unaware of the contradiction between their absolute definition of good writing as "clear" and "organized" and their equally strong conviction that good grades on writing assignments result from the coincidence of a teacher liking what the student has written.

Learning Environment

Like all the students in our sample, these freshmen designate small, discussion-oriented classes as their ideal learning environment. But their

reasons are quite different from those of more advanced students and consistent with their essentially passive approach to writing and learning. Courtney, for example, likes small classes because the teacher "goes around and
helps you and makes you understand"; similarly, class discussions are helpful
in her writing class because the teacher "tells us if what we're saying is right
or wrong." (Her interpretation of her teacher's behavior seems very much
at odds with actuality, but it is a striking illustration of the human tendency,
as Piaget described it, to assimilate events into one's prevailing world view.)
Jim also describes small classes in terms of the opportunities they provide
for individual help and direct access to the right and wrong answers that
only the teacher knows: "Class discussion gives me a lot of ideas—and you
can see if your ideas are right." For Jim, who considers himself an avid and
capable reader, class lectures are nevertheless preferable to independent
reading because he "learns more"—presumably because the teacher saves
him from having to make up his own mind about what is important.

Heather is confused by her biology class, a large lecture course, because
the text, the teacher, and the TA often don't agree, and she finds it frustrating
and nearly impossible to sort through their varied but seemingly equal
perspectives. Finding her own thought processes equally impenetrable,
Heather reports with shock and relief that she has no idea how she passed
her mid-term exam, just as she has no idea, beyond a teacher's personal
preference, why some writing assignments receive "A's." These students,
like the others in the sample, show striking consistency in what Perry and
others have identified as a "coherent interpretive framework," a way of
accommodating themselves to their world so that the values they associate
with writing become a thematic variation on the values they maintain toward
learning more generally.

Sense of Self

From these students' comments on college, writing, and learning
emerges a distinctive sense of self. We include a discussion of self-concept
in each of the profiles because our interviews made it abundantly clear that
writing development and writing instruction are intimately connected with
the developing self of the writer. Despite their unfamiliarity with the college
classroom, all four students are excited about being in college, viewing it as
a liberation from the restrictive environment of high school. Heather and
Courtney are particularly vocal about the freedom to be themselves that
they believe college offers. Courtney enjoys the freedom to wear anything
she wants and say anything she pleases, to meet new people, and "not have
titles put on you like they do in high school." Heather values the challenge
of attending a large university and feels that friends who opted for smaller,
residential colleges are, ironically, just perpetuating their high school
experience.

Unlike the AP students we interviewed, these freshmen seemed almost wholly absorbed in their devotion to defining themselves as worthwhile, unique individuals. For these students, writing, and academic affairs generally, are but one facet of a larger endeavor to chisel an independent identity from an environment in which values and standards still seem imposed from outside. The conversation in these interviews was far more abbreviated than in the interviews with AP students. Although we asked the same questions, the interviews were only about half as long. The students' egocentricity and their uncertainty about the worth of their observations result in a framing of experience in the narrowest of terms, with these students rarely seeing connections between their own thoughts and larger, more abstract themes the way the AP students regularly do. Their inability to penetrate their own thought processes, to think about their thinking, seems both a cause and effect of their still egocentric perspective. The unelaborated discourse characteristic of freshman writing is grounded in the equally sparse reflections in our interviews with these regular freshman students, a sparseness that we trace to a very uncertain self-concept in the new environment of the college class. In contrast, the AP students appear to have come to terms with many of these basic issues in establishing an identity, having been validated throughout their elementary and secondary schooling as superior and worthwhile students—genuine "college material." For the regular freshmen, however, college marks a major turning point, one of the first opportunities they have had to exercise real choice and commitment. Their initial approach to college learning, then, is necessarily entangled with other issues in personal development, and they look to their courses and professors with a more diffuse set of expectations to make learning meaningful.

Profile 2: AP Students in Honors Freshman Writing

The freshmen who had enrolled in Advanced Placement English as high school seniors express attitudes toward writing, learning, and college remarkably different from those of their nonAP fellow freshmen. While the first group seems engrossed with self-definition, this group seems comfortably self-identified as college students. Carla, Jack, Jessica, Sonia, and Don are graduates of four different high schools (one of which is a private, Roman Catholic prep school). They express a general enthusiasm for learning and agree that being "well-rounded" is a good thing, although they can't explain the cliché very clearly. Careers are important but not the only reason for being in school. In fact, only Sonia and Don name career preparation as the primary motive for college, but like the others, they also say they enjoy the experience of learning.

This group's responses focus on personal growth: "I like the challenge. Once you start learning, there's no end"; "I don't want to be ignorant"; "I don't want to be narrow-minded"; "New ideas get to be a part of you"; "College prepares you with a whole variety of experiences so that when you face something unfamiliar, it's not so terrible"; "I want to be rounded and an effective citizen. Knowing how things work makes you happier and more appreciative."

These are the students idealized by the writers of freshman English texts and liberal arts statements of purpose. They see themselves in every way as active participants in their own education—as writers, critics, discussants, citizens, and thinkers. Although they seem more mature than the nonAP freshmen, they remain fundamentally egocentric in their responses to our questions. That is, they speak very specifically in terms of how their high school and college experiences affect them personally, or they focus on personal or idiosyncratic details.

The AP English Course

These students agree that the primary purpose of AP English is to prepare for the AP exam and to move students who have already been in the honors track more quickly and through more material than the average high school student. They describe the course primarily as a literature course and their activities in it as lessons in how to "rip a book apart." The writing they could remember was almost entirely a series of in-class practice exams, and the writing instruction that accompanied it principally commentary on good and bad responses. They believe that their writing changed little— Jessica got better at using technical terms and Carla got more specific—but they grew more comfortable with the demands of writing. Similarly, they had all been good readers most of their lives, so their reading only became more analytical: they got better at finding themes, symbols, and recurrent motifs.

They either take on faith that these skills in literary analysis will prove generally useful or find them by definition valuable and even virtuous. But when asked whether they see any change in how they approach ideas or problems since taking AP English, it took considerable prompting to provoke suggestions for possible connections between reading or writing in the English class and problem-solving more generally. Jessica finally says she's learned to analyze what she hears: "I guess now I think there's something else to what people are saying." Sonia says she questions things more than she used to, but insists this is a result of reading rather than instruction.

AP English as Preparation for College

Unlike the regular freshmen, who seem to believe that learning is finite or terminal and that writing instruction is always to some degree remedial, the AP freshmen say both that AP prepared them well for college and that now that they're in college, they have more to learn about writing.

The college class itself, an elective that is strongly encouraged, has prompted this attitude. Sonia says that she enrolled because she has so little confidence in her writing. She claims that she's learned more about writing in three weeks than she did in all of high school. Don enrolled while he was waiting for his AP exam score (a 5) because he was afraid that if he didn't, he'd forfeit a spot in the course. He admits that if he could have dropped the class during the first few weeks without losing tuition, he would have, but "Now I wouldn't." Jack was convinced he had more to learn by an early writing assignment that sent students to the library to look at scholarly writing in various disciplines.

Writing

When they talk about their own writing, these students point most clearly to their personal development. They don't think of writing as a way teachers test them on material as the regular freshmen do, but as a way to accomplish some of their own purposes. Sonia, who describes herself as "not the artistic type (I write when I have to)," says of her college experience, "I've grown a whole bunch because I'm writing for me now; I put myself in the paper." Don, too, finds the writing class a source of growth: "I'm getting to explore questions I've had for years." Both Carla and Jessica value writing as a means for self-expression. "Writing is a very important part of my life," says Carla. "When I write, I bring up from my innermost self what I'm really like." Jessica agrees: "Writing is how you make *yourself* understood to someone else."

But when we frame the question as "What would you tell a high school sophomore about the importance of learning to write?" they answer first that writing is necessary for completing assignments in college and in careers. Writing is also, they agree, useful as an organizing device. Yet none of them has really recognized writing as a way of learning. Even Carla and Jessica's emphasis on self-expression belies their sense that writing is essentially reporting, rather than interpreting, information.

All but one of the AP freshmen feel that they can say something about what teachers look for in a good piece of writing. And they all assume that the teacher is looking at the persuasiveness of what a writer has done. For example, Jack thinks "teachers look for how ideas come across, what type of feeling they leave you with." Carla guesses that "originality, logical thought processes, if it's persuasive" matter most to teachers. She also remembers that her high school teacher wanted them to think of how what they said mattered, and Jessica concurs: good writing should say "something worthwhile." These two remarks about substance over suasion are unique, however, in the interviews with this group.

Except for Don, who says he really doesn't "know enough" to judge writing ("I guess what I'd do is say, do I understand this? What's it trying to say? Is it grammatically correct?"), these students feel comfortable with the criteria teachers apply, and they add their own preference for writing that has voice or personality—another version of their interest in personal expression. Carla: "I like to see the author coming through." Jack: "I like writing that has emotion and personality." Jessica: "If you turn something in and you're excited about it; it's a little original, it maybe has some humor." Unlike the regular freshmen, who write only because a teacher asks them to, these students don't see their own writing, or others' writing, as lifeless, disengaged, or remote from their own experience. They read and write fully confident that somebody cares.

Learning Environment

Like all the students we interviewed, these students prefer small classes with discussion. Unlike the typical freshman, though, they don't think of discussion as merely an opportunity to tease the right answer out of the instructor, or a chance to learn from other students' "mistakes." Instead, they value other students' contributions and enjoy the exchange of opinions, which they regard as new information, as challenges to their own thinking, as stimuli for change.

Sense of Self

This group seems happy with themselves, excited about being in college, and comfortable in their role as students. Perhaps because they have always been "good students"—and publicly recognized as such—they have adopted or internalized academic modes of discourse and academic codes of behavior without the personal redefinition that college causes the regular freshmen. Self-identified as successful students, they habitually relate what they are hearing and reading to personal experience so that learning is automatically meaningful to them. Their desire to become "well-rounded," even if they are not quite sure what that means, suggests that they will soon develop the larger frames of reference and intellectual commitments evidenced by the sophomores.

Profile 3: AP Sophomores After Freshman Writing

The sophomores we interviewed were a year away from the high school AP English course and had taken honors writing in their freshman year. They sound like the older brothers and sisters of the freshmen just out of AP. Like the freshmen, Polly, Daryl, Hong, and Mitch enjoy the diversity of social and intellectual experience that college affords them. Polly defines college as a professional, social, and economic necessity, but the three men are quite adamant in their insistence that "I didn't come here to get a job." Again like the freshmen, the sophomores express confidence both in themselves as successful students and in their college experience as worthwhile. But they articulate their ideas differently from the freshmen. Where the freshmen contextualize their responses to our questions in personal experience, the sophomores contextualize their responses in much larger, more abstract ways. As Perry and Kohlberg would predict, they have developed a habit of generalization that allows them to see connections between various disciplines, between writing and learning more generally, between college and their lives beyond, and between their own lives and the world.

The AP English Course

The sophomores, too, see the AP course as a literature course, focusing on such skills in literary analysis as locating and labeling symbols, metaphors, and themes, with very little explicit attention to writing. But they have come to see the course as too test-centered. While the sophomores agree that the AP course is the best course available in English, three of them think that the writing assigned is inadequate. After a year in college, they see clearly that much of the writing they now do falls outside their preparation for 45-minute, in-class recitations of New Critical principles. Mitch, the most outspoken critic, says, "Myself and a lot of my friends felt stuck studying for a test given months away instead of just learning something. It didn't seem like a way to spend a year."

AP English as Preparation for College

Although they enjoyed AP for the most part and believe it was the best available choice, the sophomores see it as inadequate preparation for the demands of reading and writing in college. (Polly is an exception here. She's satisfied that AP English trained her to be less wordy and to read difficult things.) The college writing course, they argue, "helps you to read and write in more diverse realms of discourse." The audience plays a bigger role for the sophomores when they talk about writing. Hong recognizes the differences among writing styles in disciplines outside English. Daryl says that the college writing course helped him to find information, do research, and most important—and a point he returns to frequently—"tie things together," to see and develop relationships between ideas and words. As Mitch says, "Writing a literary essay is real different from lots of writing you do in college; in college there's much more weight on making yours ideas hold up."

Writing

These sophomores simply assume that writing will be part of everything they do in college and in careers. Indeed, they toss it off with "Well, of course, you always have to write"—advice they could offer an inexperienced high school student. What is qualitatively different about their responses is their sense of purpose and audience. They understand teachers not as capricious individuals but as representatives of a wider circle of informed readers. Having developed to the point of being able to disengage the thought from the thinker, the sophomores talk less about making *themselves* known to others, more about making their *ideas* known to others and to themselves. Shedding egocentricity continues to be recognized as a crucial developmental task, especially to facilitate adult levels of thinking. More-over, the sophomores seem closer to thinking of writing as a way of learning than freshmen do. Hong sees that writing forces him not only to spend more time on material for a class, but also to pay more attention at a different level. Daryl says, "I use writing as a medium to get ideas out, and then I can reflect on them."

After a year's college experience, the AP graduates seem less preoc-cupied with a writer's personality and self-expression than the freshmen do. The sophomores see the quality and clarity of ideas as primary in judging a good piece of writing, and they have begun to recognize that ideas can have power and elegance, that some ideas are more important than others. In fact, they mention clarity of expression, use of transitions, and organization only as categories subordinated to the larger purposes of writing. As Daryl puts it, "Ideas are number one. Clarity and organization help you [the reader] to get the ideas. . . . Structure is important because [the reader] shouldn't have to do all the work." Similarly, Mitch answers, "Ideas come first and support. . . . Linking ideas makes them more powerful. Grammar and spell-ing are much less important to college teachers." Although one of the soph-omores mentions "conciseness and organization" first, even she says that what really counts is "drawing valid points." Another begins with clarity, defining it as a problem of organization and support, and then subordinates these criteria to what he calls "depth"—"intelligent thinking about the material."

The tension between satisfying teachers' apparently arbitrary criteria for writing and their own desire for self-expression, so evident among the regular freshmen, seems to have been resolved for the sophomores. Perhaps we can hear some residuum in Daryl's comment that "I like to not be common, but I realize that what's obvious to me might not be obvious to someone else." But what we hear most often from the sophomores is that they are comfortable and confident about their freedom to express them-selves. They have assimilated academic discourse styles and no longer find them arbitrary. And they have left behind the more dualistic perspective of the freshmen, in which so much authority for truth and right is invested in their professors.

Learning Environment

The sophomores with AP backgrounds share a preference for small classes and discussion with all the other students we interviewed. However, they seem less convinced than the freshmen that expressing themselves and hearing others' opinions are useful *per se*. Although they find discussions useful because discussions enforce involvement, the sophomores also de-mand a little more. Daryl says group work is good when all the group members are energetic; Hong qualifies his endorsement of discussions by pointing out that the professor should shape and direct discussion; Mitch points out that unless other students are willing and prepared, discussion can be a waste of time. Here, one begins to witness movement toward dialectical reasoning as Basseches has described it. The students seem unwilling simply to accept widely held convictions that discussion, by definition, is a superior way of learning; rather, they show increasing awareness of more abstractly grounded definitions of good learning.

Sense of Self

The sophomores have grown in just the ways the AP freshmen hope to. They have given definition to the notion of well-roundedness. They speak articulately, even eloquently, from personal experience. But they also locate themselves within a number of communities to which they assume certain commitments. Thus, when they talk about why they write and how they evaluate writing, they speak not only of clear self-expression but of sharing research and ideas with similarly concerned readers. Being well-rounded means seeing an issue from many angles: historical, philosophical, scientific, political, and personal. The emerging capacity for dialectical reasoning, noted in their qualified descriptions of a good learning environment, may also be recognized as a fuller sense of self. They are neither so threatened by the university that they find themselves in a "me-them" conflict, nor so familiar with it as to experience boredom or contempt. Rather, they see themselves as reasonably consistent identities who grow and change as they participate in their environment.

Profile 4: AP Student Without Freshman Writing

The four students we interviewed who had taken AP English but elected not to take a college writing course are the most anomalous of the four groups. Although they share a number of attitudes, they also diverge considerably in ways that seem to have more to do with developmental level than with class standing or school experience. Bob, a freshman, and Paul, a sophomore, have much in common with our nonAP freshmen; Nila, a freshman, and Kit, a sophomore, look somewhat like the AP sophomores who had completed the honors writing course. The unevenness of this group has much to suggest about the role of college writing in the continued development of AP students.

AP English as Preparation for College

All these students recognize the centrality of nontrivial ideas to good writing rather than simply correct presentation of personal opinion and feelings. They are all extremely confident about their ability to handle any college writing task—as Paul puts it, in his AP course he "learned every possible way to write the essay." Each of these students took AP English for the opportunity it afforded to read great literature and consider ideas and values.

They do not view writing as an essential part of the program. Both Kit and Paul took AP English for the enhanced learning opportunities they believed it would provide, not simply to pass the AP test, accumulate college credits, and waive the college writing requirement. In view of their decision to waive the requirement anyway, their previous attitudes have not carried over to college writing. All these students manifest a sense of closure toward writing—that what is to be known about writing is limited to mastery of skills, and they have mastered them. Based on the success of their freshman year, Kit and Paul are probably right—at least according to their limited definition of writing.

Learning Environment

Their attitudes toward college learning sustain this theme of self-confidence, yet they also reveal an egocentricity that closes these students off to many learning opportunities. Talking about discussion classes, Nila, Bob, and Kit all object to working with people who are not as smart as they are. Nila would prefer a one-on-one tutorial as her ideal learning environment, and Bob, like our nonAP freshmen, likes discussion primarily as a means of checking out the rightness of his own ideas. Unlike the other sophomores in our survey, who appreciate discussion for the give-and-take of being a part of a community, these students view discussion from a self-centered perspective; they like what it does for them individually.

Despite their self-assuredness, this group is the least settled in college of our four groups and seems the least able to adapt in ways that would make college learning more meaningful. Kit isn't sure why she is in college and feels that she might be wasting her time: "I don't get into things as much as I should." Nila, does not feel as challenged as she might be, yet avoids enrolling in the university's honors program or selecting the number or type of courses that would challenge her. Paul and Bob both have some vague expectations about "becoming an intellectual" or of college "forcing you to build your ideas and really think about them," but Paul still finds himself looking for "right answers" and Bob views lecture classes as the only real way to learn. The self-confidence these students express has served more as an impediment than a guide to making learning the intrinsic and self-motivating challenge that it is for AP students who continue their academic work in writing.

The differences among these students are as revealing as their similarities. Paul and Bob are more like the regular freshmen in seeing college writing courses strictly as a means of academic survival, a way to learn what professors expect. They both agree that a writing course might help them, but Bob (a freshman) prefers to wait and see what kind of grades he receives in other courses, while Paul (a sophomore) just hasn't had time. Both would give similar advice to other students; "to take writing if their grades weren't good enough." Bob and Paul place great emphasis on correctness in writing:

for Bob, correctness and quality of ideas are evenly balanced; for Paul, good grammar, good form, and avoiding plagiarism are uppermost.

Kit and Nila talk much more about writing as a way to *find* ideas, clarify thought, and come to terms with oneself. Kit feels very resistant toward the fixed five-paragraph-theme format she was required to use in her AP class and perhaps has avoided college writing assuming it would require more of the same. Nila values good writing as an indication of intellectual breadth, but she maintains the disturbing belief that when she writes she manipulates her reader into believing she knows more than she does or has worked harder than she has. For her, writing is an institution-alized form of dishonesty. Intellectually, both women consider themselves not only beyond college writing but even beyond the AP course at the time they took it. Kit, for instance, saw herself as an exceptional student in an exceptional AP program. Both women, though clearly intelligent, seem to have internalized years of teachers', parents', and peers' admiration for their accomplishments to the point that they have made themselves into static objects of academic achievement.

Sense of Self

This group gives the strong and disturbing impression of being de-velopmentally stuck. While possessing much of the immaturity of the nonAP freshmen, these students lack their openness to change, their excitement, their malleability. On the other hand, while possessing the intelligence and articulateness of the AP students, they lack their tentativeness and readiness to embrace new challenges. Unlike their peers, these able and talented students seem prisoners of their own self-definition. Their self-centeredness locks them into a restrictive set of values and makes them resist the very experiences that might help them progress.

Moral Reasoning and Writing Development: Continuities and Discontinuities

Each of our interviews ended with an exercise in moral reasoning based on one of Kohlberg's hypothetical moral dilemmas. We wanted to see how patterns in the students' attitudes toward writing and learning correlate with their reasoning about moral dilemmas, which Perry and Kohlberg regard as the most challenging area of cognitive development. Here is the dilemma we posed:

> In Europe, a woman was near death from cancer. One drug might save her, a form of radium that a druggist in the same town had recently discovered. The druggist was charging $2,000, ten times what the drug cost him to make. The sick woman's husband, Heinz, went to everyone he knew to borrow the money, but he could get together only about

half of what it cost. He told the druggist that his wife was dying and asked him to sell it cheaper or let him pay later. But the druggist said no. The husband got desperate and broke into the man's store to steal the drug for his wife.

Should the husband have done that? Why?

The students' responses to Heinz's dilemma generally align with the patterns of each group's responses to our other questions. The responses span a continuum from viewing the situation as an interpersonal problem defined by the specific characters in the story to recognizing the dilemma as a model problem and analyzing the ethical principles involved. Although the regular freshmen demonstrate most consistently the lower stages of development, and sophomores who took college writing the highest stages of development, the responses also include interesting exceptions that highlight some developmental gaps in their discussions of writing and learning and underscore the messy and ongoing nature of cognitive development.

Regular freshmen make quick decisions that seem at first to signal a dualistic, rule-bound morality: yes, he loved his wife, or no, stealing is wrong. But then they qualify their initial responses with a number of hesitations that suggest an awareness of competing claims but without any system for ranking their validity. The freshmen sound genuinely confused by the situation, skeptical that we mean it when we tell them that we aren't looking for any one "right answer." Some of them try to supply details that would make the right answer clearer—if, for example, we knew that Heinz had tried to get a bank loan first—but they can only raise the questions, not suggest consistent ways to make sense of the conflicting data.

Jim is the most certain about what Heinz should have done: "The druggist should have done things differently, but Heinz shouldn't have broken in. What would I do? I'd try more avenues." He avoids Heinz's real dilemma by postponing it; Heinz should activate all kinds of practical plans for raising the money. Shelly is similarly confounded by the dilemma: "No, he shouldn't have. I can't see myself stealing, either. I don't *blame* him maybe; he was trying to save his wife." She doesn't want to condemn Heinz because she sympathizes with him, but she can't come up with a way around the fact that stealing is wrong.

Heather and Courtney both think that they would do what Heinz did, but they don't frame their explanation according to abstract, generalizable principles. Instead, they pick up where Shelly left off—with the sense that Heinz's love for his wife ought to make some difference in how we apply rules about stealing. Heather says, "You have to look at both their motives; I'd probably have done the same thing because it's a person I really love." Courtney agrees: "It's not right, but I'd probably do it. Well, I'd probably have found another way to get the money. The main point is I'd try to keep alive someone I love; he loves his wife."[3]

Their responses to Heinz, then, parallel their responses to questions about writing. Echoing the dualistic framework that Perry has described, they cling to faith in hard work and rule-governed behavior even while they admit that they have little or no idea about how and why the rules apply. Not surprisingly, they see rules, criteria for writing as well as laws and social conventions in life, as essentially arbitrary, unsystematic, "out there," alien. The rules are part of the environment from which they are trying to define their independent selves.

The AP freshmen respond at three different levels, placing them in a wide middle range that overlaps that of the regular freshmen on one end and the AP sophomores on the other. Jack and Don both respond absolutely that Heinz simply shouldn't have stolen the drug. Don says that even though the druggist is a jerk, "he has the right to be greedy because the drug is his." Jack offers several qualifications and concludes that Heinz probably didn't mean any harm, but returns several times to the conviction that "I couldn't do it; it's never okay to steal."

Sonia and Jessica are caught up in the emotional issues of the dilemma. Sonia: "I think he's right. Your emotions always take over." When asked if emotions justify any action, she explains that you have to decide based on how many people get hurt and the weight of majority opinion. Jessica's reasoning is a little less quantitative: "It comes down to emotion. People matter more. It's a matter of survival and of human love."

Carla, on the other hand, sees the problem within a much larger context of conflicting but ordered values. Her response delineates a hierarchy of competing claims: "From a social standpoint, no [he should not have stolen the drug]. From a personal standpoint, it's his wife; he loves her. From an ethical standpoint, human life is worth more than money." Unlike her peers, she draws real-life parallels to the pro-life/pro-choice debates, perhaps the most difficult test case she could pose herself. "Laws were developed to help people live their lives in a constructive, organized manner. . . . But sometimes there's a fine line that's a case of morality. I distinguish between laws and morality."

This group of freshmen seems to vary in their responses to Heinz as they vary in their attitudes toward writing. Don, a very proficient writer (AP exam score of 5), insists on clarity and correctness in writing and prefers classes where the lecture is presented in outline form; he also turns to absolute criteria in dissolving Heinz's dilemma. Jessica wants to find the person in writing, to hear originality and humor; she also thinks that people one loves matter more than rules about stealing, although she doesn't articulate well a principle that explains why beyond the emotional imperative. Carla, who speaks most clearly about the relative worth of ideas in writing, demonstrates the highest levels of intellectual and ethical development when she argues that laws and morality are separate systems and that "human life is worth more than money."

The sophomores who took college writing have again settled into a more consistent group. Although they recognize conflict, they aren't paralyzed by it as the freshmen tend to be. Rather, they rank the various claims under the primacy of life and justice. Citing the demands to avoid infringing on the rights of others and to enhance the majority welfare, characteristics of what Kohlberg calls "contractual legalistic orientation," Polly accepts and even plays with the conflicts: "He shouldn't have, but he couldn't do anything else, so he should have. When you're talking about human life. . . . You have to weight everything, who's at greater risk. Conflict of values comes into everything; education helps [resolve conflict] if it helps you to get the facts first and then to weigh risks and benefits."

The others respond less quantitatively. The principle of human life as the highest good explicitly dictates their resolutions of the conflict between law and morality. They also discuss the problem in general terms: Heinz's dilemma is not an isolated problem of one man who happens to love his wife but comes up short on cash; it's an example of a category of human problems in which "higher laws" are occasionally pitted against other generally acceptable laws. Mitch puts the conflict clearly, if a bit cynically: "Heinz is prosecutable, but he's morally correct. The law will probably protect the druggist, but Heinz has to do it." Daryl is a bit more expansive: "Laws were made to govern people, but sometimes you have to override them, bend them or void them. . . . Letting someone die when you could save them is like killing them."

Hong, like Carla, sees this dilemma as defining the relationship between law and morality: "Heinz is putting sacrifice and life above the consequences of the law. Being morally right goes above the law. There are higher laws! We're not talking about everybody making their own laws— but life and freedom are more important." Although he thinks he would have answered the same way even in junior high or high school, Hong now sees that Heinz's dilemma raises the kinds of questions that have occupied thinkers throughout history.

Beyond the consistency of their principled thinking about Heinz, what seems remarkable about this group of responses is the capacity for generalization it reveals. In all their responses to questions about the value of writing, of various learning environments, of a college education, these sophomores fit personal, idiosyncratic experience into larger patterns of meaning.

Finally, the AP students who elected to waive college writing again present us with the most widely divergent responses. The divergence in their responses to Heinz also parallels the divergence in their attitudes to writing and learning. Paul, the most utilitarian in his attitude toward the reasons for writing and the most insistent on correctness in evaluating good writing, judges Heinz's action on very utilitarian, mechanistic grounds. "Yes Heinz was right, I put my family first. People have their own priorities in life. Stealing is dishonest; if you steal, it lowers how much a person can trust you." We asked: If he'd stolen for a Porsche, would that still be okay? "Yes, if it didn't hurt someone. If he stole from John millionaire, okay. Their claims are all about equal, except if somebody's going to get hurt."

For Bob, who is most like the freshmen in his uncertainty about the purposes of writing and college beyond immediate survival, the Heinz dilemma is also confused in the same way it is for the nonAP freshmen. His response echoes Shelly's and Courtney's: "He was wrong for stealing. But he could be justified because his wife is going to die. How could you sit there and watch your wife die?"

Kit and Nila see writing as more than a simple mechanism for reporting information: it is also a way to find ideas and clarify thought. Similarly, they see the conflict in Heinz's situation as more than a matter of simple application of rules to determine right and wrong or of indistinguishable but equal claims. Nila says, "Life is worth more than money. But that's really an oversimplification. Society teaches us to always get something in return, like the pharmacist. But if you care about people, you can't worry about the cost." For Kit, Heinz's dilemma isn't even debatable; whether or not the person is a family member, "keeping people alive is the most important." Like Hong, she can relate Heinz's dilemma to the philosophical questions discussed in her other courses.

Our interviews don't tell us much about the mechanisms that coordinate writing development and cognitive development. That is, it's unclear if the occasional unevenness expressed between attitudes towards writing and towards learning or moral reasoning follows any predictable pattern. But it's very clear that writing development and cognitive development are related and that these relations have implications for pedagogy and curriculum in writing. At the very least, teachers may better understand that when students persistently translate inventive heuristics for problem solving in writing as hard and fast rules to follow, they are assimilating writing instruction into larger—but limited—cognitive schemes. More positively, teachers might rethink the sequence and shape of assignments to encourage room for growth in students' consciousness about writing as a way to deal with increasing complexity in their lives as thinking, choosing, acting people.

Conclusions and Implications

The implications of our study extend in two directions: back to the AP English classroom and forward to college writing. College students clearly value their AP experience, primarily for its enriched intellectual opportunities to read superior literature, to contemplate important ideas, to work at a faster pace, and to interact with equally capable peers. In fact, all the AP students we interviewed asserted that the learning opportunity (and possibly the social status of an advanced class), rather than the possibility of earning college credit, was the reason they chose the AP course.

As our profiles show, however, students' intellectual development and self-reported writing development continue dramatically throughout the first two years of college. Part of this continued intellectual development involves their engagement with the richer intellectual resources of the university, and part has to do with the emerging awareness of wider and more diverse domains of discourse. Despite some students' initial skepticism, the writing course showed them that fuller uses of language than their previous experience had suggested were possible and that these uses of language were closely linked to their expanded intellectual experience. A college writing course designed specifically for AP students seizes upon the unique developmental moment of the AP student's freshman year. Kohlberg and Turiel find that late adolescence (ages 15–19) is a transitional period for moral development. The danger is that the longer people remain at a particular stage of development, the harder it becomes for them to change: "They develop stronger screens or defenses against perception of those features in their social world which do not fit their level" (Kohlberg and Turiel 448). All good teaching probably follows the prescription that Kohlberg and Turiel recommend: to confront students with the limitations of their own reasoning and to help them resolve inconsistencies. However, a writing course for AP students is especially necessary to counter the expectation that college learning is familiar territory, an extension of the "college-level work" students have already begun in AP. "Change," as Kohlberg and Turiel phrase it, "is based on the [student's] active reorganization of his experience and is stimulated by conflicts" (454). The most significant effect of college writing instruction for the AP students in our sample was their realization of writing as a making of meaning. The expectation that students become masters not just of their subjects but of their thinking confronted them with the limitations of their former approaches to knowledge and challenged them to move to a higher plane of cognition. By requiring them to think about their thinking—as one must to be fully in control of one's writing—the writing course helped students take that step toward meta-thinking so crucial to higher-order development.

The writing course probably contributes to these changes in subtle ways that have to do with more than curriculum. Perry describes with eloquence the perils of higher intellectual development, particularly the grief that accompanies losses of a simpler world view and the isolation that is an inevitable part of forging individual commitments. He asserts that "a teacher's confirmatory offering of community is necessary even at the higher reaches of development" (109)—a community of able peers and accessible faculty that is often found in larger universities only in the writing class.

The differences between the AP students who took college writing and those who skipped it seem particularly telling in this respect: though cause and effect are difficult to establish, the students who avoided college writing also lacked the intellectual gusto of the others. They seemed less able to take charge of their education to make it a meaningful experience. Although many variables could contribute to this difference, other research on the effects of college suggests that something more than individual differences or chance is at work here. In a study of students' development during their first three years of college, Terenzini concludes that "traits that students bring with them to college do not appear to be significant influences on the amount of growth that students report during their college years" (190). Another study on students in honors programs reports the positive effects of the programs' smaller environment and the increased opportunities for interaction with stimulating peers and faculty both in and out of the classroom (Pflaum et al. 418). These factors help more able students make considerable gains in interpersonal and intellectual self-esteem and become more likely to find undergraduate education a rewarding and useful experience.[4] Although the students in our study were not part of a formal honors program, the community spirit characteristic of these programs was very much part of their writing course and is generally missing in the freshman courses typical of large research universities.

Former AP students make these intellectual gains only by overcoming much of what they have learned, at least about writing, in AP. All needed to overcome the message of the AP course that they were finished developing as writers—a message that the decisiveness of the AP exam and subsequent waivers from college writing requirements unfortunately reinforce. The students who avoided college writing clearly based their decision on that message, much to their detriment as writers and as learners, while the students who took college writing still had to resolve the puzzling contradictions between what they had been taught in AP and what they were experiencing in college.

One other student from our sample suggests something of the impact of the AP program on students' attitudes and self-perception. Darla, a sophomore, took AP English but received only a 2 on the exam, too low a score to allow her to exempt freshman writing. Based on her university placement essay, she enrolled in the regular freshman course. Like the other AP sophomores, she holds a fairly sophisticated view of college learning as a way to test and develop her convictions, and she values class discussion as "brain exercise" that makes course content "part of you." She reports that when she started college "I thought I was going to drown," but "now I've found not that it's too long but too short." In response to the Heinz dilemma, she asserts without hesitation, "I would have done it, no matter whether I should or not. You've got a human life there. The choice is between obeying the law and saving a life." In her attitudes toward writing, however, Darla resembles the regular freshmen. Good writing is clear, well-organized, and covers its main points thoroughly. There's not much difference in the quality of ideas; "it's how they're presented." Not surprisingly, she finds the evaluation of writing highly subjective and inconsistent even though she has considerable confidence in her ability to figure out "what a teacher wants in a paper."

Throughout the interview, Darla returned to her performance on the

AP exam to explain her sense of herself as a writer. Though in some ways she is among the most intellectually able of our sample, she accepts the 2 as clear evidence of her failure to "learn it all." Had she received a higher score, she believes she wouldn't have needed a writing course—even though she finds that her writing improved as a result of her 101 course and that her research project for the course was the best writing she ever produced. Darla is like all the AP students in her reverence for the AP exam as the absolute arbiter of students' abilities. Although Darla's subsequent placement in the freshman course was probably appropriate, the issue is really a larger one of how students are taught to interpret the meaning of both the course and the exam and, in her case, how those meanings are then embedded in a diminished self-concept that governs her sense of worth and capability. The AP exam certainly provides useful feedback to AP teachers, students, and program planners about what the program has accomplished. But whether intended or not the exam also serves variously as a gateway or barricade to subsequent educational choices and thus may affect students' development in more profound ways than it should.

Another lesson of AP English that college students must unlearn comes from the heavy emphasis on in-class writing. This practice virtually excludes experience in drafting, revising, and editing, and in the careful reflection and gradual development of ideas that the process approach to writing makes possible. The students we interviewed had become experts in Think/Write. Accordingly, their writing behavior as they began college was narrowly constricted, mechanistic, and formula-ridden, to the extent that the very considerable personal writing that several practiced on their own was often not even considered writing. Only one student, a woman who had attended a Catholic high school, reported an AP classroom experience that was not heavily dependent upon weekly in-class drills for the AP exam. For those who had attended public schools, repeated practice tests, in some cases openly proclaimed as necessary to keep up the school's reputation of having a high success rate on the exam, seemed to be the standard mode of instruction. As a result, the most able students had acquired the most restrictive attitudes and practices concerning writing.

While college writing courses should be designed to take advantage of the enriched background of AP students, the AP course itself must also undergo change. The students we interviewed consistently reported that their AP course taught them how to produce New Critical explications and essays about theme. These may be admirable aims for a literature course, but they don't adequately prepare students for the range of reading and writing that their college years and later professional and public life will demand. (Indeed, current trends in literary studies question the adequacy even for literature courses of New Critical readings alone because of their disregard for cultural, historic, social, economic, and political contexts.) An AP course that attempts to prepare students to be careful, critical readers and writers rather than apprentice literary critics should include a much wider range of reading material and writing assignments. Such a course would also make them better readers of literature.

AP students could certainly learn more about writing if the AP course incorporated writing throughout the year, not only to demonstrate accomplishment but also to stimulate learning and engage students in a variety of rhetorical situations. That is, AP classes might engage students in *writing* rather than in *writing the AP exam*. The students we interviewed are quite certain they could have done just as well on the exam with less concentration on it in class. AP students must have opportunities to write both in and out of class, to compose both spontaneously and in successive drafts, and to complete both graded and ungraded writing activities. The notion that writing is a 50-minute event occasionally completed by typing the "final copy" is an unnecessary, unfortunate, and probably an unintended by-product of too many AP English classes.

A more satisfying curriculum, one that would predict and encourage development in writing, would include a wide variety of writing activities carried out for a range of purposes. For instance, students who keep a reading log or reaction journal will not only informally practice writing, but will read and discuss a text more actively. Having several students read from their logs at the beginning of a discussion will provide a variety of reactions to a poem, an event in a novel, a news story, a government document, an essay, or a magazine editorial. Their reactions also raise topics for more extended thinking and focused writing. These writings then become the raw material for more open-ended explorations of how readers make meaning from texts.

In closing, let us frame the issue of AP students' continued writing development in the broadest way. Our research provides strong confirmation of Piaget's interactionist perspective on the nature/nurture question, in this case the interaction of self and school environment in writing development. As the sharp differences among the profiles show, students certainly bring their own values and expectations to bear on the meanings they make of their experience. The regular freshmen make of their writing class and their college experience something very different from what the AP students do. On the other hand, what we as teachers communicate by way of our curriculum, our course requirements, our attitudes and theories about writing, and our feedback to students also becomes embedded in the meanings students make of their studies and their lives. Whether students see continued emphasis in writing as a worthwhile educational choice results from a complicated interplay of their high school experience, their university environment, and the expectations they hold for themselves. We begin to see an infinite but not unalterable regression of educational experience determining self-definition determining educational experience determining self-definition.

Although in one sense this is an all-too-obvious conclusion, in another sense it confronts us with some realities of teaching that may be discomfiting and that certainly carry significant implications. When we teach writing, we are teaching more than either a reductive set of skills or an expanded way of learning. We are also unavoidably teaching attitudes, self-perceptions, and possibilities. The implicit definitions we attach to words like "student" or "writer" have very significant and very different effects on students. The best possible outcome of the AP experience is for college freshmen to expect and look forward to new intellectual challenges and continued growth through writing, to open up possibilities rather than close them down. Jessica's conclusions about the effects of her college writing course should apply equally to AP English: "Writing is really important . . . and really helped me just to think about things you've always thought about and wonder if that's really the way they are, just the things that we've been taught in school. You think a lot [when you write] about things you take for granted." Though we may never know exactly how cognitive development and writing development are causally related, students' discoveries and rediscoveries of the constructive relationship between them is a powerful testament to the wisdom of curriculum structures that keep the two intimately tied together.

Notes

1. See, for example, Patricia Bizzell's "William Perry and Liberal Education" and "What Happens When Basic Writers Come to College?"

2. Readers who wish to obtain more detailed background in theories of cognitive development than we can provide here might consult William Perry, *Forms of Intellectual and Ethical Development in the College Years: A Scheme,* and Lawrence Kohlberg, *Collected Papers on Moral Development and Moral Education.*

3. Carol Gilligan's extensive research on women's development concludes that women conceptualize moral dilemmas like Heinz's as problems arising "from conflicting responsibilities rather than from competing rights" (19). The concern for relationships that Gilligan finds central to women's morality we heard as often from the male students as from the female students we interviewed. In neither men nor women, though, could we argue for an ethics of caring over rights. The students who defended Heinz on the basis of "emotion" or "love" appealed to his happiness or briefly to the supremacy of human love, but little more. On the other hand, the sophomore women quite consistently cast the problem in terms that Perry and Kohlberg would exemplify as the highest stages of moral and intellectual development.

Our study didn't aim to make gender-based distinctions, although we did interview approximately equal numbers of men and women in each group. A few qualifications about our limited sample seem in order, nevertheless. We interviewed mostly students who had proven themselves academic successes, those students, that is, most likely to conform to mainstream—male—intellectual values. We also provided them with a context that may have reinforced their sense that this academic problem calls for an exercise in logic.

4. See also, Alexander Astin, *Four Critical Years* and "Student Involvement: A Developmental Theory for Higher Education."

Works Cited

Astin, Alexander. *Four Critical Years.* San Francisco: Jossey-Bass, 1977.
———. "Student Involvement: A Developmental Theory for Higher Education." *Journal of College Student Personnel* 25 (1984): 297–308.

Basseches, Michael. *Dialectical Thinking and Adult Development.* Norwood, NJ: Ablex, 1984.

Bereiter, Carl. "Development in Writing." *Cognitive Processes in Writing.* Ed. Lee W. Gregg and Erwin Steinberg. Hillsdale, NJ: Erlbaum, 1980. 73–93.

Bizzell, Patricia. "What Happens When Basic Writers Come to College?" *College Composition and Communication* 37 (1986): 294–301.

————. "William Perry and Liberal Education." *College English* 46 (1984): 447–54.

Colomb, Greg. "Tacit Expectations and Student Writing: A Comparative Examination of Disciplinary Conventions in Argumentation." Presentation at the University of Chicago Institute on Cognitive Strategies and Writing. Chicago, 10 May 1976.

Freedman, Aviva, and Ian Pringle. "Writing in the College Years: Some Indices of Growth." *College Composition and Communication* 31 (1980): 311–24.

Gilligan, Carol. *In a Different Voice: Psychological Theory and Women's Development.* Cambridge: Harvard UP, 1982.

Hays, Janice. "The Development of Discursive Maturity in College Writers." *The Writer's Mind: Writing as a Mode of Thinking.* Ed. Janice Hays, Phyllis Roth, Jon Ramsey, and Robert Foulke. Urbana: NCTE, 1983. 127–44.

Kohlberg, Lawrence. *Collected Papers on Moral Development and Moral Education.* Cambridge: Moral Education and Research Foundation, Harvard University Graduate School of Education, 1973.

Kohlberg, Lawrence, and Elliot Turiel. "Moral Development and Moral Education." *Psychology and Educational Practice.* Ed. G. Lesser. New York: Scott, 1971. 410–65.

Kurfiss, Joanne. "Sequentiality and Structure in a Cognitive Model of College Student Development." *Developmental Psychology* 13 (1977): 565–71.

Perry, William. "Cognitive and Ethical Growth: The Making of Meaning." *The Modern American College.* Ed. Arthur Chickering and Associates. San Francisco: Jossey-Bass, 1981. 76–116.

————. *Forms of Intellectual and Ethical Development in the College Years: A Scheme.* New York: Holt, 1968.

Pflaum, Susanna, et al. "The Effects of Honors College Participation on Academic Performance during the Freshman Year." *Journal of College Student Personnel* 26 (1985): 414–19.

Piaget, Jean. *Genetic Epistemology.* Trans. Eleanor Duckworth. New York: Norton, 1970.

Scardamalia, Marlene. "How Children Cope with the Cognitive Demands of Writing." *Writing: The Nature, Development, and Teaching of Written Communication.* Ed. C. H. Frederiksen, et al. Hillsdale, NJ: Erlbaum, 1982. 81–103.

Terenzini, Patrick, et al. "Influences on Students' Perceptions of Their Personal Development during the First Three Years of College." *Research in Higher Education* 21 (1984): 178–94.

3

The Politics of Advanced Placement English

JAMES B. VOPAT
Carroll College

Vopat analyzes several political concerns relevant to AP English, including the influence of ETS, the difficulty of applying standardized tests to English, problems in grading the AP exams, the negative effects of economic incentives, partisanship, and questions of consumer rights.

When Robert Jameson, the "great architect" of Advanced Placement, writes, "In this universe there never was and never will be anything like the Advanced Placement Reading!" the exclamation point reverberates on a number of levels (32). Because of its phenomenal growth, the Advanced Placement program and test profoundly affect schools, colleges, and definitions of learning. This is especially true for the largest of the Advanced Placement programs, English. When those fifty-thousand-plus students take the annual Advanced Placement test in English, they are, among other things, testifying to the existence of a nationwide high school English curriculum. Because this high school curriculum is supposed to be the same as the introductory college English curriculum, the grading of the AP English test also enacts a nationwide definition of what students are supposed to learn in freshman English.

Advanced Placement promotional brochures indicate that earning the required grade on an AP exam carries the possibilities of six to eight semester hours of credit. This means that the cumulative credit potential of the yearly AP English test alone is 300,000 to 400,000 semester hours of college English credit—so there are definite economic and staffing consequences at the college level. Complicating these complications is that most of the information, statistical data, and validity studies concerning AP English have been generated and published by AP English. And standing behind, beneath, over, and around it all are three letters that have become the focus of an increasingly heated debate: ETS.

Political Issue #1: The Educational Testing Service

ETS, the Educational Testing Service, and its programs have lost a degree of public trust during the last decade. The public has become aware of serious errors in the writing and scoring of test questions as well as irregularities in the reporting of test results. Against the vigorous opposition of ETS, the state of New York enacted a truth-in-testing law in 1980. Two recent books, *The Nader Report on ETS*, by Allan Nairn, and *None of the Above*, by David Owen, accuse ETS of cultural bias, abuse of power, deception, cover-up, ageism, classism, racism, elitism, opportunism, incompetence, upholding the status quo, monopolistic practices, mental management, consumer fraud, economic exploitation of students, corporate arrogance, false advertising, lying, manipulation of facts, and strong-arm tactics.

The president of the National Organization for Women, Eleanor Smeal, has recently urged public demonstrations and the filing of lawsuits against ETS in order to force it to eliminate the alleged sexual bias of its examinations (Jaschik 30). "I do not for one minute believe," Smeal states, "that these people don't know their tests are biased." In September 1986, 36 researchers complained to the federal government that ETS had deliberately denied them access to publications that criticized the standardized-testing industry (Wilson 11). David Owen states that ETS is "probably the most powerful unregulated monopoly in America," and that "people who wish to advance in all walks of life have no choice but to pay its fees and take its tests . . . in order to pass various checkpoints in America's social hierarchy" (7). Such an omnipresent connection with ETS is, in fact, one of the goals of the corporation. A confidential 1972 ETS study, for example, describes the testing system as extending to "the millions of adolescents whose course through school and into jobs and careers is now daily affected by what does or doesn't happen to them through testing, and the millions of adults who may increasingly be affected by testing that can extend through the balance of life" (Nairn 44).

It is, I think, difficult for the individual teacher to gauge the influence of ETS or sort out and evaluate the various charges and countercharges. It is important to realize, however, that the Advanced Placement examination is the sixth largest revenue source of ETS (Nairn 488), and how you regard AP may or may not be predicated on how you feel about the Service. Perhaps who owns the store doesn't matter. Do I boycott Coors beer because the company has been charged with unfair labor practices, or do I buy the beer because I like its taste? But, of course, AP English is not a beer; it is a standardized test.

Political Issue #2: Standardized Testing

The Advanced Placement English examinations require the student to answer a series of multiple-choice questions and to write several essays of various lengths. In the Advanced Placement examinations in English Literature and Composition, the multiple-choice questions test the student's reading of selected literary passages; the examination in English Language and Composition employs multiple-choice questions that test the student's skill at recasting sentences and analyzing the rhetoric of prose passages. (See Sylvia Holladay's chapter in this collection.) The Nairn/Nader Report on ETS questions the validity, value, and objectivity of these kinds of multiple-choice formats: "The evidence indicates that multiple-choice test-taking is a specialized kind of game which rewards certain kinds of people and penalizes others for reasons apart from their ability to handle words and numbers" (83). The "kinds of people" multiple-choice testing rewards tend to come from higher income families and from schools where testing is a way of life. The "kinds of people" multiple-choice tests penalize tend to be people who think guessing is wrong. This game-like aspect of multiple choice is (unconsciously?) reinforced in AP promotional pamphlets that extol "time and options *won*" (emphasis added) through Advanced Placement scores (*Sophomore Standing* 1).

David Owen has pointed out that the word *objective* can "apply only to the mechanical grading process" of verbal multiple-choice questions such as those that comprise the first parts of Advanced Placement English. Verbal multiple-choice questions themselves are "written, compiled, keyed, and interpreted by highly selective human beings" (33). Owen has done much to demonstrate how such multiple-choice questions can be ambiguous, and how the designated correct answer isn't always correct.

Let's try a typical multiple-choice question from an AP English Language and Composition examination (1982):

> *Directions:* Revise each of the following sentences according to the directions which follow it. Rephrase the sentence mentally to save time, making notes in your examination booklet if you wish. Although the directions may at times require you to change

the relationship between parts of the sentence or to make slight changes in other ways, *make only those changes that the directions require.*

Below each sentence and its directions are listed words or phrases that may occur in your revised sentence. When you have thought out a good sentence, look in the choices (A) through (E) for the word or entire phrase that is included in your revised sentence, and blacken the corresponding space on the answer sheet.

10. Because Cesar Chavez is deeply concerned about migrant workers, he has spent much of his life fighting to improve their condition. Substitute *deep* for *deeply*

    A. over
    B. with
    C. toward
    D. at
    E. for

The correct answer, please, and don't forget you are being timed and that you are to "make only those changes that the directions require." When you substitute *deep* for *deeply* you are in a terrible mess that none of the multiple choice answers will clean up. The supposed "correct" answer "E" comes out reading: "Because Cesar Chavez is deep concerned for migrant workers, he has spent much of his life fighting to improve their condition." But, of course, it has to become "Because *of* Cesar Chavez's deep concern for migrant workers, he has . . . ." Notice, however, that the directions specifically instruct the student not to make these kinds of changes. The addition of "of" and the changing of "is" into the possessive "Chavez's" is certainly more than "slight." Technically, there is no correct answer to Question #10.

Whether Advanced Placement should hinge on such a multiple-choice dilemma as the Cesar Chavez question poses is certainly open to debate. Indeed, inasmuch as the Advanced Placement examination in English promises to be measuring the learning objectives of the nation's freshman English programs, one must also raise the issue of whether the skills needed to figure out the Cesar Chavez question are really what most freshman English curricula are about. As David Foster demonstrates in this text, teachers who have become philosophically committed to the process approach to learning and writing will find the nature and grading of the Advanced Placement English examinations difficult to defend. All multiple-choice questions are, by definition, product- rather than process-based.

There is, of course, a free-response section of the English examination, containing several questions designed to test the student's mastery of "various rhetorical modes" and ability to use "forms of discourse effectively." Leaving aside the question of whether rhetorical modes and forms of discourse remain the primary concern of freshman English courses, let's look at a sample free-response essay question:

> Question 3: A recurring theme in literature is "the classic war between a passion and responsibility." For instance, a personal cause, a love, a desire for revenge, a determination to redress a wrong, or some other emotion or drive may conflict with moral duty.
>
> Choose a literary work in which a character confronts the demands of a private passion that conflicts with his or her responsibilities. In a well-written essay show clearly the nature of the conflict, its effects upon the character, and its significance to the work.

In a paper presented at the 1982 meeting of the Conference on College Composition and Communication, former AP English reader and college professor Tom Benediktsson maintained that the wording of essay questions such as this contains obvious cues for the initiated AP student. The rewarded response to Question #3 is obviously going to be a five-paragraph theme with an introduction that restates the question, three middle paragraphs that (1) state the nature of the conflict, (2) talk about effect on character, and (3) discuss significance to the work. The fifth and concluding paragraph will briefly restate the three points. Much more than a simple essay question, #3 contains a specific organizational structure that will necessarily be successful. All the AP student really has to do is fill in the blanks. Instead of leading the AP candidate into mechanistic, formulaic response, why doesn't the question require individual thought, direction, and organizational principle? The guidelines of AP essay questions are written in such a way that students are directly discouraged from writing and thinking for themselves.

Political Issue #3: Coaching

In order to take full advantage of the cues written into the directions of Question #3, someone needs to point them out. In reading through the *Advanced Placement Course Description: English* pamphlets, I can't help wondering to what extent high school AP courses teach the annual test rather than critical verbal skills that a typical college course should be teaching. Is it learning or coaching when AP students study sample test questions and scoring guides? AP courses are promoted to be "special college-level learning experiences." Yet, when a former AP English high school student writes that her English class studied the grading rubric, rehearsed test strategy, read sample essays sent by ETS, and practiced timed writing on "specific topics" (Leman), she is not describing a "college-level" learning experience but a "special" coaching session in preparation for scoring high on the test.

There are a number of political pressures that encourage the Advanced

Placement high school instructor to coach rather than teach. First of all, the effectiveness of the classroom instruction is measured by the numbers of 5s, 4s, 3s, 2s, and 1s scored at the annual AP grading. Some school systems penalize AP teachers if a certain percentage of their students score below acceptable levels on the AP test. Parents of students are led to believe that participation in high school AP programs will result in the economic savings advanced college placement affords—or, as the AP promotional brochure states it, "If you're granted a full year of college credit, the savings could be from $3,000 to $16,000" (*Some Questions and Answers* 2). Parents quickly criticize the AP program if these economic promises do not materialize.

If the high school student performs poorly on the yearly AP exam, who is going to be blamed for this failure? Not the student because the AP student has already been designated as gifted. Not the test because it has been enshrined by the College Board and is replete with "quality controls." Indeed, it would be highly unrealistic for the AP teacher not to have the students run through the rubrics, memorize basic test strategies, scrimmage some sample test questions, and replay sample essays from the previous year's exam. (John Iorio discusses this problem at length in another chapter of this book.)

Political Issue #4: Elitism

Approximately one-fourth of the nation's secondary schools offer some type of Advanced Placement English course work. In general, these secondary schools tend to attract students from higher rather than lower income brackets. Economic profiles of the annual fifty-thousand-plus AP English candidates are not available, but because the program is designed specifically for college-bound students, it predominates and flourishes in affluent schools and indeed is especially prevalent in private preparatory schools and academies.

In AP promotional literature, the emphasis is always on the best: the best teachers, the best courses, the "very best and most talented high school students in the nation" (Main 4). AP is a type of tracking program—perhaps the largest in the nation—and, as such, becomes part of the general debate as to whether it is educationally sound to separate out special groups of students for special treatment and course work. As one AP high school student expresses it, "We were just one tight little group. . . . We got to think too much of ourselves and didn't have much contact with any nonAP students. I think it would have been better if we *had* for our own, you know, social development. And what about the way the other kids felt?" (Casserly 3). Unlike the privileged AP students, the "other kids" will not have the subsequent option of completing the four-year college degree in three years.

AP teachers are also privileged. Their students and their courses are defined as superior to other high school classes. It is a comparison that AP actively encourages: the AP course "is usually challenging and stimulating and—compared to other high school courses—often takes more time, requires more work . . . and goes into greater depth" (*Some Questions and Answers* 1). In addition, AP teachers are supposed to be given decreased course loads, thus creating a system of academic elitism within the high school teaching staff as well.

Political Issue #5: The Grading of the AP Examinations in English

The issues surrounding the grading of the AP English exam involve more than a dispute concerning what kind of learning is being measured. The AP English examination has perhaps the highest candidate success rates of any large-scale test in history. According to yearly grade distributions of the ETS, 96 to 97 percent of all students taking the AP English test emerge with a scoring designation of at least "possibly qualified" (the score of 2 or higher). The significance of this extremely high qualifying rate is that it marks a decided shift of emphasis from the original intent of the Advanced Placement program and test. What began in the late 1950s as a "concern for the academic progress of the gifted student" (Jameson 1) has become a reward system that validates mediocrity.

In the pamphlet entitled *Grading the Advanced Placement Examination in English Language and Composition*, Carl Haag writes: "It appears that in many subjects an AP grade of 2 most often corresponds to a grade of C at college; this fact suggests that AP candidates with grades of 2 should be given special consideration to make certain they are appropriately placed and credited for their achievement" (22). Only in the world of AP is the grade of "C" considered to be an "achievement." From my own three-year experience with AP scoring sessions, I maintain that by almost every academic standard—including the grading rubric—the grade of 2 is not an "achievement" but positive proof of the need for freshman English. A grade of 2 means that the AP candidate has answered fewer than half of the multiple-choice questions correctly, and that the candidate's writing is specifically characterized by the official rubric to be "weak," "distorted," "unspecific," "disorganized," and "poorly written." Even the AP English candidate achieving the unqualified "qualified" score of 3 will have missed half of the multiple-choice answers and written an essay formally defined as lacking in detail, support, and appropriate focus.

Even if we accept Haag's AP 2/grade of C correlation, it is clear that the focus of the AP program has shifted far below the needs of the gifted student. Do we seriously believe that the C student is going to actively pursue an advanced sequence of college English courses? As professor Marvin Gettleman states: "ETS would be doing the colleges a great service if it gave us hard data on whether AP students in fact use their exemption . . . to go on to take advanced electives . . . or do they mainly use the AP process as a means of escaping the minimal requirements of a liberal education?"(28).

The annual six-day scoring session of AP English itself is invariably described in superlative terms by employees of ETS and Advanced Placement. Readers are "paragons" of intellect and energy; the rapport between table leaders and readers is "impressive"; evenings between scoring sessions are filled with intellectual "discussion of one's field with teachers from all over the country." Teachers like to return year after year to the readings "because they lose their school/college badges. . . . The sheepskin curtain is down. I have sat in on and learned from many rewarding informal talk sessions after hours" (Jameson 7–11).

To an extent, Jameson's claims are true, and the AP reading marks one of those rare opportunities to sit down with various school and college colleagues and discuss the qualities of good student writing. However, such discussion had better agree with the stipulations of the already-formulated grading rubric, or no matter how enriching a time was had, you won't be asked back next year. Neither do all readers discover the six-day AP English scoring session to be as intellectually satisfying as promised. As former AP English grader Robert Crosman describes it,

> At the first I warded off brain-death by collecting "howlers" from the student-essays and stringing them together in a parody essay of my own. Then I'd sneak off "to the men's room" every hour or so and play Space Invaders, a video game that in any other setting I have always considered to be monotony itself; and finally I amused myself by writing a brilliant essay in the blank exam book of a student too demoralized even to try an answer. . . . The sad thing is that this bunch of hundreds of high school and college teachers accepted it all so meekly, eagerly even. But then we were all survivors of the College Boards ourselves, and had reasons to approve of the ends, if not the means. In fact, given the mission—to test thousands of elite high school students for possible college credit . . . could we think of a better way to produce that result? I couldn't. It's the project itself that is the hustle. (Owen 27)

I myself witnessed very bizarre and questionable grading practices in my three-year employ as an AP English grader. Movies were substituted for books; *The Hobbit* was officially acclaimed a "work of recognized literary merit"; there were rounds of peek-a-boo scoring, systematic coercion to inflate grading scores, and an essay-grading regimen so debilitating that by the fifth or sixth day many student essays were not read thoroughly.

But the most surprising thing to me about the grading of the AP English examinations was that the percentage of 2s, 3s, 4s, and 5s were figured out *in advance* of the actual essay grading, regardless of substandard performance on specified questions of the test. My assumption previous to becoming involved in the AP reading was that the AP test was a means of measuring skill and knowledge. That was before I heard about the famous "cutoff sessions" in which, after a sample of booklets has been scored, the students' "grades are cut off on lines to indicate the proportion of 5s, 4s, 3s, 2s, and

1s, to be reported" (Jameson 13). It may be statistically interesting, but it is academically questionable to decide in advance how many students will score a 3 or a 4 on a given examination. This perhaps explains why the success rate of AP English invariably hits the 96th percentile. To what extent does the grading of the AP English examinations actually serve but to validate the high school program it is supposed to measure?

Political Issue #6: Howlers

Many AP English graders collect "howlers" from the student essays they read. Even Jameson publishes a page of them in his informal history of the AP readings. An example of one of Jameson's favorite howlers is:

> Elizabeth, the heroine of the *The Scarlet Letter* by Jane Austen, committed adultery with the local doctor while her husband was away, was made to wear a sweater with a scarlet A branded on it, and produced a son who lived in sin. (11)

Crosman offers this one:

> A character who I feel was definitely evil and immoral was the captain of the whaling ship, in the suspense filled story by Charles Dickens, *Moby Dick*. (Owen 28)

For some time I have wondered about the nature of the comedy of such howlers. Tortured prose is not in and of itself funny. But when it is a learned mechanism with the blanks of the clichés filled in incorrectly—then it is, as Jameson puts it, "hilarious." For me, howlers represent a truth concerning much of the AP student essay writing. Given the time constraints of this type of standardized test, writing by necessity becomes mechanistic. Is there really a difference between howlers and the following cloned opening sentences from the student essays used to "check" readers' scoring patterns in 1979?

- Othello could be considered evil or immoral on the basis of his actions.
- Joe Christmas, one of the main characters in William Faulkner's *Light in August*, may be considered evil or immoral on the basis of his actions alone.
- Judging strictly on the basis of actions, Hester Prynne, the main character in *The Scarlet Letter*, might be considered evil or immoral.
- In Flaubert's *Madame Bovary* the character of Charles Bovary's wife, Emma, may be considered evil or immoral.
- Macbeth, the main character in Shakespeare's play of that name, may be considered evil or immoral on the basis of actions alone.

The difference between howlers and these encouraged responses is that in the blanks of the latter, the learned clichés are filled in in a way that draws less attention. Much of AP English essay writing is the type of prose George Orwell described in "Politics and the English Language"—prose consisting "less and less of *words* chosen for their meaning, and more and more of *phrases* tacked together like sections of a prefabricated hen house."

Whether howlers are a function of AP courses, social pressures, or test anxiety, they are a particular genre of AP writing, and they echo a certain student cynicism about the testing situation students have found themselves caught in. When in doubt, shove any book, character, or author into the learned mechanism and hope it runs. This undertone of cynicism extends to the graders of the Advanced Placement examinations as well. At the conclusion of each year's six-day scoring session, AP English readers put on an evening of entertainment. These skits involve songs and caricatures directed at AP students and different aspects of the reading. Here is one such song, first recited from the stage and then sung *en masse:*

> ONE, an unredeemed score.
> TWO, a waste of thirty bucks.
> THREE & FOUR are topical.
> FIVE is good but still it sucks.
> SIX will barely cover the spread.
> SEVEN will make your parents glad.
> EIGHT doth justify the bread.
> and NINE's a perfect score!
>   Score, Score, Score!
>
> [repeat *ad nauseam*]

This grading-rubric song was a great hit with readers, and as I heard it sung late into the Trenton night, I couldn't help but think that on some level it expressed a truth about the 135,000 essays just read and graded. Condensed in this one song are the unspoken realities of AP English: money, parental pressures, the meaninglessness of the grading levels, the willingness to write anything to *Score,* and the devaluation of literature and writing.

Political Issue #7: Double Credit

I have yet to hear a logical explanation of why AP students should receive double credits. Even if we agree in principle to the concept of advanced college placement, why is it necessary to award credits as well? High school students receive high school credits for taking the Advanced Placement English course. And then, on the basis of the AP test, they receive college credits again for the same course. If you carry Advanced Placement credit logic to its ultimate end, it would be possible to test out of college altogether and just receive the diploma by return mail. Let's try an experiment and continue Advanced Placement as it is, but stop awarding college credits. What would happen? My feeling is that the program would dismantle itself because the primary motivation of students is not the opportunities for advanced learning but the credits.

Political Issue #8: Money

The nonprofit status of ETS has become increasingly controversial, and as Marvin Gettleman points out, "AP testing is a million dollar business" (27). Actually, it is a multimillion dollar business. The economic issues surrounding AP English cut in a number of directions. Through a qualifying score on the AP English exam, the college-bound student can receive 6 to 8 semester hours or 10 to 12 quarter hours of college credit. Qualified scores on three or more AP exams can result in a full year of college credit. The minimal fee of the exam ($53 in 1986) makes Advanced Placement financially attractive—especially to students and parents troubled by the rising cost of a college education. Not surprisingly, the promotional materials for Advanced Placement stress economic incentive as much as academic enrichment. There are also economic incentives from the college point of view. "Colleges like the AP Program," David Owen writes, "because it enables them to give the equivalent of scholarships without spending any money" (29). The economic incentive is not so apparent from the AP grader perspective. The grading stipend works out to about $6.50 per hour. Academics are, in general, underpaid, but considering the nature of the AP reading and the millions of dollars of revenue it generates for ETS, $6.50 per hour comes close to exploitation. The most bitterly ironic economic consequence of all, however, is that credit-by-testing programs have caused a loss of college-level teaching positions. As more and more AP students use the exam as a way of simply gaining credit and sophomore standing, fewer courses and professors will be needed.

Much of the problem lies with the colleges themselves. Few college English faculties review the AP essay questions or concern themselves with matters of credit-AP score correlations. Few colleges or universities have guidelines for evaluating and monitoring AP exam grades. Few college English faculty actively participate in or have concrete knowledge of high school Advanced Placement programs. Many of the crucial Advanced Placement credit decisions are made not through academic departments but through the Admissions Department of the college or university.

Political Issue #9: Partisanship

The very same agency (AP-ETS) that sets out to design and promote AP high school English programs also designs the annual AP test and also determines the AP grade distributions and also conducts the validity studies that serve to justify the AP test and AP programs. This is a circle of self-interest, and ETS has economic resources great enough to generate all kinds of self-justifying statistical data. Unless you yourself have had some firsthand experience with Advanced Placement English, it is almost impossible to find data that support less than a "Hosanna!" One of the most serious practical problems for a critic of Advanced Placement English is that there exists no body of independent statistical data. If criticizing AP English is like David challenging Goliath, then it is David without even a slingshot handy.

Political Issue #10: Consumer Rights

The Nairn/Nader Report on ETS maintains that all ETS testing programs raise significant issues of consumer rights:

> The Educational Testing Service has created a marketplace for its services. But it is not a marketplace characterized by traditional checks and balances between sellers and consumers. It is a marketplace without adequate information, choice, competition or public safeguards (rights and remedies) for the consumers of the tests. (260)

While the ETS maintains that "it compels no one" to use its services, it does enjoy an absolute monopoly in advanced placement. AP candidates are not so much captives of ETS as those students whose SAT or LSAT or GRE scores are a prerequisite for admission to college or professional schools. But there are, nevertheless, consumer issues involved with AP. Advanced Placement test answers are not protected at the annual scoring sessions— many are used as samples for "checkings" with 300 to 400 copies made, distributed, and ultimately spread throughout the land. "Howlers" from student examination booklets are publicly ridiculed and have even been published by Advanced Placement in Jameson's booklet, *An Informal History of the AP Readings 1956–76.*

Validity studies are conducted with clear disregard for individual student rights. An AP validity study published in *College English*, for example, had 21 freshman English teachers administer a shortened version of the AP composition test to their freshman students. The 21 English teachers were explicitly directed *not* to identify the purpose or nature of the examination, and students were not informed that their responses and scores were to be sent on to ETS headquarters in Princeton. The 21 teachers were further instructed to misrepresent to their students how the test would affect their grades: "In order to provide motivation for the students, instructors were asked to inform them that the validity test would count as part of their final grade" (Modu and Wimmers 611). This is an abusive situation, but because AP-ETS is the originator and evaluator of its products, there is no realistic viable avenue for redress.

Political Issue #11: It Doesn't Matter

I have no illusions that Advanced Placement English is going to change or that it will become less popular. Standardized testing and ETS are issues of today, but they are the definition of the academic tomorrow. AP exemplifies the problems of standardized testing, period. AP is not the cause; it is the consequence. ETS—the "corporation that makes up minds," as Allan Nairn aptly puts it—is extremely wealthy and powerful, and its influence pervasive. As I finish writing this chapter, I have serious doubts that it will be published. But don't shout. ETS is our employer of the future; standardized testing our teaching methodology.

Works Cited

Casserly, Patricia Lund. *What College Students Say about Advanced Placement.* N.p.: College Entrance Examination Board, 1968.

Gettleman, Marvin E. "Foxes and Chickens: Advanced Placement History and ETS." *OAH Newsletter* Aug. 1983: 27–28.

Haag, Carl H. "Comparing the Performance of College Students and Advanced Placement Candidates on AP Examinations." *Grading the Advanced Placement Examination in English Language and Composition.* Ed. Paul Smith. N.p.: College Entrance Examination Board, 1983. 22–23.

Jameson, Robert. *An Informal History of the AP Readings 1956–76.* N.p.: College Entrance Examination Board, 1980.

Jaschik, Scott. "Feminist Leader Urges Critics of Tests to File Lawsuits and Stage Protests." *Chronicle of Higher Education* 17 Dec. 1986: 30.

Leman, Dorothy. Letter to the author. 29 August 1981.

Main, Fred C. *College Board News* Sept. 1979: 4.

Modu, Christopher C., and Eric Wimmers. "The Validity of the Advanced Placement English Language and Composition Examination." *College English* 43 (1981): 609–20.

Nairn, Allan. *The Reign of ETS: The Corporation that Makes Up Minds.* The Ralph Nader Report on the Educational Testing Service. Washington, DC: Nairn, 1980.

Owen, David. *None of the Above: Behind the Myth of Scholastic Aptitude.* Boston: Houghton, 1985.

Some Questions and Answers about the Advanced Placement Program 1986–1987. N.p.: College Entrance Examination Board, 1986.

Sophomore Standing through Advanced Placement. N.p.: College Entrance Examination Board, 1981.

Wilson, Robin. "Researchers Say They Have Been Denied Access to Critiques of Standardized Tests." *Chronicle of Higher Education* 10 Sept. 1986: 11–13.

4

AP and
the Problems of Testing

SYLVIA A. HOLLADAY
St. Petersburg Junior College

This chapter examines the problems of testing specific to AP English. The author summarizes the professional literature on testing in English, describes the two AP English exams and the evaluation procedures for each, and evaluates and poses some questions about the exams and their impact.

Just as teaching literature and composition presents its own special problems, so does assessment in these areas. The problems of testing in English—from reliability and validity to cognitive emphasis and cultural bias—have been well documented. In the Advanced Placement English program, these problems are intensified by the purpose and scope of the program. The underlying premise of the Advanced Placement program is that "college-level courses can be successfully taught to high school students by high school teachers on high school campuses" (*School Administrator's Guide* 2); thus, the purpose of the exams is to certify that AP students can perform satisfactorily at the college level. That is, the exams must certify both mastery of skills and equivalence of performance. This purpose is particularly significant because of the scope of the program: in 1985, 81,568 high school students took the AP English tests, and over 1,600 colleges and universities accepted AP exam grades to grant college credit.

This chapter examines the problems of testing in AP English. It consists of three sections: the first summarizes literature on testing in English, emphasizing problems pertinent to AP testing; the second briefly describes the two AP English examinations and evaluation procedures; the third discusses special problems of testing in AP English and poses questions about the exams and their impact.

Assessment in English: The State of the Art

Two key developments within the last 20 to 30 years have influenced how English skills are evaluated in general: (1) the growth of empirical research in reading, literary response, and rhetoric; and (2) the widespread implementation of large-scale testing programs at all levels of education, including assessment of English skills. We now know more than ever before about how to evaluate skills in English, but our knowledge is still not sufficient. For example, although we know that reading is a highly sophisticated selective process, we don't yet fully understand this process or how to evaluate it (Purves). Assessing responses to literature is even more difficult (Hayhoe 32) because understanding and analyzing imaginative literature adds a dynamic relationship between reader and text to the process of reading. Furthermore, the evaluation of writing ability is also problematic because we are only now realizing how intricate the recursive process of writing is. Research is continuing to help us refine our knowledge and procedures for assessment.

Currently, there are two popular ways to assess English skills: the controlled-response method (objective testing) and the free-response method (essay exam).

Objective Tests

The controlled-response instrument is commonly called an *objective* test, not because the test itself is unbiased but because it can be scored objectively by machine or by people without their making individual judgments as to the acceptability of a response. This type of test may include multiple-choice, true-false, or matching questions. Such items are appropriate for measuring recall of factual information and recognition of the correctness or appropriateness of rules or patterns. In English, objective testing is used with varying degrees of effectiveness to assess knowledge of facts from or about literature, reading ability, skill in literary and rhetorical analysis, ability to discern relationships, and scope of vocabulary, as well as writing-related ability, such as sentence-level skills and usage and mechanics skills (spelling, grammar, punctuation, capitalization).

Statistically, any test should have both *reliability* and *validity*. An objective test is statistically reliable; that is, it can be scored consistently and fairly. However, the use of objective measures to test reading and writing is controversial. Controlled-response questions on reading, especially on the reading of literature, force "the reader to select the best of another's responses to the work in question rather than one's own" (Mellon 85) and too often become "guess what the test writer is thinking" questions (Purves, "Competence" 84). Multiple-choice questions cannot accommodate personal or ambivalent responses, even though there is always uncertainty about authorial purpose and tone, as well as a range of valid interpretations. In assessing writing, a controlled-response test can only indirectly measure ability. Because it does not directly assess composing processes or application of writing skills, it is low in validity; that is, it does not measure all the skills or processes it is intended to assess.[1] Writing teachers often express concern that this type of testing overemphasizes the discrete skills of writing—spelling, usage, grammar, error recognition—and de-emphasizes the more important rhetorical and communicative aspects of writing—organization, coherence, effectiveness of content or style. Clearly, because objective testing has sufficient reliability but not sufficient validity for assessing reading and writing, used alone it is not a suitable device for measuring English competence or equivalence.

Essay Tests

The free-response or essay test, the second type of assessment instrument used in English, elicits a writing sample; thus, it directly measures writing ability. It has validity as an instrument that assesses ability to compose and communicate in writing. It also has validity in assessing ability to understand and analyze literature if we view writing as a way of learning and of demonstrating learning. But maintaining reliability in free-response testing is more difficult than in objective testing because free-response evaluation requires judgments from individual raters. The major problems of essay tests usually result from difficulties in being consistent in defining writing tasks and scoring writing samples.[2]

The design of appropriate writing tasks is one of the most controversial aspects of direct writing assessment. The writing task—the testing assignment and instructions for students—serves as a springboard or prompt for what students write. Sometimes the task is called a stimulus because its purpose is to encourage writing that fits the expectations of the test designers. A typical writing task specifies length of time for writing, type and number of writings expected, topics or subjects for writing, and criteria by which the writing will be evaluated.

Test developers must first decide how much time will be allowed for a writing and how many samples of what types will be expected during the allotted time. Although conditions for testing should be as near those of realistic writing situations as possible, other considerations, such as total time available for test administration, usually determine the time limit. The amount of time allotted for production of a single essay response usually varies from 20 minutes to an hour. The decision on the number of samples is influenced by the time available: the more time available, the more samples students are usually expected to write. Because of inadequate time for recursive planning and revising, time limitations can adversely affect all students, especially inexperienced, anxious, bidialectical, and bilingual students.

However, test constructors should consider other more important factors in determining how many and what type of samples to include in a writing assignment. One factor, for example, is that a single writing may not adequately sample the abilities of a student (Ruth and Murphy). Also, different modes of writing (such as personal experience narration, argument, or literary interpretation) may require different types of cognitive and rhetorical responses from students. Research on modes and cognitive processes is inconclusive at this time, and we have no method of determining comparability of modes. Based on what we do know, however, most assessment experts recommend that a test specify two or more different tasks requiring different types of information in order to alleviate some of the detrimental effects of basing writing assessment on a single sample in a single mode.

Another unresolved issue in designing writing tasks is whether to include a full rhetorical context—subject, writer's role, and audience. Although experts disagree, Brossell and Hoetker conclude that "there is no research base for the common belief that students will write better and more easily to a topic that includes a full rhetorical context" (14). Furthermore, complete scenarios increase the information-processing required of students facing severe time limitations (Brossell, "Rhetorical Specification"), and decrease chances that the topic will be within the range of their experience (Lloyd-Jones; Charney; Hoetker and Brossell). Also, complete scenarios affect evaluation by increasing the difficulty of comparing separate topics on one test as well as on tests given at different times (Brossell and Hoetker; Hoetker).

Determining the difficulty level of a topic, another consideration in devising writing tasks, is one of the greatest challenges in writing assessment. We have little research on how to determine the difficulty level of a topic or how to make sound comparisons among different prompts and different ways of stating prompts (Charney; Ruth and Murphy; Hoetker and Brossell). This lack of a system for classifying essays and essay topics often leads to charges of unreliability or inconsistency in direct assessment of writing (Hoetker; Charney). In light of these problems, topics must be stated as clearly as possible, without emotionally laden words or hidden ambiguities, and must be field-tested before being used as assessment tools.

Scoring also poses a major problem in establishing reliability for essay tests. There is no correct answer in free-response essays as there is in closed-response items. Evaluating a writing sample requires judging whether a student exhibits competence or excellence in writing. There are five wide-spread methods of evaluating writing samples:

1. error count (tallying deviations from the conventions of standard written English);
2. analysis of syntactic fluency (describing sentence structure, in T-units, for example);
3. holistic evaluation (determining a single score that represents an overall impression of writing ability);
4. analytic scoring (determining a series of separate scores on specifically identified aspects of a piece of writing—for example, organization, word choice, or punctuation); and
5. primary trait scoring (using a scoring guide created specifically for a writing task).

Each can be useful for different purposes, but holistic scoring is the method most often used to assess competence or equivalence. Certain safeguards produce acceptable reliability of holistic scoring: carefully trained readers, a scoring guide that reflects the test population and the consensus of readers, anchor papers to illustrate the levels of the scoring guide, periodic checks of readers' scores to reinforce standards, and independent evaluations of each paper by at least two readers.

White effectively summarizes scholarship on measuring writing ability:

> The issue of multiple-choice versus essay testing of writing has become a bit dated since the development of relatively reliable and cost-effective holistic scoring procedures. Insofar as a test seeks to measure actual writing ability, the issue can be more generally defined as a conflict between direct and indirect measures. Traditionally and logically, an indirect measure is preferred only when it shows clear advantages over the direct measure. Until recently, advocates of indirect (usually multiple-choice) measurement of writing ability could point to the high cost and low reliability of scoring writing samples as compared with the low cost and high efficiency of multiple-choice answer sheets. Now the argument has shifted: The high development costs of multiple-choice tests under truth-in-testing laws, the lower validity of such tests, and the damage to curriculum such tests cause by devaluing actual writing—all these suggest the weaknesses of multiple-choice measurement in the field of writing. ("Pitfalls" 68)

Assessing reading ability is equally as controversial as assessing writing ability. Multiple measures (for example, multiple-choice questions, cloze passages, oral recall, written recall, written response) are advocated for effective reading assessment, but the method most often used to assess comprehension is simply a series of questions on a brief passage (Johnston). Reading experts disagree about the suitability of essay writing as a test of comprehension or understanding. Some experts agree with Whimbey and Blatt and Rosen who claim that essay responses are appropriate in both instruction and assessment because writing helps students articulate and order what they have read. Other scholars further argue that written discourse is the *best* way to demonstrate comprehension.[3] Still others, such as Ashby-Davis, argue that any technique that requires a test-taker to perform both as reader and writer has questionable value in assessing reading ability. Mellon summarizes reactions to this form of assessment:

> Open-ended essay questions allow full freedom for the expression of response, but impose the additional burden that the persons answering must compose their responses in some organized fashion. Broadly speaking, they must in effect produce one literary work in response to another literary work, and in so doing must strike off from the original work in any one of an indefinite number of possible directions, more or less ignoring all the others. (*National Assessment* 85)

Attempting to assess reading by asking students to write an essay compounds the problems of both student and evaluator.

Assessment in English need not be based on either objective or essay tests; it can be based on both. Because controlled-response and free-response methods assess different skills and abilities in reading and in writing and because they are scored differently, a combination of objective and essay questions is preferable. This combined method not only increases the reliability of assessment but also provides a more complete evaluation of a student's ability than one or the other singly, thus increasing the amount of information on which to base an evaluation (Conlan; White, *Teaching*). The current consensus and general practice is to use both.

Advanced Placement Testing in English

The credibility of the AP Program depends upon the credibility of its examinations. In no other discipline is this more true than in English, due primarily to the diversity of introductory college courses in composition and literature and the difficulties and uncertainties of assessing skills in English. On one, three-hour AP exam in English, candidates must demonstrate themselves sufficiently capable in writing, reading, and literary interpretation for course exemption and advanced placement in college.

There are two parallel AP exams for English, one for each AP course offered: English Literature and Composition (the older and more popular) and English Language and Composition. Both exams emphasize reading and writing skills considered essential for advanced study. The two exams are linked by common questions—a set of multiple-choice questions on a passage of discursive prose and an essay question calling for analysis of the rhetorical features of another prose passage. Each three-hour exam allows students 75 minutes to complete 60 multiple-choice questions, and 105 minutes to complete three essay questions. These two sections of the exams are intended to complement each other by measuring different skills. Performance on the essay section counts 60 percent of the total grade, and the multiple-choice section 40 percent. A student performing acceptably on the free-response or essay section must answer about 60 percent of the multiple-choice items correctly to obtain a total grade of 3 (on a scale of 1 to 5), the score for exemption at most colleges and universities.

Multiple-Choice Testing in AP English

Multiple-choice questions were not used on the AP English exams in the early years of the program; rather, assessment was based completely on free-response essays. Controlled-response multiple-choice questions were later added for several reasons: they can be scored quickly and economically; they increase reliability; and they help discriminate among students (Jones and Wimmers; Albrecht; Paul Smith). Currently, three types of controlled-response questions appear on the AP tests: (1) questions on surface features of language (such as grammar, syntax, or diction); (2) questions on literary or poetic effects of a passage; and (3) questions on understanding the subject and the main point of a piece (Jones and Wimmers 28–31). These items are scored with a correction factor to compensate for guessing, and the section counts 40 percent of the total score (*Advanced Placement Course* iii).

Essay Testing in AP English

The essay or free-response section of the AP English exams, used since the program was established in 1954, requires students to demonstrate skill in composition by writing three essays of various lengths in various rhetorical modes. In addition to the rhetorical analysis question that appears on both the Literature and Composition and the Language and Composition exams, additional essay questions specific to each course appear on each exam. The Literature and Composition exam calls for critical and analytical essays on literary principles or selections. The Language and Composition exam requires personal essays, argumentative essays, or analyses of rhetorical features of a prose passage.

To evaluate the AP essays, scorers use the modified holistic scoring method—general impression scoring with a ranking guide and illustrative anchor papers. A chief reader assisted by experienced readers determines tentative standards for rating the essays and selects representative papers for each level of the scoring scale. Readers then practice using the tentative scoring guides and anchor paper until the majority are consistently applying these standards in rating papers. Each essay is scored independently, and group leaders continually check the readers' ratings so that no one strays from the original agreed upon criteria and anchor papers. The Advanced Placement program attempts to control reliability in evaluating the writing samples by using scoring guides on a scale of 0 to 9, by training and monitoring readers, and by ensuring reader and writer anonymity (Albrecht 3; Paul Smith 3).

Determining the Total Score for an AP English Exam

A student's overall exam score is established by combining ratings on the three essay questions and the multiple-choice section. These scores are weighted according to formulas determined in advance by the AP development committee to yield a single raw composite score for each candidate. The chief reader converts composite scores into the five-point scale by which AP grades are reported: 5 = extremely well qualified; 4 = well qualified; 3 = qualified; 2 = possibly qualified; 1 = no recommendation.

Some Questions and Conclusions About AP Testing

The College Board claims to make AP certification in English valid and reliable in several ways: by basing AP courses on typical college courses, by placing both secondary and college teachers on test development committees and scoring teams, by providing ETS testing specialists to assist subject matter experts, and by encouraging communication among all those directly involved in the AP program. Despite these good intentions, however, problems still exist. Certainly, any testing program of this magnitude and complexity raises questions and concerns.

The AP English exams raise interwoven psychometric, educational, cultural, and political concerns. Several of these result from the current state of assessment in English, others from the specific nature of the AP exams, and still others from the politics of teaching and testing. The exams elicit several questions to which there may be no firm answers at this time.

QUESTION:
Should multiple-choice questions be used on AP exams, or should these questions be eliminated because the pedagogical and philosophical harm outweighs their psychometric benefit?

One area of concern about AP English exams is the use of controlled-response questions to evaluate students' knowledge and understanding of language, rhetoric, and literature. The College Board added multiple-choice questions to increase exam reliability, and its published statistics indicate high reliability of this section of the exams: .81 in 1981 and .86 in 1982 on the Literature and Composition test (Albrecht 4), and .83 in 1981 and .85 in 1982 on the Language and Composition exam (Paul Smith 4).

However, objective testing is not universally accepted as a measurement tool by all testing experts. These experts have five main objections:

(1) multiple-choice questions sacrifice validity because they don't directly measure abilities in English; (2) they only approximate what a writer actually does as he or she edits a piece of writing; (3) the correlation between student performance on multiple-choice tests and essays is too low; (4) this type of testing contradicts current theory in psycholinguistics and in reading theory; and (5) it has an undesirable impact upon interpreting and teaching English.

One of the most significant of these objections is that controlled-response testing in language and literature conflicts with the widely accepted transactional paradigm in reading and literary theory. Louise Rosenblatt and other reader-response critics argue that a literary work is a transaction between reader and text; thus, meaning is an event, a process that transforms participating entities. Stanley Fish adds, "Interpretation is not the art of construing but the art of constructing. Interpreters do not decode poems; they make them" (327). Iser claims a work is actualized as a result of the interaction between text and reader and that the reader receives a message by composing it (10). Weaver sees "no sharp separation between observer and observed, reader and text, reader/text and context" (312), and Fish further asserts that the identification of context and the making of meaning occur "simultaneously"—that "text, context, and interpretation all emerge together" (313, 340). Thus, a reader identifies a word and its letters more or less simultaneously (Frank Smith), defines words in nonlinear transaction with other words (Weaver), and interacts with a text to make meaning (Rosenblatt). According to this organic process theory, a text does not exist without a reader, and both reader and text are transformed by their interaction.

This emerging paradigm has important implications for teaching and testing. This view of reading and literary response suggests that teachers and evaluators should emphasize the whole, not the discrete parts; stress process, not product; respect the experiences that students bring to reading; and accept meaning that students construct. But controlled-response testing runs counter to all of these principles.

In assessing skills in language and literary analysis, test items that list several possible answers but give credit for only one inescapably reinforce the idea that there is *one correct way* to interpret and respond to language and literature. AP question writers do attempt, however, to get at multiple meanings by using "not" and "except" to require students to select a single element that is not true or is not part of a pattern (Jones and Wimmers 19), and also by using "best" or "most" or "primarily" to force students to discriminate among several possible choices (4). Here are some examples of this type of item stem:

- Which of the following does *NOT* indicate . . . ?
- All of the following reinforce the imagery *EXCEPT* . . . .

- The speaker's tone is *best* described as . . . .
- The image suggests *primarily* . . . .

But because they know that they will be evaluated by questions with single correct answers, students are inclined to believe in and search for the right word or sentence pattern in language, or for the correct theme or tone or connotation in literature. Teachers often reinforce these attitudes and practices by presenting their own interpretations and preferences as correct. In evaluation of language skills, items requiring candidates to choose one of five options for rephrasing a sentence clearly strengthen the mania for correctness in language use. In assessment of reading skills and literary responses, multiple-choice questions not only contradict reader-response theory but also deny students the joy and respect of interpreting literature on their own (Mellon; Purves, "Competence").

Granted, readers may draw conclusions that aren't supported by the text, and writers may use some forms of language that are inconsistent with current conventions. Granted also, responding to language and literature involves judgment, and an expert's judgment—whether that of test developer or teacher—is usually considered better than that of relatively inexperienced students. But which is more important for students? Should they be led to think there is one correct way to think, speak, and respond to literature and language, a way they can discover if they look in the right places or ask the right questions? Or should they be allowed to develop and exercise individual critical skills based on personal experience, evidence, and clear thinking? Current linguistic and literary theory tells us that the pedagogical and philosophical harm of controlling students' responses to language and literature seems to overshadow psychometric benefits.

QUESTION:

Are three essays in a period of 105 minutes the best or most advisable method for evaluating writing ability, or should a portfolio of each student's writing over time be collected and evaluated?

The AP exams require students to write three essays in different rhetorical modes in 105 minutes. The College Board considers composing a critical essay a suitable test of a student's ability to respond to literature and to analyze the features of a particular work because "in writing an essay, a student must ask questions of the text as well as answer them" (Jones and Wimmers 3). They point out, too, that some things—such as tone, shifts in insight or perception, and ambivalence in meaning—cannot be measured by multiple-choice questions (35). And they further argue that students are "free to comment on the nuances, ambiguities, and contradictions that make the reading of literature such an interesting experience" (3). However, the issue is whether three essays written in this amount of time is the *most* appropriate method of assessing the abilities of AP students.

Portfolios of student writing are now recommended as a method for directly assessing writing ability. Roberta Camp of ETS has developed systematic procedures for using the writing portfolio in assessing development in writing. Peter Elbow recommends portfolios as an alternative to proficiency exams. Ruth and Murphy call the writing folder a "promising development" for "measuring growth in writing ability that can account for variations in the complexity of the task that the student attempts"; they add that holistic scores are "insufficient" to identify such "variations" (419). Nevertheless, some experts consider portfolios to be impractical:

> If we had but money enough and time, we would measure writing ability by collecting, over a period of several months, a number of samples of a student's writing, produced in reaction to various stimuli and written under various conditions—some impromptu exercises strictly timed and some untimed essays done at home, for example. This collection would then be evaluated by as many different trained evaluators as we could manage, and the score achieved might then provide, if all goes well, an extremely accurate picture of that student's writing ability. But since we have neither enough money nor enough time to do that kind of extended evaluation, we usually compromise. . . . Which sort of compromise is best? The answer lies in our priorities, our concerns, and, sad to say, our budgets. (Conlan 116)

The AP exam compromise is, as it should be, more demanding than the common competency task requiring one essay in 50 or 60 minutes. The triple free-response tasks on AP exams offer students an opportunity to show their abilities in more than one mode of writing (although we have no way of determining comparability of modes). For example, the 1982 Literature and Composition exam incorporated these three writing tasks: (1) analyze the language of the poem "The Groundhog" by Richard Eberhart, (2) analyze the rhetorical strategies of an argument by Adlai Stevenson, and (3) explain how violence contributes to the meaning of a literary work of the student's choice. Likewise, the 1982 Language and Composition exam required three distinct tasks: (1) explain reasons for agreement or disagreement with a stand on human happiness expressed in a passage; (2) analyze the rhetorical strategies of Stevenson's argument; and (3) describe a place. However, such writing prompts require a great deal of language and information processing, as well as recall and writing in a relatively brief time (35 minutes is suggested for each essay). The abstract passage on human happiness is approximately 400 words long, while the political argument by Stevenson is about 500.

Would a portfolio of a student's work provide a fairer sampling of writing ability? That is, would more samples of a wider variety written in various situations over months of time provide more valid assessment than three 35-minute essays? Would the folder show a student's growth more accurately? Would some timed and some untimed writings reveal a clearer picture of a student's ability? Would the writing portfolio be less dependent upon a student's comprehension of passages on which essays are to be based? Perhaps we cannot answer these questions until we have more research on comparing modes, writing tasks, and writers' responses. But for an exam program as significant as AP, it seems the time and money spent evaluating portfolios would be worthwhile—fairer to students and more credible to college faculty.

QUESTION:

Do standards for evaluating writing samples reflect the opinion of the group leaders, or are they reached by consensus of the entire group of readers?

The criteria for rating AP writing samples are developed and implemented with great care to make scoring as reliable as possible. First, over a period of two years prior to the administration of a test, the AP development committee and the chief reader develop and refine standards for evaluating essays. Second, the chief reader, assisted by question leaders and table leaders, rigorously trains readers in the use of grading standards and the accompanying grading scale for each question. The goal of this training is to meld the individual reader's professional assessment with the standards developed by the reading group (Albrecht 3; Paul Smith 3). During the training session, reader consensus on standards is supposed to be reached and a sense of community established. This procedure seems paradoxical. How can readers reach consensus on criteria established earlier by the development committee and the chief reader? Can leaders of a training session meld individuals' standards to those of a group and at the same time allow them to arrive at consensus?

It is doubtful that scoring standards represent a consensus of the total community of readers in such a large and prestigious testing program especially considering the rigorous training necessary for reliability in evaluation. In any large reading of essays, especially one such as the AP reading, chief readers and assistants may cut off discussion on scoring and make dogmatic statements in the interest of time and efficiency. Furthermore, some readers may be so intimidated by the size and prestige of the scoring process that they go along with criteria as presented without raising reasonable points of disagreement. And we might wonder if a consensus of over 300 people with diverse backgrounds, experiences, and biases is advisable or even possible. For the purposes of AP testing, which should take precedence: uniform criteria to ensure fairness to students or a sense of community among readers? Is it possible to have both?

QUESTION:

Given the current state of direct assessment of writing, should the chief reader alone determine which composite score equals a satisfactory performance, or should this decision be made by a group of experts?

For the AP exams, the chief reader is responsible for converting students' composite scores into the five-point scale. To make these determinations, he or she evaluates performance section by section for the current examination, calibrates the exam against results of preceding years, and analyzes patterns of performance (Albrecht 27; Paul Smith 21). In most testing programs, it is accepted that this year's score of 6 on an essay may represent the same level as last year's 7 or next year's 5; this variation is most likely if a scoring guide or rubric is not constant, as is the case of AP exams. Giving one person—the chief reader—so much significant decision-making responsibility causes concern.

Presently, there is no known way to determine the difficulty level of a writing task and no statistical formula to equate modes, topics, and essay responses. In the last decade, we have made little progress in agreeing among ourselves as professionals on a definition of "good writing"—agreement essential for reliable and valid holistic scoring. At the request of the Special Interest Group on Writing Assessment, a group of ETS test developers and researchers has formulated guidelines for free-response testing to ensure consistency, fairness, and accuracy in scoring examinations. Several states, such as New Jersey, Florida, and California, have developed descriptions of levels of writing for the same purpose.

Much work remains for psychometricians, as well as theorists and researchers in rhetoric and composition, if the discipline is to develop acceptable procedures for strengthening validity and improving reliability of essay tests. Perhaps there is a need for professional standards and procedures in this area; or perhaps uniformity and codification of a process as individualized as writing is undesirable. But until such issues are resolved, several questions remain: Should the crucial final decision of who receives a satisfactory AP score be made by one person, no matter how highly qualified? Or should he or she be assisted by a group of informed experts? Would consensus of a group be fairer to candidates and more acceptable to college faculty?

QUESTION:

Should the two English exams be considered equivalent, or should credit for literature be given for the literature course and exam and credit for composition for the composition course and exam?

In 1954, the AP Literature and Composition course and exam were first offered. In 1978, the Language and Composition course and exam were developed to accomplish something that the established Literature and Composition sequence did not: to offer students advanced coursework in "that other college-level English option in language, rhetoric, and expository writing" (*Advanced Placement Course* 2). Both exams emphasize common skills in reading and writing; they have the same length and format; they are administered at the same time so that students can take only one or the other; and they are linked by some common questions. The College Board's twofold purpose in these practices is to encourage colleges to treat students taking either exam in a similar manner and to discourage colleges from requiring both exams for one year's credit (*Advanced Placement Course* 2).

These practices, however, cause college administrators and faculty problems in deciding how to award college credit for AP study in high school. Should a student who has taken the Literature and Composition course receive college credit for freshman composition or for world literature? Should a student who has spent a year focusing on literature receive the same credit for freshman composition as the student who has spent a year focusing on language and rhetoric? If there is a need for separate study and testing, isn't there a need for separate credit?

Can we assume, as many English teachers do, that students who read and write well about literature can also read and write well about other subjects? Or that students who read and write well in science or history can also understand and explicate literature? The chief reader for the 1981–82 Language and Composition exam seems to think so: "These shared or similar features [in the two exams] reflect the obvious fact that the formal study of ordinary language differs little, if at all, from the study of literary language, and is no less demanding" (Paul Smith 11). However, Mellon, speaking for the NCTE Committee to Study the National Assessment of Educational Progress, refutes this position: "Writing about literature constitutes a particular kind of rhetorical task, and students ordinarily require special instruction in order to perform it" (85). It seems that, to be consistent with other educational practices, college credit should be granted for the specific area of intensive study and performance in the AP program.

QUESTION:
Do college and university officials decide to grant AP credit in English because the exams correlate with their courses, or do they accept AP scores because competing institutions are doing so?

The College Board recommends that in determining if AP credit will be granted college and university officials and faculty compare AP English courses and exams with their own courses in composition and literature. AP English courses are developed as typical college courses, but with the wide diversity in freshman English courses, there is no guarantee that the AP exams fulfill the objectives of a specific college course. For example, an AP course with an emphasis on literature would not correspond to a college freshman composition course with a writing-across-the-curriculum emphasis. Do college officials usually investigate AP programs and try to correlate the AP objectives with their own? Or do they decide to grant AP credit for reasons other than academic ones? In a period of declining enrollments, are administrators more concerned about losing students to nearby colleges than with students' preparation for the college curriculum?

QUESTION:

Does the AP curriculum and testing program reflect our diverse American society, or is there a hidden curriculum?

What we teach and how we test reflect our values as a society (Lederman 41; Lunsford 8). If we value reading and writing ability as critical skills for success in our culture, then we will teach reading and writing. If we believe the business of an English class is reading and writing, we will use instruments that assess these skills directly, not indirectly. If we believe in the traditional canon of "the best that has been thought and said," as does William J. Bennett (3), then we will teach the well-known and highly regarded works of our Western heritage. The AP exams appear to reinforce this traditional canon. The majority of the works used or referred to on the exams were written by male Anglo-Saxon writers, now dead. Why are so few of these writers contemporary? Why are so few female? Why are so few black? Where are the Orientals, the Chicanos, and the Indians? If we believe in a pluralistic society, we must value the writings of all the diverse groups of America, and we must include them in our courses and on our tests.

QUESTION:

Are AP English courses more important than the tests, or is the curriculum driven by the tests?

According to the College Board, AP English course descriptions are not meant to be prescriptive; rather, they are intended to suggest the range and quality of the courses (*Advanced Placement Course* 3). The English exams are designed to assess "common skills in reading and writing that are necessary for advanced study in the field" (1). Those involved assert that they are aware of the difficulty in finding an appropriate balance between *describing* and *prescribing* (1). White cites the AP program as an example of the "mutual support" teaching and testing should give each other and asserts that the "courses generated by the tests are more important than the tests themselves" ("Pitfalls" 58).

It seems likely that high school teachers might try to anticipate the expectations of test developers and teach to the test so that their students will make good showings. (See John Iorio's chapter in this book.) They will stress the traditional canon in literature, and they will train students to make supposedly correct choices in language and literature. Furthermore, the current AP program clearly emphasizes literature more than it does rhetoric; naturally, the majority of AP teachers will tend to do the same. Nevertheless, many college students would profit from more intensive study of effective writing in areas other than literary analysis. Do the AP English tests truly reflect AP English courses, our diverse society, and current professional opinion, or do the tests determine course content and affect the curriculum?

The AP English exams intensify problems and uncertainties in the assessment of reading, writing, and literary response. Current procedures in AP testing raise serious questions about the intent and the credibility of the program for exemption from college courses. Changes in current practices in the AP program and procedures in AP testing would make this program more equitable for students and more credible for faculty and administrators.

Notes

1. See for example, Cooper and Odell; Myers; Stiggins; Larson; White; Greenberg et al.
2. See Myers; Hoetker; Stiggins; Charney; Larson; White; Conlan; Brossell.
3. Petrosky; Petersen; Jensen; Langer and Smith-Burke; Horner; Stotsky.

Works Cited

Advanced Placement Course Description: English. N.p.: College Entrance Examination Board, 1986.

Albrecht, Robert C. *Grading the Advanced Placement Examination in English Literature and Composition.* N.p.: College Entrance Examination Board, 1983.

Ashby-Davis, Clair. "Cloze and Comprehension: A Qualitative Analysis and Critique." *Journal of Reading* 28 (1985): 585–89.

Bennett, William J. *To Reclaim a Legacy: A Report on the Humanities in Higher Education.* National Endowment for the Humanities, November 1984.

Blatt, Gloria T., and Lois Matz Rosen. "The Writing Response to Literature." *Journal of Reading* 28 (1984): 8–12.

Brossell, Gordon. "Current Research and Unanswered Questions in Writing Assessment." *Writing Assessment: Issues and Strategies.* Ed. Karen L. Greenberg, Harvey S. Wiener, and Richard A. Donovan. White Plains, NY: Longman, 1986. 168–82.

———. "Rhetorical Specification in Essay Examination Topics." *College English* 45 (1983): 165–73.

Brossell, Gordon, and James Hoetker. "Development and Field Test of Items and Topics for the College-Level Academic Skills Test in Writing." Report for the College-Level Academic Skills Project Office, Florida Department of Education, December 1983.

Charney, Davida. "The Validity of Using Holistic Scoring to Evaluate Writing: A Critical Overview." *Research in the Teaching of English* 18 (1984): 65–71.

Conlan, Gertrude. " 'Objective' Measures of Writing Ability." *Writing Assessment: Issues and Strategies.* Ed. Karen L. Greenberg, Harvey S. Wiener, and Richard A. Donovan. New York: Longman, 1986. 109–25.

Cooper, Charles R., and Lee Odell, eds. *Evaluating Writing: Describing, Measuring, Judging.* Urbana: NCTE, 1977.

Fish, Stanley. *Is There a Text in This Class?* Cambridge: Harvard UP, 1980.

Greenberg, Karen L., Harvey S. Wiener, and Richard A. Donovan, eds. *Writing Assessment: Issues and Strategies.* New York; Longman, 1986.

Hayhoe, M. J., "Reading and Literature." *Directions and Misdirections in English Evaluation.* The Canadian Council of Teachers of English, 1985.

Hoetker, James. "Essay Examination Topics and Students' Writing." *College Composition and Communication* 33 (1982): 377–92.

Hoetker, James, and Gordon Brossell. "A Procedure for Writing Content-Fair Essay Examination Topics for Large-Scale Writing Assessments." *College Composition and Communication* 37 (1986): 328–35.

Horner, Winifred B., ed. *Composition and Literature: Bridging the Gap.* Chicago: U of Chicago P, 1983.

Iser, Wolfgang. *The Act of Reading: A Theory of Aesthetic Response.* Baltimore: Johns Hopkins UP, 1978.

Jensen, Julie M., ed. *Composing and Comprehending.* Urbana: National Conference on Research in English, 1984.

Johnston, Peter H. "Assessment in Reading." *Handbook of Reading Research.* Ed. P. David Pearson. New York: Longman, 1984. 147–82.

———. *A Cognitive Basis for the Assessment of Reading Comprehension.* Newark, DE: International Reading Association, 1983.

Jones, Robert J., and Eric Wimmers. *Multiple-Choice Testing in Literature: Advanced Placement English.* N.p.: College Entrance Examination Board, 1983.

Langer, Judith A., and M. Trika Smith-Burke, eds. *Reader Meets Author—Bridging the Gap: A Psycholinguistic and Sociolinguistic Perspective.* Newark, DE: International Reading Association, 1982.

Larson, Richard L. "Tests of Minimum Competence in Writing." *SLATE Starter Sheet.* Urbana: NCTE, 1985.

Lederman, Marie Jean. "Why Test?" *Writing Assessment: Issues and Strategies.* Ed. Karen L. Greenberg, Harvey S. Wiener, and Richard A. Donovan. White Plains, NY: Longman, 1986. 35–43.

Lloyd-Jones, Richard. "Primary Trait Scoring." *Evaluating Writing: Describing, Measuring, Judging.* Ed. Charles R. Cooper and Lee Odell. Urbana: NCTE, 1977. 33–66.

Lunsford, Andrea A. "The Past—and Future—of Writing Assessment." *Writing Assessment: Issues and Strategies.* Ed. Karen L. Greenberg, Harvey S. Wiener, and Richard A. Donovan. White Plains, NY: Longman, 1986. 1–12.

Mellon, John C. *National Assessment and the Teaching of English.* Urbana: NCTE, 1975.

Myers, Miles. *Procedures for Writing Assessment and Holistic Scoring.* Urbana: NCTE, 1981.

Petersen, Bruce T., ed. *Convergences: Transactions in Reading and Writing.* Urbana: NCTE, 1986.

———. "Writing about Responses: A Unified Model of Reading, Interpretation, and Composition." *College English* 44 (1982): 459–68.

Petrosky, Anthony R. "From Story to Essay: Reading and Writing." *College Composition and Communication* 33 (1982): 24–25.

Purves, Alan. "Competence in Reading." *The Nature and Measurement of Competency in English.* Ed. Charles R. Cooper. Urbana: NCTE, 1981. 65–94.

———. "Evaluating Growth in English." *The Teaching of English: The Seventy-Sixth Yearbook of the National Society for the Study of Education.* Part I. Ed. James R. Squire. Chicago: U of Chicago P, 1977. 230–59.

Rosenblatt, Louise M. *The Reader, the Text, the Poem: The Transactional Theory of the Literary Work.* Carbondale, IL: Southern Illinois UP, 1978.

Ruth, Leo, and Sandra Murphy. "Designing Topics for Writing Assessment: Problems of Meaning." *College Composition and Communication* 35 (1984): 410–22.

School Administrator's Guide to the Advanced Placement Program. N.p.: College Entrance Examination Board, 1985.

Smith, Frank. *Understanding Reading: A Psycholinguistic Analysis of Reading and Learning to Read.* New York: Holt, 1971.

Smith, Paul. *Grading the Advanced Placement Examination in English Language and Composition.* N.p.: College Entrance Examination Board, 1983.

Stiggins, Richard J. "A Comparison of Direct and Indirect Writing Assessment Methods." *Research in the Teaching of English* 16 (1982): 101–14.

Stotsky, Sandra L. "A Proposal for Improving High School Students' Ability to Read and Write Expository Prose." *Journal of Reading* 28 (1984): 4–7.

Weaver, Constance. "Parallels between New Paradigms in Science and in Reading and Literary Theories: An Essay Review." *Research in the Teaching of English* 19 (1985): 298–316.

Whimbey, Arthur. "Reading, Writing, Reasoning Linked in Testing and Training." *Journal of Reading* 29 (1985): 118–24.

White, Edward M. "Mass Testing of Individual Writing: The California Model." *Journal of Basic Writing* 1 (1978): 18–38.

———. "Pitfalls in the Testing of Writing." *Writing Assessment: Issues and Strategies.* Ed. Karen L. Greenberg, Harvey S. Wiener, and Richard A. Donovan. New York: Longman, 1986. 53–78.

———. *Teaching and Assessing Writing: Recent Advances in Understanding, Evaluating, and Improving Student Performance.* San Francisco: Jossey-Bass, 1985.

PART II

The AP English Programs

5

Establishing and Administering an Advanced Placement English Program

DIANE Y. KANZLER

Southeast High School
Bradenton, Florida

Kanzler presents a helpful primer for beginning and maintaining an AP English program. She discusses administrative concerns and the responsibilities of the principal, department chair, and AP teacher in establishing the program.

The most important responsibility of the schools is to provide students with meaningful options that will enhance their educational experience and prepare them for the variety of opportunities ahead. The Advanced Placement program has demonstrated through its durability and consistent growth that it is such an option. As director Harlan P. Hanson observed on the program's silver anniversary, "Able students, like their teachers, *can* find delight in college-level instruction while still in high school and can then proceed to advanced collegiate studies on the basis of common external examinations" (49). The advantages of instituting an Advanced Placement

English course are numerous, but its primary focus is, of course, the students' needs:

> This program has always had a dual purpose: to provide a deeper educational experience for the able student in the secondary school, and to enable exceptional students to earn college credit for courses taken in high school. Although the second of these two objectives receives the most publicity, the first has been more important to American education. (Fenton 235)

Interested educators can gain a better definition of "a deeper educational experience" by reading the pertinent materials produced by the College Board, particularly *Advanced Placement Course Description: English*, the "acorn" booklet, which describes the two English courses (the traditional Literature and Composition and the more recent Language and Composition) as well as the pamphlet *Beginning an Advanced Placement English Course*.

In terms of actual course implementation, the College Board states, "The school need not request the College Board's special permission. . . . It need only appoint an AP Coordinator; file a Participation Form; and order, administer, and return the examinations [contracted to the Educational Testing Service] in the spring" (*Guide* 6). Certainly, this procedure seems simple enough. However, at the outset, the local school board must approve any efforts to investigate and later to initiate an Advanced Placement program. The board may actually originate the proposal or may affirm the individual school's plans. As community representatives, the board can envision the benefits for students and may become part of the process as planner and provider. Nevertheless, the individual school maintains most of the responsibility for planning and implementing an Advanced Placement English program.

Preliminary Steps

The process of initiating the program should begin at least a year prior to offering the first course and should enlist the input of faculty, students, and parents. This communal approach fulfills an important public relations function and helps the Advanced Placement English program become a mutual effort and investment rather than an administrative decree.

In a faculty meeting early in this preceding year, the principal (or appropriate representative, such as a curriculum coordinator) should provide the faculty with a general description of the tentative English course and solicit their input. Because the English department will be most deeply involved, the faculty must be informed to enable them to answer questions from students and parents and to provide initial impressions on the feasibility of the course from varying viewpoints. While the course is in the earliest planning stages, the principal or coordinator will be able to address any reservations, fears, or misinformation that may exist. Additionally, suggestions and innovative ideas can be incorporated into the process at the outset. As the planning progresses, updates will keep the faculty informed and the dialogue active.

Similarly in the fall the school should devise a brief course description, an introduction to Advanced Placement, and a questionnaire for underclass students and their parents to determine their degree of interest in and support for the proposal. Such a questionnaire and *meaningful* follow-up will accomplish several aims. Students and their parents will have the opportunity to become part of the process, not passive recipients of institutional actions. Many will be interested in investigating other course offerings in English and the entire curriculum. Parent and student will work together on course selection and an educational plan from an informed stance. The school will benefit from the public relations, while the Advanced Placement English course will receive support and input. Quite a few students will view the future AP course as a goal, an honor for which they can plan and work, thereby enhancing their studies as underclass students.

Likewise, the school should provide frequent progress reports on the AP program and a method for parents to provide input to the school. One of the most effective vehicles for this activity is a regular school newsletter that includes information on curriculum developments, school events, and other school matters, as well as questionnaires. Not only will this newsletter help everyone become better informed but it will provide avenues of input from all concerned parties.

Curricular Concerns

The initiation of an Advanced Placement program in any discipline necessarily involves an examination of the existing curriculum. The AP course must work in harmony with and be a logical step in the curriculum for the appropriate students. As the College Board explains in the booklet, *Beginning an Advanced Placement English Course*:

> Twenty years ago it was easier to generalize about the typical high school and college English curriculum than it is now. Today's richer diversity of goals, methods, subject matter, and students is a challenge to the AP English Program, which is intended to "articulate" high school and college curriculums by training motivated high school students to do college-level work and to reward them for their achievement with credit and placement in higher-level college English courses. (4)

Edwin Fenton discusses this articulation within the curriculum in his examination of the honors programs available for the "superior student." He states that a fully successful advanced placement program should be built on a carefully devised sequence of courses beginning, at the latest, in the tenth grade. . . . Experience now indicates that no advanced placement program can be fully successful unless it is built on a firm foundation of honors work extending throughout a student's high school career. (239)

The curriculum coordinator and the English department should ensure that the courses taken by academically able students meld logically and sequentially. The objectives and accompanying activities of English honors courses in the earlier grades are the foundation and must be scrutinized. As Fenton stresses, the tenth grade is the crucial year for enactment since much of what students will learn in the eleventh and twelfth grades will be based on what they have learned previously.

As a result, implementation of the Advanced Placement English course will enhance the English department's offerings by providing more choices and addressing the needs of motivated, gifted students who might find the existing English offerings less than challenging. In addition, the investigation into the curriculum, its standards and requirements, will reap positive results. While the AP course receives attention, the entire English curriculum and other areas of the school's course of study will undergo re-evaluation. Many will benefit. Again, the students are the focus here, and the school must seriously examine feasible options that best serve the students while making Advanced Placement the last stage in a logical progression.

Administrative Concerns: The Principal

The process of investigating and sharing ideas in order to implement the Advanced Placement English program will serve the administration, especially the principal and department chair, as well as strengthen the curriculum. Hanson observes, "Just as the program obliges [administrators] to address the issues necessary for stronger students to be well served, it also gives them a way to discover that they are not alone and to share what they have learned" (50). Because of the cooperative nature of this process, principals are not the only agents mandating change. Nevertheless, they have concerns and responsibilities that are vital to the Advanced Placement English program and that are primarily theirs, although in some schools, the department chairpersons share these. The duties of the principals include appointing the AP coordinator, creating a budget for the new course, scheduling time for teacher preparation during the school year and summer, and selecting the course instructor.

The logical choice for AP coordinator is the guidance counselor who also serves as the director of testing for the school. The coordinator will serve as the liaison between the school and the College Board and administer the Advanced Placement tests in the spring. When appointing the coordinator, the principal should provide this person with the following materials available from the College Board: the "acorn" booklet; *Information for Coordinators: Advanced Placement Examinations* (free for one to five copies); *Using the PSAT/NMSQT to Help Identify Advanced Placement Students* (free single copy); and *School Administrator's Guide to the Advanced Placement Program* ($10 and necessary). While fulfilling the duties required by the Advanced Placement program, the counselor-coordinator will also become a valuable resource within the guidance department, familiarizing the other counselors with the AP program to facilitate future student counseling and registration.

A principal's primary concern in initiating any program is cost, and planning in this area will necessarily include the input of the department chair and AP instructor. The expenditure for beginning an AP English course is relatively modest, about $1,500. This figure should cover supplies and books, with some monies allotted for the preparation of the AP instructor. This is based on a single class of 15 to 18 students, a size strongly recommended by the Advanced Placement program and AP teachers because of the intensive level of study and writing demanded of all participants. Bolstered with the community support already garnered, the principal can petition the school board for a special allocation to finance the proposed course to avoid draining funds from other English courses in the existing program. Another funding concern is that the AP course utilizes college-level texts that are generally absent from state-adopted lists. Therefore, textbooks must be purchased from a separate fund within the school budget.

Funds for the preparation of the instructor should be incorporated into this budget. The principal should provide the teacher with the time and money to cover fees and substitutes so that he or she can visit nearby schools that have successful AP programs, attend local AP workshops, and participate in a regional two-week summer institute, the last two sponsored by the College Board. These activities are invaluable in preparing a teacher for the new AP course, and their effects will be felt throughout the school, as will be discussed later in this chapter.

Certainly the most important responsibility of the principal is the selection of excellent teachers. Indeed, this is critically important to the Advanced Placement English course: "No school should begin an advanced placement program without a distinguished teacher in each subject it undertakes" (Fenton 237). The principal will be able to select this distinguished teacher in the late fall only after department meetings have familiarized the English faculty with the nature and demands of the course. Interested teachers should submit applications, and the principal should make the appointment based upon the teacher's enthusiasm for the projected course and successful experience in teaching gifted students, two factors that overwhelm most other considerations.

The Department Chair

In the earliest stages, the chair works very closely with the rest of the administration, defining the nature and scope of the AP course as well as the support from faculty, students, and parents. Obviously, the chair will work most intensely within the department on disseminating program information, establishing a positive attitude toward the course, directing an examination of the existing English curriculum, and juggling teaching schedules for the approaching year. Other duties include assisting the principal in selecting an instructor, working on the budget, and gradually effecting good public relations among the faculty for the program.

In early fall department meetings, the chair should introduce the English faculty to the two AP English courses. An effective resource during these discussions is a copy of the "acorn" booklet for each teacher. After other groundwork has been completed, the department will be a strong voice in deciding how to structure the AP program to best meet the needs of the students and meld with the English curriculum. Should the Language and Composition course be offered to juniors and the Literature and Composition to seniors? Or should the department offer only one of these courses? The department must work to provide the most meaningful options to gifted students. This principle must be repeatedly invoked to avoid resentment from members who may believe the course to be a permit allowing a colleague to raid classes in search of good students. The AP program depends upon cooperation and close coordination among all English department members, especially those who teach students identified as possible members of the AP class.

The open exchange within the English department and within English classes will facilitate discussion with students and parents regarding the proposed course. The parent-student questionnaires can become a more meaningful means of communication when amplified by class discussion. The English class, then, can be a major forum in formulating and clarifying the nature of the AP course and other areas of the curriculum.

The chair should assist department members in a thorough examination of the existing English curriculum, commencing in the early fall after the dust has settled from the opening of school. This review should emphasize, but not be limited to, the sequence of reading and writing skills taught in the ninth through eleventh grade honors courses, as these are the firm foundation required by the AP program. This review will help the faculty strengthen the English curriculum in terms of proper sequence and relevance of skills taught on all levels.

Certainly, the chair must be involved in the application process for the position of AP instructor. If the chair is an applicant for the position, he or she will have an obviously limited role. If not, then he or she can serve as the principal's contact person and provide input on the decision. Following the choice of the AP English instructor, the chair will face the usual job of juggling teacher schedules following spring registration. The introduction of the Advanced Placement course won't add anything dramatically new to this process. One consideration, however, will be to schedule the course during a period that won't conflict with some of the other courses taken by gifted seniors. Frequent aggravations in the scheduling dilemma come from single-section courses that must be scattered throughout the day to enable students to take the most appropriate courses and not have to abandon one due to a conflict. The chair must keep these issues in mind and begin looking over the schoolwide master schedule, addressing this issue at meetings with other department chairs, the principal, and guidance personnel to arrange classes to best meet students' needs.

Many other responsibilities will naturally occur throughout this formative school year and beyond. The English chair will work on the budget with the principal and the instructor, the primary ordering agent; serve as ambassador for the course with the faculty, students, and parents; take an increasingly larger role, along with the instructor, in informing the faculty and department of developments and progress of the course and its students; present insights into the course, perhaps through presentations by successful AP instructors from nearby schools; and generally keep all avenues of dialogue open so the program is well presented.

The AP Teacher

"The most important variable in the [AP] program's success is the quality of the teacher..." (Fenton 237). To be chosen as an Advanced Placement English instructor is certainly an honor—and an incredible responsibility. This person, again, is chosen because of demonstrated excellence and enthusiasm in working with academically able students. The teacher, much like the department chair, should take an active role in promoting the program, ordering materials, and assisting in student registration, as well as personally preparing for the course through study, workshops, institutes, and contact with other AP teachers.

Advanced Placement instruction is one of the most exciting opportunities for intellectual and professional growth, again proving that the benefits of the AP program aren't limited to students:

> An obvious reason for the Program's growth is that it appeals to teachers, and for good reasons. Although for school teachers the AP Course in English usually demands wider and deeper reading, more scrupulous course organization, more challenging teaching, as well as the more public prospect of an "outside examination," the rewards of engagement in a course and program that associates them with a national group of teachers and scholars are very real. (Smith 116)

Two important aspects of teacher preparation are the Advanced Placement workshop held locally in the late fall/early winter and a regional two-week summer institute. Not only is the information presented at these meetings invaluable but the teacher will also meet experienced AP colleagues, a source of support, advice, and direction for the arduous process of planning and implementation. Some of these colleagues may teach in nearby schools, enabling the neophyte instructor to spend a day or two watching a successful AP program in operation. Of particular benefit to the new teacher is the opportunity to examine materials used in some AP classes and to discuss them with instructors. The teacher may also find supplementary materials compiled by local districts, such as one resource book for AP English teachers created by teachers and supervisor Dr. Mary Henderson of Sarasota County, Florida, or another created by the Division of Communication Skills in the North Carolina Department of Public Instruction. The Advanced Placement booklets from the College Board suggest a variety of materials recommended by teachers throughout the country, but it is increasingly difficult to obtain sample texts from publishers and even more difficult to take the time to review them all. In matters of ordering materials, the instructor should be the dominant voice while working within the budgetary framework established by the principal and the department chair.

Close contact with other AP teachers can help the instructor resolve a multitude of concerns about implementing the course, selecting useful materials, and devising a syllabus. All teachers can attest to the professional and intellectual excitement of sharing ideas and innovative experiences with fellow teachers. Advanced Placement is no different. Well supplied with advice on curricula and materials, the AP instructor can then begin some of the final and most important steps in establishing this and future classes.

Registration: Students, Parents, and Teacher

Throughout this prefatory school year, administration, faculty, parents, and students have been working in concert toward establishing the Advanced Placement English course. Therefore, as registration looms in the spring, all parties will be able to work from informed positions as they prepare for the senior (or junior) year and the AP course. Many school personnel are involved in the process, but the AP teacher will probably be the one to direct many of the steps involved in formulating the first and subsequent classes.

The AP teacher should speak to all eleventh grade honors classes at least two weeks prior to their actual registration in order to give a general view of the course (to which students have already been introduced) and to answer any remaining questions. Interested students should then fill out an application form and return it to the AP teacher. The form should include a written course description and request the following: previous English courses taken and grades earned, approval from the student's English teacher and parent (signatures should be required), current and projected extracurricular activities, after-school employment and number of hours worked per week, PSAT verbal score (if available), and a brief statement from the applicant expressing reasons for wishing to enroll in the course.

The AP teacher should then notify these students of an hour-long meeting, perhaps before or after school, in order to obtain a writing sample under controlled conditions, much like the AP exam itself. Topics for writing may be based upon readings or themes covered in the junior English class or may use topics from previous AP examinations. The writing sample provides an actual sample of the student's own writing and indicates whether or not any serious deficiencies exist. It is also a further affirmation of the student's commitment to the course.

The applications and student writing samples should then be reviewed by a committee of interested English teachers including the AP instructor, the junior (or sophomore) English teacher(s), and the department chair. This committee can then decide which students should take the course. The decision to counsel a student against enrolling should be based on one or more of the following reasons. A student's writing samples indicate severe deficiencies. A student applied because of peer or parental pressure while lacking the writing and critical thinking skills necessary. A student with marginal writing capabilities is so heavily involved in extracurricular activities and/or jobs that his or her enrollment would be unwise. These borderline students may also have low PSAT verbal scores, casting serious doubt on their ability to succeed in the course. Many teachers and counselors familiar with the AP program find that a PSAT verbal score of 50 has a high correlation with success in the AP course and on the AP examination. Of course, any reliance on a single test score as a requirement for enrollment is inadvisable.

Each student must be individually counseled by the AP instructor or by his or her current English teacher about the results of the preregistration process. The reasons for discouraging a student from enrolling in the course should be clearly explained, yet not etched in stone. The teacher-advisor must inform borderline students of the reasons for serious reservations about their enrollment in Advanced Placement English. However, if a student with potential possesses enough motivation, he or she shouldn't be denied a place in a class.

Enrollment in the Advanced Placement English class is an honor, an acknowledgment of ability and achievement. As such, the school may choose to invite students and parents to an evening reception in their honor, hosted by the principal, AP coordinator, English department chair, and the AP teacher. The parents have been involved throughout the process and will not need a lengthy information session about the program. However, in addition to recognizing parents for their cooperation, the school will have further reasons for this function, some of which are

- to address questions parents may still have about the program;
- to remind parents of the fee for the examination at the end of the year and the availability of fee reductions for students with actual need;

- to impress parents once more with the amount of study and dedication the course requires;
- to encourage parents to continue an active interest in the AP program throughout the upcoming year through dialogue with the school and their children; and
- to effect positive public relations.

The reception's coordinator should consider ordering some materials through the College Board to further enhance this function. The 13-minute color film or videotape, *AP: Option for Excellence*, can be rented for $15 from the College Board Film Library, c/o RHR Filmedia, 9 East 38 Street, New York, NY 10016, (212) 686–9833. The following pamphlets are also appropriate for this meeting: *Some Questions and Answers about the Advanced Placement Program* (up to 50 free copies), *What College Students Say about Advanced Placement* (single free copy, inquire about more), and *Sophomore Standing through Advanced Placement* (up to 50 free copies).

A Final Note

Clearly, considerable work is required to establish an Advanced Placement English program. When the course becomes a reality, students and teacher alike will embark on one of the most challenging and exciting experiences available in a high school curriculum. Not only will the participants benefit, so will the school:

> Most secondary schools have noted that when they introduce advanced placement courses, the work of the entire institution is affected. The existence of college-level courses for superior students in certain subject fields has almost invariably set a standard of performance which has affected both content and teaching in other courses. (Paschal 26)

Cooperation between students, parents, and teachers will contribute to making the Advanced Placement English course a reality, a promising option available to the academically able. As noted by one of these gifted students who experienced a variety of programs for superior students, "On balance, we believe that AP is one of the best options around for an individual student to start exercising some control over his education. If AP courses are not offered at your school, start agitating" (American 87). With foresight, professional planning, and a continuing open forum, students won't have to agitate to obtain viable options in their education. The schools will have anticipated their needs and will have responded.

Works Cited

Advanced Placement Course Description: English. N.p.: College Entrance Examination Board, 1986.

American Association for Gifted Children. *On Being Gifted.* New York: Walker, 1978.

Beginning an Advanced Placement English Course. N.p.: College Entrance Examination Board, 1976.

Fenton, Edwin. "Honors Programs in the Secondary Schools." *The Superior Student in American Higher Education.* Ed. Joseph W. Cohen. New York: McGraw, 1966. 219–52.

A Guide to the Advanced Placement Program. N.p.: College Entrance Examination Board, 1983.

Hanson, Harlan P. "25 Years of Encouraging Able Students." *Education Digest* 26.7 (1981): 48–51.

Paschal, Elizabeth. *Encouraging the Excellent.* New York: The Fund for the Advancement of Education, 1960.

Smith, Paul. "Language, Literature, and Advanced Placement." *Journal of Education* 162.2 (1980): 114–25.

6

The AP Literature and
Composition Course

JAN GUFFIN

North Central High School
Indianapolis, Indiana

Guffin discusses the curricular objectives of the Literature and Composition course, presents alternative ways to organize the course, distinguishes between planned and impromptu writing assignments, and lists some typical obstacles to an effective course. The author provides several useful handouts and writing assignments.

The focus of this chapter is the Advanced Placement course in English Literature and Composition. It discusses the goals of the course, the student audience for whom it is intended, typical formats for organizing it, the integration of language skills, resources for teachers and students, and additional considerations for those about to institute such a course or those seeking to enrich an existing course.

The course title itself raises a couple of important questions: Does *course* mean a syllabus for a single school term or a course of study over a longer period of time? Does *English Literature* mean the literature of England or literature written in or translated into the English language? In effect, the title means any or all of the above. In some schools, for example, a single course syllabus serves as a capstone to previous accelerated courses and focuses specifically on helping students refine their skills in critical reading and writing. In other schools, the title stands for a broader course of study: the sequence of courses that accelerated students take over a three- or four-year period, at the end of which they may or may not elect to take the AP examination. In some cases, the course focuses exclusively on the literature of England or Great Britain; in others, it includes not only works written originally in English but also works in translation. The College Board, in fact, does not prescribe a rigid course outline or list of works to be studied; instead, it describes the general goals of the course and invites participating schools to determine the most appropriate format and content for their respective locales.

Course Goals

What are these common goals? How do they relate to the purpose of the course? For what student audience are they intended? Though the goals have remained essentially the same since the AP program was first established, they are updated every year or two in College Board publications. These goals are most succinctly stated in *The College Board Examinations in English Language Skills and Literature*:

> The AP Examination in Literature and Composition assumes the student's deliberate and systematic preparation in college-level English. In addition to being skilled in reading and analyzing literature, students should have experience in writing not only expository essays but also critical essays related to literary topics. It is assumed that students have learned to use varying modes of discourse and are able to recognize the assumptions and effects of various rhetorical strategies. Students are expected to have studied intensively a few representative works of recognized literary merit from several genres and periods. (9)

In the most practical sense, one might argue that the course exists to prepare students for an external exam, and perhaps some students and teachers do think of the course in this way. In other words, if at the conclusion of the course, students are able to demonstrate by external examination an ability to read and respond to literature in a way comparable to that of college sophomores, they have satisfied the most obvious purpose of the course. Experienced AP teachers, however, would likely urge a more philosophical view of course preparation and insist that the examination, though important, is but one of several important long-term goals, such as the following:

- to learn at a rate commensurate with one's ability;
- to deal with material that intellectually mature students find engaging;

- to refine reading and writing skills important for success, not only in college but also in the professional world;
- to cultivate habits of reading, writing, speaking, and thinking which characterize lifelong learning and enjoyment. (Corey et al. 2–3)

The business of learning and teaching in an AP course emerges from somewhere between the practical and the philosophical. Students and teachers read a variety of texts of recognized literary merit, respond to them in different ways—through class discussions, informal and formal writing assignments, oral presentations, and library research—and eventually develop by consensus the standards of critical appraisal that enable an individual to read, understand, and enjoy literature. This process also means adopting concrete learning objectives, such as improving one's comprehension by

- asking pertinent questions about the assumptions and implications of a given work;
- describing how language contributes both literally and figuratively to the meaning of a work;
- drawing conclusions about the themes of a work, appraising them and speculating independently on related ideas;
- describing the relationship between form and content in a literary work; and
- reflecting on and evaluating what one has read. (Corey et al. 5–6)

And this means coming to

- view writing as a developed discipline that includes collecting information, formulating ideas and determining their relationships, drafting paragraphs and arranging them in an appropriate order with transitions between them, and revising what has been written;
- responding in writing clearly and fully to questions about a literary work;
- using the conventions of standard written English with skill and assurance; and
- writing appropriately for different occasions, audiences, and purposes (persuading, explaining, describing, interpreting). (Corey et al. 6)

AP Students

Criteria for selecting students for such a course vary from the exclusive use of standardized test scores to policies of open admission. Selection criteria depend necessarily on such factors as the size of the student population, the availability of qualified teachers, a system-wide policy for accelerated students, and the role of parents in determining school programs. In simplest terms, it's fair to say that successful AP students are those who consistently perform above grade level on standardized tests or who demonstrate that they are capable of doing more challenging work in reading and writing than most of their peers are.

But these are only base-line considerations. More important than empirical data are the attitudes and intellectual behaviors of students likely to succeed in the course. Typically, they aren't satisfied with the obvious or superficial in their study of literature; they enjoy examining ideas and come to accept that some questions may remain unanswered or that there may be several defensible answers to the same question; and they are capable of reflecting on what they read. With comparable patience and skill, they are able to work with language at both concrete and abstract levels, moving, for example, from examining specific literary passages for considerations of diction to the more global features of a text, such as theme, character, and style. They are also students who can develop skill in responding to different literary genres and who come to demonstrate poise in explaining the relationships among subject, speaker, and audience in a literary work. Being able to express oneself creatively is not a prerequisite to participating meaningfully in the course, though possessing the curiosity and the courage to attempt different kinds of expression enhances growth in responding to and using language.

Organizing the Course

With such goals and students in mind, there are numerous possibilities for organizing a course. Most typically, teachers organize the Literature and Composition course by genre, theme, or time period, perhaps because teaching materials for these formats are readily available. Each of these plans has its merits in helping students achieve the goals of the program and in preparing them for the exam.

Organizing the course by genre, for example, forms a natural basis for comparing factors that affect the relationships among speaker, subject, and audience in one genre or another. How, for example, do lyric poets and dramatists affect their audiences in different ways? It also permits students to explore the evolution of a given genre and speculate on its current and future status. When students are able to understand the prominence of the novel as an art form in the nineteenth century, for instance, and can relate its prominence to the proliferation of discursive prose in the twentieth century, they are in a position to raise intelligent questions about the needs and tastes of readers in their own generation. And focusing on one literary genre at a time allows students to become increasingly familiar with major authors and works in that genre, thereby sharpening their awareness of the critical standards usually applied to a given genre and helping them become better critics themselves.

Organizing the course by themes, on the other hand, may promote a fuller understanding of how artists working in different genres undertake artistic renderings of similar ideas. Seeing how a poet, a playwright, an essayist, a short story writer, and a novelist each interpret the conflict of human wills, for example, eventually enables students to analyze why one artist is better served by poetry and another by drama when dealing with a similar theme. The thematic plan also illustrates the universality of literary ideas by showing the timeless and timely qualities of works written in different times for different audiences. Moreover, it helps illustrate how a single important idea is integrated into and shaped by a genre, thus enabling both students and teacher to further examine a given theme by bringing to the course examples from current art or their own experience.

Organizing the course chronologically offers still other possibilities. The chronological format, more than the other patterns, lends itself to the study of a writer and his or her times. Looking more closely at authors in the context of the social, political, and intellectual history that surrounds their work enables students to understand the evolution of literary art, as well as the idiosyncrasies of thought or style in a given work. Students following a chronological format come to understand more deeply the uniqueness of a Conrad story, a Dickinson poem, or a Hemingway novel by looking carefully at the life and times of these writers and perceiving the imprint of their personalities on their work.

If time, inventiveness, and resources permit, teachers naturally need not feel constrained to organize the course in any of these three ways. Those who rely on paperback books instead of anthologies, for example, may choose topical ideas (such as The Seven Ages of Man or Archetypal Women through the Centuries) as organizing principles for the course. Or they may choose to showcase certain writers, such as Nobel laureates, or writers known for the advances they made in various literary genres, or writers who were famous rebels during their times. The limits on how a course is organized are often those which we as teachers impose on ourselves. So long as the course objectives promoted by the College Board and the AP development committee (itself made up of teachers from schools and colleges) are consistently addressed in a given course, students will become enthusiastic and astute readers.

A helpful way to keep these objectives before students is to consider growth in the study of literature and language as a recursive experience that integrates the arts of language: reading, writing, speaking, and listening. Figure 6–1 illustrates this idea. At the center of the circle are the course format and materials chosen by the teacher. Around the circle are the kinds of language activities likely to be found in any AP literature course: close and survey reading, as well as in- and out-of-class writing. Collectively, these elements provide a matrix that suggests not only a balance of one kind of reading or writing against another, but also linkage of one activity to another. (I explain these activities briefly in Corey et al. 7–8; a fuller discussion appears in *Academic Preparation in English* 29–32.)

The ideas of recursiveness, integration, and balance in course design

**Figure 6–1　Curricular/Instructional Considerations for AP English
Literature and Composition**

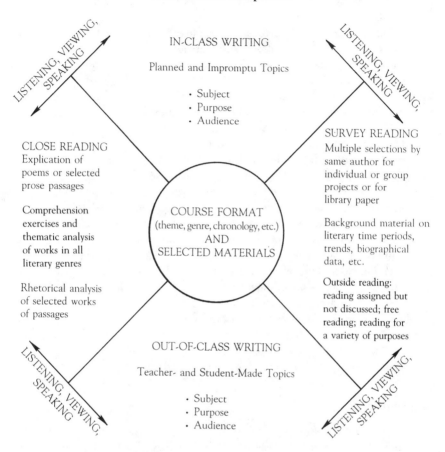

IN-CLASS WRITING

Planned and Impromptu Topics

- Subject
- Purpose
- Audience

LISTENING, VIEWING, SPEAKING

LISTENING, VIEWING, SPEAKING

CLOSE READING
Explication of
poems or selected
prose passages

Comprehension
exercises and
thematic analysis
of works in all
literary genres

Rhetorical analysis
of selected works
of passages

COURSE FORMAT
(theme, genre, chronology, etc.)
AND
SELECTED MATERIALS

SURVEY READING
Multiple selections by
same author for
individual or group
projects or for
library paper

Background material on
literary time periods,
trends, biographical
data, etc.

Outside reading:
reading assigned but
not discussed; free
reading; reading for
a variety of purposes

LISTENING, VIEWING, SPEAKING

OUT-OF-CLASS WRITING

Teacher- and Student-Made Topics

- Subject
- Purpose
- Audience

LISTENING, VIEWING, SPEAKING

may be clarified by the format, materials, and class activities of a sample
class. For example, imagine the school year divided into six grading periods
of equal length. During the year, the teacher wishes to progress chronologically through a survey of world literature. This chronological format relieves
the teacher to some extent of worrying about representative time periods;
the more difficult task will be to ensure that all genres receive sufficient
attention.

Once representative works have been charted for each grading period,
the teacher can proceed to a more difficult challenge: planning integrated
activities for each grading period. A mix of in-class and out-of-class writing,
and of close and survey readings is ideal. The teacher should introduce some
impromptu in-class writing assignments (students come to class knowing
they will write but not knowing the topic) and some that are planned (students come to class to write on material they have read, discussed, and

reviewed over a period of several days). Out-of-class writing should include papers written on specified topics and others on topics generated by the students themselves.

Figure 6–2 shows the results of such careful planning and illustrates what recursiveness, integration, and balance come to mean in practical terms. Though it seems simplistic to reduce any course to a mix-and-match teacher exercise, it is at least fair to say that an AP Literature and Composition course should maintain integrity as a college-level course yet reflect the teacher's orientation toward the study of literature and writing.

The approach described here favors variety in course content and student activity at the expense, one might argue, of devoting sufficient attention to the students' learning to write a literary essay. Or one might argue that it favors survey reading at the expense of in-depth reading of a greater number of works. One might even argue that the notion of language growth as a series of recursive experiences integrating a variety of language activities need not be so geometrically orchestrated. However, through my own experience, I have come to believe strongly that courses that focus exclusively on either breadth or depth of experience in literature or on mastering a single kind of discourse do a serious disservice not only to the AP students but also to literary art. What makes the language of English universally appealing and useful is its liveliness and dynamism. To fragment it for purposes of simple mastery is to minimize or ignore its most brilliant properties. If AP students hold the greatest promise for preserving and expanding the utility and the art of English, they deserve to experience the language in all its forms—again, and again, and again.

Resources

Regardless of the plan devised for the course in Literature and Composition, the teacher will discover high school textbooks sorely lacking in materials and assignments. If one is lucky enough to have fellow teachers with whom to interact, there is no better resource for trying out new ideas and refining old ones. Many teachers are not so fortunate, however, and they virtually work in a vacuum, either because of the smallness of their schools or their colleagues' lack of interest. In such a case, the College Board itself is the next best resource. Each year, the College Board sponsors one-day workshops across the country attended by teachers who share similar questions and interests and workshop leaders experienced in teaching AP Literature and Composition. Participants at these workshops can count on a lively exchange of ideas about curriculum and instruction, as well as on obtaining effective assignments that other teachers have tried. The College Board also shares former AP test questions with workshop participants. These questions naturally help acquaint students with the kinds of questions they will encounter on the exam, but, more importantly, they also provide the teacher with ideas for questions to be developed at home.

Reading

Grading Period	1	2	3	4	5	6
Close	Drama: Tragedy Folk Epic Lyric Poetry Prose Satire	Literary Epic Short Fiction Autobiography	Drama: Tragedy Nonfiction Lyric Poetry Short Fiction	Drama: Comedy Tragedy Nonfiction Prose Satire Lyric Poetry	Lyric Poetry Narrative Poetry Novel Short Fiction	Novel Drama: Tragedy Lyric Poetry
Survey	Drama Short Fiction	Short Fiction	Drama Nonfiction	Novel		Short Fiction

Writing

	1	2	3	4	5	6
In-Class: Planned	Unit Test Essay	Unit Test Essay	Semester Exam Essay Editorial Persona Essay	Unit Test Essay	Essay on Flaubert	Final Exam Essay
Impromptu	Rhetorical Analysis of Prose Passage	Configurations Essay		Analysis of Lyric Poetry	Rhetorical Analysis of Prose Passage	Essay on U.S. Census
Out-of-Class: Teacher-made Topic		Inductive Essay on Maxims (Expressive/ Transactional)	Letter to Famous Author (Expressive/ Transactional/ Persuasive)	Library Work Begins	Library Paper Due (see novel, above)	Analysis of Poetry (Transactional/ Analytical)
Student-made Topic	Essay on Place (Expressive)	Creative Writing: Poetry	Creative Writing: Prose	Literary Analysis (Transactional/ Analytical)	Essay on Definition (Transactional/ Persuasive)	

Certainly, a teacher who merely recycles old exam questions through-out the semester or year still offers students some benefit. To do only this, however, underestimates what AP students are capable of doing and ignores the learning that can take place only in the classroom, but which can't be used, for one reason or another, on a national exam. (See John Iorio's chapter in this text.) In integrating exam questions into the course, the teacher should keep in mind several questions: What link to reading, to discussion, to the real world does a given assignment provide? What level of critical thinking is demanded of students to experience new insights about a literary work, about themselves, about what they have studied in preceding weeks, or about what they will study in subsequent units? How flexible is the assign-ment in allowing students to generate original ideas? In other words, is the assignment so narrow that all papers will reflect the same supposedly right answer, or are the assignment's learning objectives, though specifically re-lated to those for the AP course and exam, general enough that students can satisfy them with some of their own ideas?

Sample Writing Assignments

The assignments that follow illustrate how effective assignments can open out towards the other language arts, invite original responses, link students' thinking to reading and discussion, and prepare them adequately for a good performance on the AP exam in the process.

Planned Assignments

The first two assignments might be considered *planned* topics because they ask students to write about literature they have read carefully, discussed at length in class, and thought about on their own. These assignments il-lustrate two kinds of planned topics: one for writing in response to a series of works, the other in response to a novel. In the first case, students have read works by six authors on six quite different subjects. In preparation for their in-class essay, they have reviewed their class notes to remind them-selves of major ideas found in each work, of stylistic features noted during discussion, and of details of the selections they might use to develop their essays. The assignment itself asks students to use critical reading/writing skills to produce a new idea from the information they have gathered—to reorganize it in a way to show interrelationships not previously discussed. The value of this kind of assignment is in its ability to engage students in the process of classifying information in a way that provides new insights on individual selections and on the selections as a group. Since the process of classifying this information relates directly to reading and classroom discus-sion, it seems less artificial to students than, say, a question that asks the same thing about material they aren't familiar with. Such an assignment also provides a positive alternative to the predictable question that asks students to feed back to the teacher major points about each work discussed in class.

PLANNED TOPIC #1

The six selections listed below can be grouped into various categories, each group designating some category under the general subject of *power*. Arrange these selections into no fewer than two such groups, no more than three (you may list a given selection more than once). Then write an essay in which you elaborate on the works you have categorized in *one* of your groups, explaining, in effect, your rationale for organizing them as you have. In your explanation, consider parallels and/or contrasts among the works in a single group.

Antigone   *Confessions of St. Augustine* *The Poetics*
Apology of Socrates *Dinner with Trimalchio*   *Medea*

POWER

Group I	Group II	Group III
(category/ kind of power)	(category/ kind of power)	(category/ kind of power)
Works	Works	Works

The second writing assignment functions similarly, but it is geared towards a single work in a single genre. Some teachers opt not to have students write about a novel once it has been studied in depth simply because the essay question is likely to require nothing more than giving back to the teacher what has been said about the novel during class discussion. Such a question serves no real purpose other than to give students practice in a writing pattern they have probably already mastered. The question here, however, asks the student to rethink the novel in a different way. Students will have talked about the conclusion of the novel, no doubt, but probably not in relation to the novel as a whole in the same way the question asks them to. By looking back over the novel to determine what is revealed, students write their way to a larger understanding of the book and test their ability to produce a logically organized, fully developed essay that uses the resources they bring to class from previous study.

PLANNED TOPIC #2

One mark of a superior novel is that its conclusion serves a dual purpose. Whereas in a lesser work the conclusion merely *resolves*, or brings to a close, the conflicts of the story, in a superior work, the conclusion both *resolves* and *reveals:* it brings to a close the conflicts, but it also reveals to the reader the significance of those conflicts in relation to a major theme(s) of the work. Write an essay in which you explain how the conclusion to the novel you have read serves this dual function.

Impromptu Assignment

The following impromptu question asks students to exercise quite different skills. Here, after looking closely in class at passages by Erasmus, Melville, Cellini, and Franklin, students are given a new passage and asked to apply what they have learned about rhetorical strategies in their previous study. This passage might be considered too easy to appear on the AP exam itself, but it serves beautifully as a classroom exercise. It is an abbreviated version of Deems Taylor's essay on Richard Wagner in *Of Men and Music*.

IMPROMPTU TOPIC #1

Study the following passage carefully. Then write an essay in which you (a) identify Taylor's apparent aim and (b) explain in detail the major rhetorical devices he employs in meeting that aim.

The Monster

He was an undersized little man, with a head too big for his body—a sickly little man. His nerves were bad. He had skin trouble. It was agony for him to wear anything next to his skin coarser than silk. And he had delusions of grandeur.

He was a monster of conceit. Never for one minute did he look at the world or at people, except in relation to himself; in his own eyes he was the only person who existed. He believed himself to be one of the greatest dramatists in the world, one of the greatest thinkers, and one of the greatest composers. To hear him talk, he was Shakespeare, and Beethoven, and Plato, rolled into one. And you would have had no difficulty in hearing him talk. He was one of the most exhaustive conversationalists that ever lived. An evening with him was an evening spent in listening to a monologue. Sometimes he was brilliant; sometimes he was maddeningly tiresome. But whether he was being brilliant or dull, he had one sole topic of conversation: himself. What he thought and what he did . . . .

The name of this monster was Richard Wagner. Everything I have said about him you can find on record—in newspapers, in police reports, in the testimony of people who knew him, in his own letters, between the lines of his autobiography. And the curious thing about this record is that it doesn't matter in the least.

Because this undersized, sickly, disagreeable, fascinating little man was right all the time. The joke was on us. He was one of the world's great dramatists; he was a great thinker; he was one of the most stupendous musical geniuses that, up to now, the world has ever seen.

People couldn't know those things at the time, I suppose; and yet to us, who know his music, it does seem as though they should have known. Listening to his music, one does not forgive him for what he may or may not have been. It is not a matter of forgiveness. It is a matter of being dumb with wonder that this poor brain and body didn't burst under the torment of the demon of creative energy that lived inside him, struggling, clawing, scratching to be released; tearing, shrieking at him, to write the music that was in him. The miracle is that what he did in the little space of seventy years could have been done at all, even by a great genius.

Is it any wonder that he had not time to be a man?

Deems Taylor

Impromptu/Planned Assignment

The second impromptu question is best considered in relation to the out-of-class assignment with which it is paired. These two assignments were used in the same unit on the eighteenth century, the impromptu at the beginning of the unit and the out-of-class paper near the end. Near the beginning of this unit, without having talked much about the use of language to express either universal laws or particular ideas, students were asked to name a configuration and to provide a rationale for the name. This task serves two important purposes: by engaging students with language in a novel way, it relieves them of worrying about providing a right answer and allows them to concentrate on the rhetoric of their own prose; and without their knowing it, it prepares them for a close look at how language was used by Neoclassical writers, not merely to achieve elegance, but also to express a world view about which they felt great certainty.

IMPROMPTU TOPIC #2

Read the following statement about our tendency to use language in a personally meaningful way:

> Learning that people and things have names is man's basic lesson in his acquisition of language, and once he begins to grasp the naming idea, his demand to know the names of things is almost limitless. This desire to get things "pinned down" and so to feel at home with them seems to be a natural phenomenon (at least within historic time), even when nothing demonstrably practical appears to depend on it.
>
> Dorris Garey

After studying the configuration pictured below, give it a name. Then write a well-developed essay in which you explain your reasons for naming it as you have and discuss the possible significance of the thing you have named.

After these papers were returned and responses discussed at length, the students were ready to approach the literature of the unit with an increased awareness of language precision. They then read Pope's *Rape of the Lock*, a substantial portion of his *Essay on Man*, a play by Molière, and Voltaire's *Candide*, and looked at the turns of phrase of LaRochefoucauld and LaFontaine. Finally, they were given the following out-of-class assignment and a full week to complete all three steps. Step 1 of the assignment asks students to reduce the already economical phrasing of LaRochefoucauld to a single word, and then to elaborate in their own prose on the topic they pulled from the original.

STEP 1: PREWRITING

Directions: Each of you has been assigned one maxim. Now do the following:

1. Choose a partner to work with.
2. Copy each of your maxims below:
   a. _____
   _____
   _____
   b. _____
   _____
   _____

3. Reduce each maxim to one word that identifies the general topic of the maxim. (Example: deceit, vulnerability, etc.)
   a. _____
   b. _____

4. Collaborate with your partner to write an original, succinct, elegantly phrased, memorable, and quotable maxim that deals with each of the topics you named in section 3 of step 1. Copy each of your new maxims below; sign both of your names.
   a. _____
   b. _____

5. Hand in your paper at the end of the period.

Step 2 takes the students from the specific, seemingly trivial details from *Harper's* "Index" to a general statement about their own culture, based on combining the bits of data which appear in random order.

STEP 2a: PREWRITING
Moving from Specific to General

Attached is a list of random facts about American behavior, drawn from various issues of *Harper's* magazine. Assume the role of a twentieth century *moraliste*. Consider these behaviors in relation to one another, and group them in three or four categories. Then join a discussion group in which you brainstorm generalizations about at least two categories. On this sheet write the category, the generalization, and the numbers of the facts that pertain to each generalization.

Category: _____
Generalization: _____

_____

_____

Facts that pertain: _____   _____   _____   _____   _____

_____   _____   _____   _____   _____

Category: _____
Generalization: _____

_____

_____

Facts that pertain: _____   _____   _____   _____   _____

_____   _____   _____   _____   _____

Category: _____
Generalization: _____

_____

_____

Facts that pertain: _____   _____   _____   _____   _____

_____   _____   _____   _____   _____

Facts about Americans: *Harper's* "Index"
(February, August, October, November, 1985)

1. Budget per episode of *Miami Vice:* $1,500,000
2. Budget of the Miami vice squad unit in 1984: $1,161,741
3. Number of high school marching bands that ordered the sheet music for "Barbara Ann" in 1985: 3,000
4. Percentage of black men with college degrees who work for the government: 33%
5. Percentage of black women with college degrees who do: 45%
6. Percentage of black children who live below the poverty line: 46.7%
7. Percentage of women executives with MBA's who say their pregnancies were planned: 93.8%
8. Percentage of other women executives who say this: 73.3%

9. Amount U.S. Government spent on paper shredders in 1984: $4,000,000

10. Portion of all goods sold in U.S. today that is imported: 1/5

11. Percentage of Americans who say news portrays politicians "too favorably": 46%

12. Who say it portrays sports stars "too favorably": 54%

13. Percentage of Americans who say Monday is their favorite day of the week: 3%

14. U.S. spending on health care in 1960, expressed as a percentage of the gross national product: 5.3%

15. Today: 10.6%

16. Price of a "terrorist-proof" Mercedes 500 at Washington's Counter Spy Shop: $208,000

17. Portion of American households made up of a single person in 1955: 1/10

18. Today: 1/4

19. Percentage of men who say they are happier since their divorce: 58%

20. Percentage of women who say this: 85%

21. Percentage increase since 1980 in number of lawyers who specialize in divorce cases: 100%

22. Percentage of federal district court judges appointed by President Carter who are millionaires: 4%

23. Percentage appointed by President Reagan who are: 22.5%

24. Percentage of Fortune 500 companies that tested employees and job applicants for illegal drug use in 1982: 10%

25. Percentage that test today: 25%

26. Number of Fabergé Imperial eggs owned by Malcolm Forbes: 11

27. By the Kremlin: 10

28. Weekly sales per square foot near the cash registers in the average supermarket: $22.80

29. Per square foot elsewhere in the store: $7.76

30. Percentage of men between the ages of 55 and 59 who were retired in 1970: 10.5%

31. Who are retired today: 20%

32. Number of Americans who commute from a suburb to a city to go to work: 13,900,000

33. Who commute from one suburb to another: 26,900,000

34. Americans arrested for spying from 1965 to 1975: 7

35. Since 1975: 42

36. Portion of the personal mail sent in 1984 that consisted of greeting cards: 1/2

37. Copies of *The Catcher in the Rye* checked out of public libraries in Chicago and never returned: 7,500

38. Rejection rate of applicants for the 1985 kindergarten class at Manhattan's Trinity Episcopal School: 85%

39. For the 1985 entering class at Stanford University: 86%

STEP 2b: PREWRITING:
Moving from General to Specific

Re-examine the generalizations your group produced using the facts from *Harper's* magazine. Using one of the generalizations, write freely, trying to think of a sobriquet for the America or the American people of the 80s. You may create a new word to reflect the generalization, an acronym, an anagram, a palindrome, or use a short hyphenated phrase. Then write a rationale for why Americans should henceforth be known as _____ .

The final step of the assignment takes students back through prewriting activities, now on their own, and asks them to take a good look at the culture in which they're living and make an assertion about it that they can support with reference to empirical data.

STEP 3: WRITING ASSIGNMENT
Persuasive Aim

Objectives:

1. To relate Neoclassical thought to contemporary life
2. To use language for expanding and reducing ideas
3. To consider the relationship between literal and figurative uses of language
4. To improve diction and tone
5. To practice inductive and deductive reasoning
6. To practice the persuasive aim
7. To practice documentation

Materials:

1. Prewriting materials done in class
2. Two lists of facts from *Harper's* magazine
3. *English Language and Writing Skills*: Chapter 16, Chapter 17 (pp. 348–51), Chapter 19 (pp. 513–17)
4. Class notes on anagrams, palindromes, etc.

Procedure:

1. Use the same procedure we followed in class to arrive at a sobriquet for the America (or the American) of the 80s.
2. Your audience is made up of the same people who would read *Harper's*: college educated, interested in our culture, curious about the ideas of others, and appreciative of the power and the mystery of language.

3. When you have a name to write about and your evidence from *Harper's*, which you will use to develop your thesis, draft a paper that asserts that your new term is sufficiently meaningful to be adopted as a new nickname for our culture.
4. As you develop your paper, keep in mind what appeal(s) you are using (logical, emotional, ethical) and what tone you seek to maintain.
5. Try to persuade your reader by using material from *Harper's* in the body of your paper.
6. Edit your paper for standard written English; check documentation carefully.

FACTS
(from *Harper's*: February, August, October, November, 1985)

1. Percentage of fifth-graders who say they think a lot about hunger and poverty in the U.S.: 52%
2. Percentage of ninth-graders who say this: 31%
3. Percentage of refrigerators in American households that are either white or almond: 90%
4. Average number of new recipes tried in American households every month: 1.6
5. Percentage of Americans who say there should be a law against interracial marriage: 27%
6. Percentage of families in New York City with annual incomes over $50,000 that are black: 7%
7. Of families in Chicago: 20%
8. Legal fees paid by CBS to outside counsel in 1984: $10,400,000
9. Net profit of the Turner Broadcasting System in 1984: $10,620,000
10. Percentage of Broadway tickets that are bought by companies and deducted as a business expense: 20%
11. Of tickets for National Hockey League games played in the United States: 62%
12. Percentage of fathers who were in the delivery room when their children were born in 1973: 27%
13. In 1983: 79%
14. Percentage of American adults who can't swim: 47%
15. Percentage of Americans who never go to the movies: 39%
16. Acres of land purchased for national parks by the Reagan Administration: 57,169
17. By the Carter Administration: 419,492
18. Cab fare from New York City to Los Angeles: $5,550
19. Percentage of American sixth-graders who cannot locate the U.S. on a world map: 20%
20. American adults who read below the ninth-grade level: 60,000,000

21. Applicants for the 1,600 places in Stanford's class of 1988 who had straight-A averages: 2,368
22. Number of homosexuals discharged from the U.S. military in 1983: 1,796
23. Amount the military spent in recruiting and training the homosexuals it discharged: $22,500,000
24. Percentage of Americans who rank Detroit as the nation's worst city: 64%
25. Percentage increase since 1980 in number of Houston businesses filing for bankruptcy each month: 276%
26. Percentage increase in joint ventures undertaken by U.S. and Japanese companies since 1980: 100%
27. Percentage of Americans who say they support the 55 mph speed limit: 76%
28. Percentage of drivers on interstate highways who exceed the 55 mph speed limit: 60%
29. Average number of minutes a customer spends test-driving a new car: 25
30. Average amount Americans spend to remodel their kitchens: $4,448
31. Percentage of Americans who eat their evening meal between 5 p.m. and 8 p.m.: 87%
32. Rank of steak and potatoes among Americans' favorite foods: 1, 2
33. Rank of watching television among activities people look forward to during the day: 1
34. Rank of Rover, Spot, and Max among most popular names for dogs: 1, 2, 3

Together, these two assignments illustrate how the teacher in the AP Literature and Composition class need not be constrained by preparing students merely to answer certain kinds of questions on the exam. If, by using language in ways that are relevant to their reading, students can deepen their insights of the literature and steadily improve their own control over thought and word, then they will naturally progress toward being able to respond to whatever question they are asked, whether on the exam or later in the college classroom. In the process, they are likely to enjoy their study of literature and composition more than if they were simply asked repeatedly to respond to the same kind of literary exercise in writing.

Avoiding Pitfalls

Still, who has ever taught a course that didn't have its pitfalls? And how often are those pitfalls of our own making? Listed below are some of the traps that I and other AP teachers have fallen into over the years. These rather simple concerns are often the first ignored and, eventually the first regretted:

Student Pitfalls

1. Despite their intellectual promise and their ability to verbalize orally, students in AP English courses need just as frequent practice in reading, writing, speaking, and listening and just as much, perhaps more, teacher response, as do their peers in less challenging courses.

2. Despite their academic promise, AP students are human. Frequently they are the students in a school who undertake more than others, not merely in terms of course work but also in terms of school activities. Sometimes, they revise their priorities, and classwork comes in last. When that happens too often, they need to be reminded of it and helped to reestablish their priorities.

3. Because AP students tend to be busy in and out of school, they may need help in organizing their time to stay on task. Because, too, they are often mature students that adults can relate to, it is easy to develop a personal relationship with a class, which gets in the way of work which needs to be done. These students tend to be expert at negotiating teachers into different due dates or eliminating an assignment altogether. Teachers need to be wary at times, wise at others—the pop quiz, incidentally, is still in style.

Teacher Pitfalls

1. It is easy to think of all students in an AP class as potential English majors. They're not, and treating them this way is a disservice to them.

2. Teachers should not earn points for having a certain number of students who score high on the AP exam. Though good scores may reflect good teaching, poor scores don't always mean the opposite. Schools that fund the Literature and Composition course on this kind of accountability should rethink their reasons for having the course at all.

3. Teachers sometimes overteach their own weakest area. This is especially apparent in the teaching of poetry, a genre that many teachers love, but worry about teaching well. The result is sometimes a degeneration into the teaching of nomenclature by overemphasizing the recognition of figurative language and other stylistic features and failing to view the poem as a literary whole with form and content, speaker and subject, style and tone. We do students no good when we drill them on laundry lists of poetic terms. Recognizing figurative language is itself of little value beyond enabling students to come closer to explaining *how* it functions in a given piece.

4. The teacher, unfortunately, is just as vulnerable as students in letting a course get out of control. Allowing ourselves to concentrate too heavily on our own favorite authors or works can work to everyone's disadvantage. Before we know it, we've taught a course in the nineteenth-century novel and forgotten that our students need exposure to literary works in a variety of time periods. It is equally easy to rationalize ourselves away from those things we find most difficult. If we don't happen to like seventeenth-century

poetry, we can find five or six quick reasons why our students wouldn't profit from reading it; yet down deep, we know that looking at the language of Donne, Marvell, or Taylor is in and of itself a rewarding, though rigorous, experience for the students.

5. There are just as many ways to rationalize not covering all of the material in a course. When March rolls around and we find ourselves still working on December's calendar, it's time to reflect on our own planning skills. The real hazard here is that, even though a teacher might justify all that has been taught, he or she runs the risk of jeopardizing students when it is time for them to take their exam. If they have not had sufficient exposure to authors, works, or time periods, they may come up short for want of practice.

6. Though it is to everyone's advantage to use the library in the Literature and Composition course, it's of no great consequence to make little research scholars out of AP students. Time spent consulting numerous secondary sources merely to justify an interpretation of a literary work would be better spent giving students practice in justifying their own interpretations, becoming comfortable with a text, and talking about it intelligently—before being able to quote critics.

7. Above all, try to avoid making the AP Literature and Composition course so serious and stressful an experience that teachers and students fail to enjoy it. Test or no test, literature is for our passions; we should exercise them in the best way we can with our students.

Ultimately, teachers and administrators must examine carefully their reasons for wanting an AP course. If the basic reason is genuine—to better meet the needs of students who show potential for advanced study in language and literature—then the examination will find its own place in the larger scheme of considerations concerning student placement, course organization, teaching materials, and instructional strategies. The AP exam will, in effect, become one more opportunity for capable students to demonstrate with pride their long-term growth in the language arts.

Works Cited

Academic Preparation in English. N.p.: College Entrance Examination Board, 1985.

Advanced Placement Course Description: English. N.p.: College Entrance Examination Board, 1986.

The College Board Examinations in English Language Skills and Literature. Princeton, NJ: Educational Testing Service, 1986.

Corey, Robert D., and Barbara Pollard, with Jan Guffin. *Teacher's Guide to Advanced Placement Courses in English Literature and Composition.* N.p.: College Entrance Examination Board, 1985.

Taylor, Deems. "The Monster." *A Complete Course in Freshman English.* Ed. Harry Shaw. New York: Harper, 1959. 958–61.

7

The Language and Composition Course

GARY A. OLSON

University of South Florida

ELIZABETH METZGER

University of South Florida

The authors describe the Language and Composition course and its objectives. They argue that the course should mirror the typical freshman English course in its emphasis on the writing process. The authors discuss several curricular concerns, including types of writing assignments and resources available to AP teachers.

Teachers and administrators sometimes don't make clear distinctions between the two exams and courses of study in AP English. The Literature and Composition course (often called the "old course") helps students acquire the ability to read closely, understand the conventions of literary discourse, develop an appreciation of literature, and write articulately about it. Students are exposed to representative literary works from several genres and time periods. The Language and Composition program (the "new course"), on the other hand, helps students learn the general critical, analytical, and writing skills that help them become competent, college-level writers. Students are exposed to the modes of discourse and the techniques of good writing, and their reading usually focuses on discursive prose, often about subjects from many different academic disciplines.

Although students learn composition skills in both AP English courses, the "old course" is primarily a college-level introduction to literature, while the "new course" is a college-level composition course. This distinction is especially important because some colleges and universities distinguish between the two: they award credit for the first course in their freshman English sequence to those students who have performed well on the Language and Composition exam, and credit for the second course to students who have performed well on the Literature and Composition exam. That is, many college administrators are becoming cognizant of the fact that the Language and Composition course more accurately reflects the typical freshman English course.

Unfortunately, some schools have offered the Language and Composition course as a survey of American literature and the Literature and Composition course as a survey of British literature. Such an arrangement is a perversion of the intent and nature of the AP English program. The 1987 booklet, *Advanced Placement Course Description: English*, clearly defines the Language and Composition course, claiming that "it should reflect an awareness of the most useful theories of language and composition available" and that "it should encourage students to develop an individual style adaptable to different occasions for writing in college" (4). In fact, this same booklet suggests that students taking one of the courses are likely to have different "abilities and interests" from students taking the other: "Students choosing AP English Language and Composition should enjoy studying and writing various kinds of analytic or persuasive essays on nonliterary topics," while "students choosing AP English Literature and Composition should enjoy studying British and American literature of various periods and genres" (3). Clearly, the Language and Composition course should be a *freshman composition* course.

The objective of the Language and Composition course is to help high school students develop the capability of composing college-level prose. Students who demonstrate their abilities by scoring well on the AP exam may receive official credit for one or two freshman composition courses in college. The AP exam in Language and Composition consists of 58 objective questions (constituting 40 percent of the exam) and three essay topics (constituting the remaining 60 percent of the exam). Students are allotted 75 minutes to complete the objective questions and 105 minutes to write the essays. The course itself typically covers eight areas of study:

- levels of diction from formal to casual
- organized study of sentence structure
- varieties of sentence types

- relationships of sentences within paragraphs
- modes of discourse (narration, description, etc.)
- aims of discourse (informational, persuasive, expressive)
- rhetorical strategies (logical, emotional, and ethical appeals)
- relationships among author, subject, and reader

Ideally, the maximum enrollment in a Language and Composition class should be 15 students but certainly no more than 25. Such a low enrollment is likely to distress budget-conscious school administrators, but they should be made aware that the Language and Composition course is special. If the course is handled properly, students will be generating *many* writing assignments throughout the year, and it is extremely difficult to respond to them all if there are more than 25 pupils in the class. Every effort should be made to convince administrators that if the Language and Composition course is to be truly advanced and contain the necessary *quality* of instruction, the enrollment must be kept low.

Selecting Students

When establishing a Language and Composition course in your school, identify the most able and ambitious students. Weaker students will find the typical AP class much too demanding to compete in successfully. Many AP administrators suggest that a school should make acceptance into the AP class an honor. To do this, you might consider establishing a formal application procedure, in which students must write a persuasive letter of application or an essay describing why they wish to enroll in the course. Either document (especially if written in a controlled setting) can be used as a diagnostic instrument for assessing which students show the most potential for competing successfully in the course. Also, written teacher recommendations, especially those supplied by a teacher of a course a student has taken previously, are helpful in determining the student's past performance and in ascertaining the student's potential for succeeding in a rigorous college-level writing course. Although some schools use scores from standardized tests to screen students for AP classes, these are less reliable than writing samples in indicating students' ability to compose effective prose. Standardized test scores should be used, if at all, only in connection with other methods.

Many schools supplement the screening process with an information meeting for students interested in enrolling in the AP course. You can use the information session to explain the nature, aims, and objectives of the composition course. For example, you can inform students that the course is a rigorous, college-level class in language and composition skills, not in the study of literature, and you can give them a general overview of the course's content. Such an information session is useful as a screening device because it helps students understand what the course will entail and thus enables them to withdraw from consideration if the course requirements seem too stringent.

If you conduct the application and screening procedure toward the end of an academic year, you will be able to assign summer reading to students accepted into the class; this will help prepare them for the rigorous study ahead. Perhaps you could assign readings in a rhetoric textbook (not a grammar handbook) and an anthology of discursive prose essays. Thus, students will enter the AP class already familiar with some of the course material.

The success of any screening system for AP may depend in part on familiarizing parents with the program. It's wise to meet with the parents of all AP applicants to stress that while admittance into the AP course is an honor, failure to be admitted does not signify that their children are inferior or unsuited for college work. In other words, parents, too, must understand that students *compete* for a place in the AP class and are not automatically admitted. The best forum is an information meeting, held before students are selected. This session may be separate from the one for students, or the two may be combined. The meeting should demonstrate to parents that the course will demand of students a commitment to the rigors of the course, including extensive reading and writing.

The Writing Process

The Language and Composition course is a challenge to teachers and students alike. There is no such thing as a *standard* AP course with an established curriculum; each course is as unique as its individual teacher. However, if the Language and Composition course is to mirror a college-level freshman English course, it should exhibit a continual attention to and preoccupation with the writing process. Students must learn to view the act of writing as an ongoing process involving several activities, including *pre-writing, organizing, drafting, revising,* and *proofreading.* If students are truly to become college-level writers, they must develop the ability to apply their compositional skills to any rhetorical situation, not just to the AP exam. The official *Course Description* states: "The course will include both the reading and analysis of varieties of discursive prose and the study of the process of writing—from the discovery of the topic to the preliminary drafts to the final edited draft" (4). The Language and Composition course should provide students with instruction and practice in all aspects of this process.

Prewriting

Most composition specialists agree that prewriting—generating information about a paper's subject, purpose, and audience and *thinking* about this information before actually writing a draft—is one of the most important facets of the composing process. Substantial class time, therefore, should be devoted to discussing and practicing prewriting techniques. That is, students must know how to use brainstorming, freewriting, the journalistic questions, and even heuristics to generate information about their subject and audience before they begin to write a paper. Group prewriting activities are especially helpful in familiarizing students with the techniques of generating information and in stressing their importance to the writing process.

Brainstorming, perhaps the easiest of prewriting techniques, entails thinking of every possible detail about a subject and audience and recording these details in a notebook. This simple method of gathering details is effective because it helps students *see* their ideas on paper and encourages them to *think* about a paper before beginning it. After brainstorming, students can ask the *journalistic questions* (who? what? when? where? why? how?) about their subject and add any new information to their prewriting notes. You should also encourage students to *freewrite*—that is, to write as rapidly and spontaneously about the subject as possible for a predetermined time span (usually five or ten minutes). During freewriting, students write continuously, without lifting pen from paper. The advantage of freewriting is that it helps students draw on what might have remained beneath the conscious level at which brainstorming tends to function. They may then extract details from their freewriting and add them to their prewriting notes.

Organizing

AP teachers should also spend time showing students how to arrange and organize their information before drafting. The old-fashioned outline, with its Roman and Arabic numerals, has come under fire recently for being too rigid and artificial, and perhaps with good cause. However, with or without an outline, students must recognize the necessity of imposing some type of order on their prewriting material before composing a draft. Many composition instructors find that an effective method of teaching arrangement is to encourage students to rewrite their prewriting information as an ordered list of items. Students often perceive this procedure to be much more practical and effective than the traditional outline. Finally, it's important that students understand organizing to be a flexible activity; they shouldn't feel bound to their original organizational plan if they discover a more appropriate one while drafting or revising. A writer's original organizational plan is only a way to provide *direction* while drafting; a writer should not feel compelled to stay with the plan if it doesn't work.

Drafting

It is perhaps best to teach AP students to invest more time in *prewriting* and *revision* activities than in composing the first draft. Often, beginning writers view drafting as an overwhelming activity, usually because they try to carry out too many operations at once. Many composition theorists suggest that it's best to encourage students to compose a draft as fast as possible after they have adequately prewritten and arranged their material. There is no need for writers to get stuck on matters of correctness or style while drafting. When writing a draft, students should not, for example, spend ten minutes trying to think of the correct word in a particular sentence or the best phrase in another. Encourage them instead to write the draft quickly, leaving fill-in-the-blanks when they are stumped. The objective of drafting is to compose a draft that can then be reworded and reshaped during the revision process. This procedure eliminates the strain for writers to perform everything—generating ideas, organizing them, and writing about them in perfect prose—in one sitting. It is also helpful in preparing students for the essay exam component of the AP test since it helps them learn to write rapidly while avoiding writers' block.

Revising

It is essential to stress to AP students the importance of the revision process. Once students have produced a draft after prewriting and organizing, they should be prepared to reshape the paper. Too often, students believe that the first draft is the final one. Encourage students to rewrite a draft several times, critically analyzing their prose, sentence by sentence. The best writers are frequently the most proficient editors, so it is advisable to spend a considerable amount of time on revision techniques. Many AP teachers conduct revision workshops in their classes before each paper is due; in these sessions, students exchange papers and make editorial comments on them. This practice helps students acquire a critical eye, and, as Robert Reising and Benjamin Stewart demonstrate in their chapter in this collection, it helps shift some of the burden of evaluation to the students themselves.

One technique for helping students understand the importance of revision is to ask the class to devise a *revision checklist* that students can then use when revising their papers. Devising a checklist helps student contemplate and discuss the kinds of issues central to revision. Here is a brief revision checklist that students may use as a model:

REVISION CHECKLIST

1. Have I made my main point clear enough?
2. Does my introduction contain sufficient information to orient my readers to my subject?
3. Have I directed my paper to a specific audience?
4. Have I organized my paper in a logical way?
5. Have I included every important detail about my subject?
6. Have I eliminated irrelevant details?
7. Have I maintained a consistent point of view?
8. Is my *exact* meaning clear in each sentence?

9. Does my conclusion put my subject in perspective for my readers?
10. Have I spent enough time revising my paper?

Proofreading

Finally, students should be aware that proofreading is distinct from revision. While in the revision process students frequently engage in wholesale rewriting and reconceptualization of their drafts, during proofreading they should be concerned with matters of correctness: grammar, spelling, punctuation, and neatness. Too often, student writers are overly concerned with these matters *while they are drafting,* thus stifling creativity and originality. Although these considerations are important, they shouldn't be a priority too early in the process.

Perhaps it's best to advise students to make several proofreading passes through their papers: once for grammar, once for punctuation, once for spelling. Making separate passes helps students concentrate on the exact things they are looking for. In addition, you may want to show students an old proofreaders' trick: make one pass through the paper reading backwards—first the last sentence, then the second-to-last sentence, all the way through to the first sentence. This procedure helps writers de-program their texts from their minds so that they don't read *what they think* is on the page rather than what is really there.

Writing Assignments

Throughout the school year, students should have practice in writing different types of papers (personal, persuasive, and perhaps even research papers) and should write in-class as well as out-of-class essays. The in-class assignments could mirror the AP exam experience. In fact, ETS will provide you with sample exam topics used in past years. Here, for example, is an essay question used on the 1980 Language and Composition exam. Students were allotted 35 minutes to compose the essay:

> Public officials or individual citizens have frequently attacked or suppressed works that they consider harmful or offensive. Select a book, movie, play, or television program that some group could object to on the basis of its action, language, or theme.
>
> In a well-organized essay, discuss possible grounds for such an attack and then defend the work, arguing, on the basis of its artistic merit or its value to the community, that it should not be suppressed.
>
> Avoid plot summary.

Here is a sample question from the 1987 exam. Again, students were allotted 35 minutes for their response:

Just as every individual has an idiolect—a language that varies in minute ways from the language of every other person—so every group has a sociolect or language of its own. That language may differ from other varieties of the same language in its pronunciation, inflections, syntax, vocabulary, or the manner and conditions in which it is used.

Write an essay describing some major features of the language used in one specific group that you know well—an occupational, ethnic, social, or age group, for example. Your essay should indicate what purposes these features serve or what influences they reflect. You should assume that your reader is not familiar with the language you describe.

Using ETS exam topics will help prepare students for the type of writing they will undertake on the AP exam. However, as John Iorio argues in this collection, overemphasis on exam topics can be counterproductive. Timed, in-class essays should be only one of many types of writing assignments.

More important than in-class essays are assignments that allow students the opportunity to work on a paper through the entire writing process, from prewriting to multiple revision to proofreading. Many composition specialists agree that students' success depends in part on how well the teacher constructs the writing assignment. Erika Lindemann writes, "Because each composition represents a response to a specific 'invitation' to write, the problems in many papers may be the fault, not of the writer, but of the assignment" (203). In other words, students need clear, specific, detailed assignments, not the typical, vague injunction: "Write about your best friend." According to Eleanor Hoffman and John Schifsky,

A good writing assignment recognizes all the student's needs and his developmental maturity. It provides needed guidance from the prewriting through the writing through the rewriting stages. It provides a definite route through the assignment, a route which allows many choices but which enables the student to arrive at his destination. A productive and useful writing assignment requires planning that structures the assignment for both teacher and student. Thus, when designing assignments, the teacher of writing, in fact any teacher, must take such variables as aim, audience, mode, tone, organization, style into consideration if he hopes to construct an assignment that: 1) leads the student to do purposeful writing, and 2) enables the instructor to develop useful criteria for evaluating the student's writing. (42)

Thus, the most valuable kind of writing assignment provides students with a full rhetorical context, including a realistic purpose and audience. Often called *cases* or *scenarios,* these assignments ask students to respond to specific rhetorical situations. Here is one such scenario taken from an essay reader used in many freshman English classes:

> The principal of your former high school has asked you to return and address this year's graduating class. For convenience, you plan to write your speech in essay form. You have decided to compare and contrast the "high school experience" with the "college experience." In what ways are they similar? How do they differ? Your purpose is to help younger students profit from your experience. (Ray et al. 139)

Here is another example from the same text:

> You have just been appointed entertainment editor of your campus newspaper. Your main task is to review records, films, and restaurants that students might be interested in. You have decided that in your first essay you will classify the *types* of restaurants in your community. This article may be serious or humorous, but you will want to make sure that you devise a classification system that will account for all eating establishments in the area, even though you won't, of course, be able to mention every one. You may want to make your classes amusingly descriptive: dives, greasy spoons, black-tie joints, and so on. Your audience is made up of students, administrators, and faculty members who read your school's newspaper. (244)

Notice that each scenario places students in a realistic situation, provides an identifiable audience, and establishes a clear purpose for writing. Such full-context assignments mirror the way real writing is encountered in the world at large.

Clearly, designing effective writing assignments demands a great deal of care and thought. To assist teachers in preparing assignments, Lindemann provides the following heuristic:

A HEURISTIC FOR DESIGNING WRITING ASSIGNMENTS

1. *What do I want the students to do?* Is it worth doing? Why? What will the assignment tell me about what they've learned? How does it fit my objectives at this point in the course? Does the assignment assess what students can *do* or what they *know?* Am I relating their work to the real world (including academic settings) or only to my class or the text? Does the assignment require specialized knowledge? Does it appeal to the interests and experiences of my students?
2. *How do I want them to do the assignment?* Are students working alone or together? In what ways will they practice prewriting, writing, and rewriting? Are writing, reading, speaking, and listening reinforcing each other? Have I given students enough information to make effective choices about the subject, purpose, form, and mode?

3. *For whom are students writing?* Who is the audience? Do students have enough information to assume a role with respect to the audience?

4. *When will students do the assignment?* How does the assignment relate to what comes before and after it in the course? Is the assignment sequenced to give enough time for prewriting, writing, and rewriting? How much time in and outside of class will students need for each stage? To what extent will I guide the students' work? What deadlines do I want to set for collecting the students' papers (or various stages of the project)?

5. *What will I do with the assignment?* How will I evaluate the work? What constitutes a "successful" response to the assignment? Will other students or the writer have a say in evaluating the paper? What problems did I encounter when I wrote my paper on this assignment? How can the assignment be improved? (208–09)

Another type of writing assignment that many AP teachers use is the daily journal. Students are asked to write a certain amount (usually a full or half page) in a notebook every day. They can choose their own subject so long as each journal entry is a focused discussion on one subject. You grade the journal only on quantity (keeping up with the correct number of pages), not on correctness or any of the usual concerns teachers traditionally have when grading formal papers. This procedure offers students the necessary practice in writing (without anxiety over a grade) that is so essential for developing writers. At the year's end, each student's journal grade can be factored into his or her cumulative grade as equal to one or two paper grades. Not only does a journal provide a medium for students to express their thoughts on paper regularly, but it is an excellent sourcebook for future paper topics, and thus can be used as a prewriting device.

Although current research shows that the best writing assignments are *rhetorical*—providing students with a purpose, audience, and context—occasionally students can benefit from *a-rhetorical* exercises. For example, you can ask students to analyze professional and student essays for audience, purpose, writer's role, subject. Or, you can have students examine pieces of writing for connotation and denotation. Also, you might have students experiment with changing their point of view, altering their stance in a piece of writing and playing devil's advocate with their own papers—in effect, writing from an opponent's point of view.

Responding to Student Papers

Since students in the AP class will be writing a substantial amount of prose throughout the year, AP teachers carry an especially heavy burden in providing qualitative responses to all assignments. In fact, one essential aspect of the process approach to teaching writing is that students must write and often submit several drafts of each assignment. One method of reducing your response time while increasing the quality of your responses is to use a cassette recorder to respond to student writing. In this procedure, students are asked (or given the option) to provide a cassette tape which is submitted with each writing assignment. You then record your responses on tape rather than spending valuable time writing your remarks on students' papers. The taped response allows you to discuss with students the various options in their papers, helping you guide their revision efforts. Responding by tape has several advantages:

- It saves time.
- It allows for a more detailed, qualitative response.
- It allows for communicating in a friendly, constructive tone.
- Students seem to enjoy it.

You may find this method awkward the first few times you use it since it takes practice to coordinate the many tapes and papers, but soon you will find it to be a useful, effective procedure. For detailed information about this technique, consult "Beyond Evaluation: The Recorded Response to Essays" (Olson).

The Objective Component

It is perhaps more difficult to prepare students for the objective component of the AP exam than for the written portion; however, after a full year of practice with the composing process, students should have enough linguistic sophistication to perform well. Each objective question on the exam asks students to choose the correct answer from a field of five possibilities. The exam questions are usually of two types. In the first, students are given a sentence and are asked to alter its structure in a specific way. Here is an example:

1. Thorough critics review books only after they have read every-
   thing else written by the author.
   Begin with "To be a thorough critic. . . . "
   A. you had read
   B. reading everything
   C. they must have read
   D. they would read
   E. you must read

In the second type of question, students are asked to read a paragraph or two and then answer questions that test students' comprehension and knowledge of style and rhetorical devices. Here is a sample:

2. All of the following are ideas considered in the passage EXCEPT:
   A. Good and evil are inseparably joined.
   B. Man must be free to acquaint himself with all kinds of ideas.
   C. The cultivation of real virtue depends on freedom of choice.
   D. Heretical ideas can easily be identified and repressed.
   E. Innocence protected from evil cannot be called virtue.

To score well on the first type of question, students must understand how to mold and remold language. The editing workshops and increased attention to revision will help students acquire this skill. Another helpful technique is sentence-combining exercises done as a class activity. Most AP teachers are familiar with sentence combining, and much has been written about its effectiveness. Perhaps one of the most appropriate sentence combining texts for the AP class is William Strong's *Sentence Combining: A Composing Book.* Through sentence combining, students learn about the flexibility of language and how to test various linguistic options.

To score well on the second type of question, students must demonstrate keen analytical skills. If you use prose (nonfiction) anthologies in your AP class, you should spend time analyzing the essays in terms of *content, style,* and rhetorical *fluency.* That is, the essays shouldn't be used simply as models; students should learn to read critically as part of becoming good writers.

Resources

There are no standard texts for the Language and Composition course. Frequently, Language and Composition teachers assign a prose reader, a rhetoric-handbook, and perhaps a sentence-combining text. There are a bewildering number of texts to choose from, and no one text is inherently better for an AP class than another. One AP teacher we know uses Mc-Crimmon's *Writing with a Purpose* (a rhetoric), Ray's *The Process Reader* (an anthology of nonfictional essays), and Strong's *Sentence Combining: A Composing Book.* Many AP teachers find out what texts are used by nearby colleges and universities in their freshman English classes and then try to adopt identical or similar texts; we highly recommend this approach.

There are many professional resources available for the writing teacher, including articles in *English Journal* and other composition journals. One valuable source for the AP teacher is Erika Lindemann's *A Rhetoric for Writing Teachers.* Although this book is directed mainly toward instructors of college-level composition, it contains a wealth of theoretical and pedagogical information that will help AP teachers conduct a successful Language and Composition course. Another excellent text is Stephen and Susan Judy's *An Introduction to the Teaching of Writing*. Both of these texts present practical pedagogical techniques useful in AP classes. If you are interested in learning more about the theory behind these approaches, consult David Foster's *A Primer for Writing Teachers*. Below is a list of works recommended by the College Board. Although some of these texts are dated, many are helpful.

Useful Works on Composition

Barzun, Jacques. *Simple and Direct: A Rhetoric for Writers*. New York: Harper, 1976.

Berke, Jacqueline. *Twenty Questions for the Writer: A Rhetoric for Reading*. 3rd ed. New York: Harcourt, 1981.

Donovan, Timothy R., and Ben W. McClelland. *Eight Approaches to Teaching Composition*. Urbana: NCTE, 1980.

Duncan, Robert. *Writing, Writing*. Portland, OR: Trask House Books, 1971.

Elbow, Peter. *Writing without Teachers*. New York: Oxford UP, 1975.

———. *Writing with Power: Techniques for Mastering the Writing Process*. New York: Oxford UP, 1981.

Gibson, Walker. *Tough, Sweet, and Stuffy: An Essay on Modern American Prose Styles*. Bloomington, IN: Indiana UP, 1966.

———. *Persona: A Style Study for Readers and Writers*. New York: Random, 1969.

Guerin, Wilfred, et al. *A Handbook of Critical Approaches to Literature*. 2nd ed. New York: Harper, 1979.

Hall, Donald. *Writing Well*. 3rd ed. Boston: Little, 1979.

Joos, Martin. *The Five Clocks*. New York: Harcourt, 1967.

Lanham, Richard A. *Style: An Anti-Textbook*. New Haven, CT: Yale UP, 1974.

Macrorie, Ken. *Telling Writing*. 4th ed. Portsmouth, NH: Boynton/Cook, 1985.

Murray, Donald M. *A Writer Teaches Writing*. Boston: Houghton, 1968.

Roberts, Edgar V. *Writing Themes about Literature*. 4th ed. Englewood Cliffs, NJ: Prentice, 1977.

Strunk, W., Jr., and E. B. White. *The Elements of Style*. 3rd ed. New York: Macmillan, 1978.

Trimble, John R. *Writing with Style: Conversations on the Art of Writing*. Englewood Cliffs, NJ: Prentice, 1975.

Zinsser, William. *On Writing Well: An Informal Guide to Writing Nonfiction*. 2nd ed. New York: Harper, 1980.

(Course Description 4)

A Final Note

If you integrate the writing process thoroughly into the Language and Composition curriculum, and you yourself participate actively in the process, your students are likely to learn techniques that will not only ensure their success on the AP exam but, most importantly, will enable them to compete well in college and beyond.

Works Cited

Advanced Placement Course Description: English. N.p.: College Entrance Examination Board, 1987.

Foster, David. A Primer for Writing Teachers. Portsmouth, NH: Boynton/Cook, 1983.

Hoffman, Eleanor, and John Schifsky. "Designing Writing Assignments." English Journal 66 (1977): 41–45.

Judy, Stephen N., and Susan J. Judy. An Introduction to the Teaching of Writing. New York: John Wiley, 1981.

Lindemann, Erika. A Rhetoric for Writing Teachers. New York: Oxford UP, 1982.

McCrimmon, James M. Writing with a Purpose. Ed. Joseph F. Trimmer and Nancy Sommers. 8th ed. Boston: Houghton, 1984.

Olson, Gary A. "Beyond Evaluation: The Recorded Response to Essays." Teaching English in the Two-Year College 8 (1982): 121–23.

Ray, Richard E., et al. The Process Reader. Englewood Cliffs, NJ: Prentice, 1986.

Strong, William. Sentence Combining: A Composing Book. 2nd ed. New York: Random, 1983.

8

Evaluating Students' Work in AP Courses

R. W. REISING

Pembroke State University

BENJAMIN J. STEWART

Pine Forest High School
Cumberland County, North Carolina

The authors argue that although an AP English class demands a substantial amount of writing from students, teachers need not be overburdened with evaluation problems. The authors outline several methods of formative and summative evaluation that AP teachers can use to help them respond to students' papers while reducing their own workloads.

Teaching Advanced Placement English isn't easy. In an effective AP course, students write many papers and drafts of papers, substantially increasing the work load of the AP teacher. Every Advanced Placement English course is fundamentally a course in writing. Whether the course focuses on Language and Composition or Literature and Composition and regardless of its grade level or intensity, it carries a mandate to place writing at its center. Whatever else the AP English experience is, it is one requiring substantial writing.

Yet, the fact that writing is central to AP doesn't necessarily mean that AP teachers need be flooded with student papers and paper evaluation problems. Research in rhetoric and composition over the past several decades suggests that treating writing as a process as well as a product permits an abundance of student prose while leaving the teacher free of burdensome, and ultimately self-defeating, assessment responsibilities. This research provides no panaceas, but it does present perspectives on evaluation—and strategies for it—that promise growth in writing. AP English students, indeed, all students, can improve their writing skills when the quest for a polished final product respects the process of composing it.

The process approach of teaching writing demands that a teacher's attention shift from the finished product to the writing activities that students must experience to arrive at an effective product. This shift requires new and exciting teaching strategies that help even talented AP English students discover ways of making meaning on paper. Students creating texts can usually benefit far more from strategies than from sermons, from interactions with classmates as a draft emerges than from red-penciling after a paper has been completed, and from usage exercises inspired by their own prose than from grammar drills required by curriculum guides. In short, attention to the process of writing improves students' writing in general. For AP students who internalize the process, the benefits will extend far beyond the AP English examination to any writing situations they will encounter.

Respect for process as a pedagogical approach introduces a teacher to a host of evaluation devices suitable both for evolving drafts and for final copy products. In other words, a process orientation allows for *formative*, or ongoing, evaluation, as well as *summative*, or final, evaluation. Because Advanced Placement English generally represents the freshman-level composition courses taught in colleges and universities, AP teachers must use both of these forms of evaluation to prepare students for the writing standards of higher education. Simultaneously, AP teachers must also prepare students to perform well on timed writings for the AP examination. Facing AP teachers, then, is the problem of presenting a curriculum that features both timed-response essay writing and the composition requirements of the traditional college-level class. A balance of in-class and out-of-class writing assignments is crucial to meeting these twin demands.

Formative Evaluation

Although summative grading demands a fixed judgment about the quality of a piece of writing, formative evaluation does not. Instead, it provides guided responses that assist a writer with future drafts. The primary assumption of all formative evaluation is that a particular draft isn't yet appropriate for public scrutiny or final grading, that its content demands refinement, and that material must be added, deleted, rearranged, or refocused. Formative evaluation, therefore, accompanies and supplements the revision and editing activities that help writers improve their text.

Formative evaluation consists of reactions and feedback from a variety of sources committed to offering assistance: peers (both individual and group), the writer, and the teacher. It's important to recognize that the AP teacher is not alone in helping to improve students' writing skills; students themselves must shoulder a sizable portion of that responsibility. In fact, current composition research shows that peer- and self-evaluation are valuable in effecting writing improvement.

Peer- and self-evaluation, however, don't diminish your role as teacher; in a process-attuned setting, you simply assume different, but no less critical, duties. Organizing and coordinating formative responses is a time-consuming obligation; effective peer- and self-evaluation occur not in an anything-goes classroom but in a disciplined, well-orchestrated one. The pedagogy of process assumes that you will train students to become evaluators, provide them with opportunities to practice evaluating texts, and monitor all assessment activities. Since evaluation requires objective and sophisticated thinking, it can't be left to chance; overseeing and grading are necessary.

One effective way to monitor students' attempts at evaluation is to use checklists that you or members of each peer group have devised. After an evaluation session, students can use the checklists to rate the quality of their peers' responses to their papers. For example, the checklist might ask students to rate their readers on a one-to-five scale on such criteria as the following: "My reader shows insight into the concepts in my paper," and "My reader's responses are relevant to my topic," and "My reader's responses are irrelevant," and "My reader remained passive during most response opportunities." Thus, students evaluate not only one another's papers but also their peers' responses to them.

Peer Evaluation

Peer evaluation allows students to work as one body analyzing and discussing reproduced copies of student writing, or as response groups of four or five, or as editors for one another's papers in groups of three or four. Regardless of the organization of the peer group, however, it is wise to specify the criteria you expect in an evaluation. When, for instance, you have assigned several drafts of an essay, the class as a group may consider focus and organization in the first draft; response groups may address paragraphing in the second draft; and writing partners may treat grammar and punctuation in the final draft. Each type of peer evaluation should include an evaluation form or checklist that allows students to provide their peers with detailed responses to their papers. The collective impact of such feedback is to alert students to specific strengths and weaknesses in their papers while encouraging them to consider and internalize criteria crucial to successful revision. Everyone benefits. Since each student is both writer and responder, he or she cannot avoid moving toward a better command of the features of a given writing assignment. Simultaneously, you, as teacher, don't emerge as the lone audience and judge.

Most AP teachers will want to devise their own peer evaluation forms. However, Chapter 7 of *Writing for Learning in the Content Areas* (by Wolfe and Reising) contains several evaluation forms and checklists that you can adopt for peer evaluation. Preceding those materials is a discussion of the important role of peer evaluation in process-sensitive writing pedagogy, always desirable if students are to be guided toward the writing competence expected in AP English.

Holistic Scoring

Holistic scoring deserves a special place in AP English pedagogy because it is the scoring method employed in rating the timed essays on the annual AP examination. Although created for summative evaluation, it is also effective in formative evaluation, and both teachers and students can easily come to appreciate why.

Holistic scoring allows you to assess how well a student can write a complete composition. It assumes that the effectiveness of a paper is dependent upon the interaction of such diverse factors as purpose, tone, audience awareness, organization, diction, syntax, and usage. When grading holistically, you form an impression of that effectiveness, not by totaling the sum of component parts, but by responding to the merits of the paper as a whole. After forming an impression of the paper's effectiveness, you usually will want to assign a letter (*A*, *B*, *C*) or a number (1 through 9) to the paper.

Essential to the holistic method are a specific writing prompt (that is, the writing assignment itself) and a rubric (or scoring guide) keyed to that prompt. The prompt and rubric are usually teacher designed and reflect the goals of a particular unit of instruction. It is sometimes beneficial, however, to allow AP students to create the rubrics for certain assignments to help them determine and understand what appropriate criteria for evaluation should be. Such a practice admits students into the community of writers that, after all, they are trying to emulate. In addition, the various sample prompts, rubrics, and discussions available from the College Entrance Examination Board (CEEB) can prove invaluable in developing proficiency in holistic scoring.

Training AP students in holistic scoring is relatively easy. First, students can practice evaluating CEEB materials and essays composed by students in a previous year. After completing such evaluation, the students can record the results on a blackboard for everyone to study and discuss. After practice, students will gain a consensus in their evaluation. Once a class has been trained to score holistically, students can evaluate drafts of their peers' papers. Class discussions centered on what makes certain papers more effective than others are generally quite instructive and allow you to guide students in discussions about organization, inferences, syntax, diction, and style. Learning to evaluate one another's papers helps students master those skills and strategies necessary for composing well-written, free-response essays similar to those on the AP examination. (For additional information on holistic scoring, see our subsequent discussion on Summative Evaluation.)

Self-Evaluation

Self-evaluation is another important formative method. It also requires specific teacher guidance in identifying assessment criteria and in instructing students in their application. Since AP students should be aware of their own accomplishments, self-appraisal provides them with an immediate opportunity for satisfaction or for feedback for subsequent and usually self-motivated revision. You can ask students to rate their own drafts on a checklist, and you can ask them to freewrite (rapid, spontaneous composing) for ten minutes, discussing the strengths and weaknesses of their own papers. This information will be of use to students when they revise their drafts. Various assessment guides are useful with self-evaluation, just as they are with peer evaluation. Again, *Writing for Learning in the Content Areas* offers several illustrations of checklists and other forms proven effective in self-evaluation.

Teacher Evaluation

Although it is generally accepted that intensively graded papers with excessive teacher comments impede a writer's development, guided and focused teacher feedback is essential. Many composition specialists believe that marking every error or problem on a student's paper can easily overwhelm and then discourage the student; more appropriate are comments directed to several selected areas that the student should work on. Selected comments identify what a writer did well in a draft, explain why certain problems hamper effective discourse, and suggest a variety of strategies for improving communication.

Teacher evaluation can provide formative feedback on an AP course, as well as on the performance of its individual students. That is, you can accumulate data concerning the growth of students as writers while measuring differences among student writers. Such information is important in determining the make-up of response groups. For example, you may get the best results when formulaic writers are paired with creative and free flowing writers. Each writer may learn by revising from feedback provided by a peer with a contrasting style.

An additional teacher evaluation technique that promotes revision strategies is focused pupil-teacher conferences. Such conferences are comparatively short (usually about one to three minutes), and they isolate selected problems. Although they permit an exchange and clarification of ideas, they are most helpful when the teacher can lead writers to diagnose their own rhetorical and stylistic problems and then to design strategies for solving them. Central to this process, of course, is your guidance in helping students analyze their own papers.

Formative evaluation is essential to an effective, process-oriented course. Instead of merely presenting lessons in rhetoric, you can individualize your instruction by addressing important rhetorical elements—sense of audience, purpose, and structure. With this as a starting point, assessment methods like peer evaluation and the focused conference can provide feedback to stimulate your students to discover and articulate for themselves their composition intentions. The several drafting and revising activities encourage an awareness of writing as an organic act in which writers ask important heuristic questions about their own prose. Thoughts shape writing; writing shapes thought. Writing process becomes learning process and, with each revision, you will be guiding AP writers to focus on concerns which allow prose to emerge into an effective final product.

Summative Evaluation

Summative evaluation renders a final, fixed judgment on a piece of writing. Unlike formative evaluation, it isn't intended to assist a writer in revising a paper but to grade him or her on a completed writing task. Summative evaluation represents the end of a writing assignment, the sum of its effectiveness; it is, therefore, most appropriate for assessing product rather than process. Yet, occasionally it can prove revealing when applied to a draft of a paper—probably not an initial effort but a second or third draft, one that reveals a writer's thinking and skills in a nearly finished form.

Four types of summative evaluation are appropriate for AP English courses: *holistic, analytic, primary trait,* and *focused holistic scoring.*

Holistic Scoring

As we have mentioned, holistic scoring is an effective method of formative evaluation, but it has long been popular in summative evaluation, for which it was initially developed. It is particularly desirable when you must grade a large collection of papers and return them quickly. The method admits of no procrastination or pondering; papers are read rapidly and impressionistically. In addition to efficiency, holistic scoring provides excellent validity and reliability.

Employed by a skillful teacher, holistic scoring alerts students to their respective rankings among peers who have attempted the same writing assignment. Usually, you will want to create groupings of three, four, five or more and place each paper into one of these groups. The more groupings you create, the finer or more exact the distinctions you can draw. We can recommend no magic or special number; holistic scoring can result in as many as 15 gradations within a class of 15 AP writers. Fundamentally, holistic scoring rates a given set of papers not on specific writing features but on the totality of all writing features; differences emerge among the papers only because different totalities are discernible, one more effective than another.

Analytic Scoring

Analytic scoring is a method of evaluation that measures written performance based on an evaluation of a paper's component parts. It involves analysis of specific features of a paper or the specific skills necessary to produce a successful paper. These criteria must be isolated and scored individually. In using analytic scoring, you should first enunciate the objectives of a writing task and determine how certain performances will be demonstrated. Since it is impractical to analyze and evaluate every component of a writing sample, you should give careful consideration to selecting those factors that will be evaluated and to assigning an appropriate point value to each factor.

Analytic scoring is most useful when designed to assess the ability of a student to master the objectives of a particular instructional unit (for example, structural concerns, syntactic considerations, or conventional usage). Focusing on specific features of a student's paper helps you isolate its strengths and weaknesses. By identifying the specific factors to be assessed, an analytic scale can be tailored to characteristics of various modes of writing (such as exposition, narration, argumentation) and thus can be used to assess individual writing skills in a wide range of traits.

Although validity, reliability, and efficiency are sometimes difficult to gain and maintain in analytic scoring, the method offers one primary advantage: students learn exactly where their writing strengths and weaknesses lie. Analytic scoring, because it focuses on a paper's specific components, is far more instructive to students than holistic scorings; hence, pedagogically, it is more effective.

But AP teachers need to be warned: analytic scoring can be reductive and so detailed that it risks inundating writers with more information than they can accommodate. The key to successful analytic scoring lies in selectivity, in wisely choosing those features, substantive as well as mechanical, which you know to be important to your students' development as writers. Below is a sample analytic scale:

SAMPLE ANALYTIC SCALE

	Low		*Middle*		*High*
General Merit					
Ideas	2	4	6	8	10
Organization	2	4	6	8	10
Wording	1	2	3	4	5
Tone	1	2	3	4	5

	Low		Middle		High
Mechanics					
Usage	1	2	3	4	5
Punctuation	1	2	3	4	5
Spelling	1	2	3	4	5
Handwriting	1	2	3	4	5

(Adapted from Cooper 7)

Primary Trait Scoring

Primary trait scoring isolates a particular type of discourse and examines it as a member of its class. In an AP course, which typically demands a variety of tasks, a student may write to persuade, request, instruct, inform, and so on. The aims of each of these tasks differ, as do the focuses, though every piece of writing should be sensitive to its audience, subject, and voice. Primary trait scoring directs attention to the trait or traits relevant to the mode of discourse being examined, and a specific scoring guide can help you monitor the relevant trait. Developed by the National Assessment of Educational Progress, primary trait scoring assesses the goals of a particular writing task (for example, a letter to a local newspaper arguing for the enactment of a certain law). By analyzing the strengths and weaknesses that primary trait scoring reveals in a paper, you can emphasize such rhetorical and situational-specific features as audience, speaker, and purpose, and simultaneously highlight concerns you deem pressing.

You can quickly create useful scoring guides if you wish to experiment with primary trait scoring. For a particular assignment, you need only identify the primary traits important to its execution. Once identified, those traits govern and focus the guide. Minimally, the guide should contain the following: (1) short analyses of the trait in question, with appropriate rationales; (2) samples of papers that have been scored, appended to explanations of why each sample was scored as it was; and (3) the rating scale you will use (for example, 1 to 5).

Although written over a decade ago, Richard Lloyd-Jones's "Primary Trait Scoring" remains enlightening to those teachers who desire a detailed description of primary trait scoring and its pedagogical possibilities.

Focused Holistic Scoring

Similar, but perhaps less specific than primary trait scoring, is focused holistic scoring. This method, developed for use in the Texas Assessment of Basic Skills, combines features of holistic and primary trait scoring. While you evaluate a writing sample holistically, you simultaneously address precisely defined elements of a particular mode of discourse.

In contrast to holistic scoring, this criterion-referenced method rates writing samples in terms of predefined criteria instead of merely ranking them against one another. While it retains the holistic features of responding impressionistically to all aspects of a composition, it also provides you with opportunities to focus on writing skills or strategies that you can reinforce with future instruction if such attention is necessary. For example, three criteria that you might monitor in focused holistic scoring are organization of ideas, clearly defined purpose, and attention to audience.

As with primary trait scoring, focused holistic scoring is readily available to the AP English teacher. All you need do is evaluate holistically and purposely allow that evaluation to be conditioned by predetermined criteria, such as organization and subject-verb agreement. What emerges are two or more groupings of student papers, each characterized by how effectively students handle certain features of discourse.

New Directions in AP English Evaluation

Among the most innovative of evaluation methods now available in AP English are portfolios, contracts, and journals. Portfolios require that students collect and submit all their written work, including successive drafts of each paper, at the end of a term. They then receive one grade on a combination of process, including the amount of serious revising and risk-taking that is obvious, and product, defined as completeness, neatness, correctness, and coherence of final drafts. In other words, rather than grading assigned papers periodically all year, you grade each student's portfolio at the year's end. This procedure frees you from the burden of evaluating hundreds of papers all year. But most importantly, the portfolio allows students to take the initiative to rework their papers as many times as they wish—a process that often results in high quality papers.

The contract, too, represents a break from tradition in assessment. The contract is an agreement that you and each student sign at the beginning of the term, specifying the requirements of the class and the grading criteria you will use. (See sample contract in Figure 8–1.) One benefit of the contract is that it gives students more responsibility for controlling their own work during the term. Because the contract is a nontraditional approach, it would be wise to alert parents of AP students via a letter prior to its use. (England 18).

Portfolios and contracts accommodate creative evaluation in AP English and represent innovation at its best, but so does an even older strategy: journal-keeping. Not only does expressive, or personal writing continue to warrant regular, if not daily attention in the AP classroom, but it deserves to be a factor in student evaluation. One valid way to make it such is to reward both quantity, the number of pages or entries submitted at semester's end, and product, a paper or two directly inspired by journal writing that have been taken through the total writing process. Grading the former merely demands that teachers count pages; the latter, that they grade only finished versions of papers that have evolved over time, and through multiple drafts, from cognitive or affective seeds planted in journals.

Figure 8–1 A Sample Grading Contract

THREE GENERAL POINTS:

1. Everyone who completes the minimum amount of writing minimally well will receive a "C" in writing.
2. No one will receive a "D."
3. Any student who does not complete *all* minimum requirements minimally well will receive a grade of "F."

IN ORDER TO EARN A GRADE OF "C" IN THIS COURSE FOR EACH NINE WEEKS, YOU MUST:

1. Place in your folder a minimum of *five* pieces of writing;
2. Submit a revision of at least *three* of those pieces of writing;
3. Submit a second revision of at least *two* pieces of writing;
4. Submit one piece of your choice for *grading* during the last week of the course.

IN ORDER TO EARN A GRADE OF "B" IN THIS COURSE, YOU MUST:

1. Submit a minimum of *seven* pieces of writing;
2. Submit a revision of at least *four* pieces of writing;
3. Submit a second revision of at least *two* pieces of writing;
4. Submit one piece of your choice for *grading* during the last week of the course.

OR, as an alternative, you may elect to

1–A. Complete all requirements for a "C" as stated above;
2–A. Submit for final grading *three* pieces of writing, *two* of which must be judged to exceed minimum achievement as established and discussed in class.

IN ORDER TO EARN A GRADE OF "A" IN THE COURSE, YOU MUST:

1. Complete requirements (1–4) above for a "B" grade;
2. Complete requirement 2–A above as listed for the "B" alternative. Students who earn "A's" will be expected to exceed minimum expectations in quantity *and* quality.

ADDITIONAL SPECIFICATIONS, DEFINITIONS, CLARIFICATIONS, AND EXPECTATIONS:

1. Each original and revised submission must be dated by the instructor before placement in folders.
2. No more than two pieces—original or revised—may be placed in a folder during a single week.
3. At least one half of all work submitted must be submitted by week four of each grading period.
4. Original submissions and any subsequent revisions must be stapled together in folders.

5. The average "expected length" of writing submitted will be approximately 500 words.
6. All pieces submitted should be carefully edited and revised, using editorial and proof-reading practices as demonstrated in class.
7. Final course grades will be determined after evaluations of the writing submitted during the last week, and after documentation that all other specifications for a given grade have been followed.
8. Only two designations (an "*" for superior work, that which exceeds minimum expectations for the course, and a "+" for acceptable work, that which meets minimum expectations for the course) will be made on these papers.

I understand how I will earn my grade in writing in this course and agree to have my grade determined according to the steps outlined.

Name _____

Date _____

I understand the grading procedures to be used to determine a course grade in writing.

Parent/Guardian

Signature _____

Date _____

(Adapted from England 18–19)

It is easy to see forward-looking evaluation in AP English as a welcome merger of the old and new, of proven assessment strategies that assume ever greater validity because of respect for writing as process and for what research says about process. The problems of evaluating students' work in AP courses cease to be burdensome when teachers respect how writing emerges from the human mind.

Works Cited

Cooper, Charles R. "Holistic Evaluation of Writing." *Evaluating Writing: Describing, Measuring, Judging.* Ed. Charles R. Cooper and Lee Odell. Urbana: NCTE, 1977. 3–31.

England, David A. "Teaching Writing Processes and Determining Grades." *The Quarterly* 8.3 (1986): 18–27.

Lloyd-Jones, Richard. "Primary Trait Scoring." *Evaluating Writing: Describing,*

Measuring, Judging. Ed. Charles R. Cooper and Lee Odell. Urbana: NCTE, 1977. 33–66.

Wolfe, Denny, and Robert Reising. *Writing for Learning in the Content Areas.* Portland, ME: Walch, 1983.

9

Preparing Students for the AP Examination
Dangers and Opportunities

JOHN IORIO
University of South Florida

The author argues that when AP teachers focus exclusively on preparing students for the AP examination, they subvert the integrity of the course. He presents a case for teaching a true college-level course that focuses on essential critical and analytical skills.

The Advanced Placement examination and its rubric have become paradigms of writing standards and expectations. And those who have never taken seriously Quintilian's warning about teaching from models would probably see nothing wrong or limiting in choosing the test as the ultimate model. The increasing popularity of the test is one measure of its success. But such success incubates weakness, and respect for the program quickly passes into subservience. Like all Platonic paradigms, its presence is a judgment, imposing its silent will on the schools it seeks to help. My purpose here is to point out the pernicious effects of focusing on the test in Advanced Placement courses—that teaching for the test is reductive, self-defeating, and ultimately a betrayal of educational integrity and student development. At the same time, I wish to suggest alternatives to the tyranny of the test that would allow both the curriculum and Advanced Placement to benefit the student.

Testing: Promises and Dangers

There is in the nature and process of any test a basic antagonism to the nature and process of education. While education addresses itself to the whole person, tests are reductive; while education is liberating, tests are confining; while education operates best in a leisurely world, tests create a frenetic ambiance. For cooperation, tests substitute competition; for inclusiveness, exclusiveness; for integration, fragmentation. Finally, tests may seem so important that they give students and teachers the illusion of being the goal of education. And yet, tests are an indisputable and integral part of the educational process. They help set standards, measure progress and achievement, and provide a quick and easy read-out of a student's intellectual development. In the case of Advanced Placement, the tests also purport to assign students their proper place in college. (See Sylvia Holladay's chapter in this text.)

So, periodically, 400 to 500 teachers and professors from Hawaii to Maine make their way ritualistically to Rider College to score the examination. They read holistically from 8:30 a.m. to 5:15 p.m. for six days. The rubric, a sacralized set of standards to which each reader must conform and by which each paper is judged, sits before them like some Delphic offspring to be consulted from time to time to guard against heterodoxy. After six days the reading ends. Readers depart, many of them ready to carry their reborn faith in the process to distant regions, while silent computers calculate the academic fate of thousands of students.

Since AP is a conduit to educational rewards and prestige, pressures mount for schools and teachers to shape their AP courses around the AP test. The pressures come from many sources. The positive achievements of Advanced Placement courses in the schools and among teachers cannot be discounted. According to a College Board survey that sampled the views of 1,513 teachers from 600 high schools,

> nine in ten AP teachers surveyed believed schools that offer college-level AP courses can help raise the standards of education through a school or school system. Eight in ten say these courses provide incentives, goals, and models to students who are younger than AP students. Half of the teachers believe these courses can help improve the quality of teaching in grades that precede those in which students may take the AP courses. ("AP Teachers" 7)

Responding to the survey, College Board president George H. Hanford said, "After 30 years of use, Advanced Placement has emerged as a dynamic model of educational excellence—a tried and tested educational program that can and does inject energy and intellectual rigor into secondary schools" ("AP Teachers" 7). Such enthusiasm, coupled with the momentum of success, yearly reinforces the increasing number of teachers and schools embracing the Advanced Placement program.

The pressure of prestige is also present. Principals look to AP courses to raise standards or to decorate a lackluster curriculum. Schools like to announce the number of students who have gone on to advanced courses in college. Teachers vie for AP courses, knowing that being anointed as Advanced Placement teachers and assigned courses more sophisticated than the general run of offerings confers upon them an enviable aura.

Similarly, more and more students demand the test. After all, they have been turned into eager consumers by the promise that they will take advanced courses, perhaps receive college credit on the basis of the test, and be spared the agonies and boredom of freshman English. Is there a student who would not want to enter college with such advantages?

There is also money to be considered. Eliminating courses and shortening the time spent in college can save hundreds, even thousands of dollars. Many parents cannot ignore a special interest in their children's passing the test. In these days of high college costs and trade school sentiment, the elimination of any course not clearly seen as contributing to the marketability of the student is viewed by many parents with the highest sympathy.

Everyone benefits from the test, it seems. The tide of assent is inexorable. What then are the problems?

The central problem, it seems to me, often lies with teachers themselves. Trained to AP conformity, impressed by clear-cut results, seeking rewards and fearing failure, some teachers return to their classrooms ready to teach the test as if it were a newfound evangelical truth. Such teachers have been known to spend an entire year leading students through past AP tests. They give minimal attention to substance, concentrate on the kind of writing honored by AP, use AP tests as the basis of writing exercises, and impose AP criteria as expressed by the rubric. Other teachers may arrive at this behavior when they discover that the success of a course, unfortunately, is measured by the number of students passing the test with high scores. Their initial enthusiasm and commitment to course integrity begin to wane. They may at first introduce a test or two, but occasional dalliance soon becomes compulsion as pressures mount, and they are lured to what shimmers as the most promising hope—teaching for the test. However teachers arrive at such behavior, it is unconscionable. Teaching for the test short-circuits the student's education while holding out the promise of easy reward—the academic equivalent of instant gratification.

But there are other dangers fundamental to the AP test itself. Often these dangers are obscured by the glitter of success, the rigidity of ritual, and the fervor of mass consensus. But they are there—reductionism, reflexivity, compromising of course integrity, and a rigid, mechanical approach to language and literature.

We tolerate tests because, veiled as they are in fairness and objectivity, they seem to be the most effective instrument in the evaluation process. By extrapolation and deduction we can use a test to determine the range of a student's learning. Teaching for the AP test, however, circumvents the purpose and process of the test. It gives us a false reading of a student's achievement, thereby giving us misplacement instead of advanced placement and allowing some students to pass who sorely need a college-level course. It contributes to the negative, even cynical attitude of students who believe that circumventing courses and hard work is the mark of high acumen. In the end, students may discover that what has been circumvented is their own education.

This reductionism allies itself with the reflexivity that takes place when the test is taught or when it becomes the aim of a course. After the reading at Rider College, many teachers take the examinations home with them. Certainly, not all of them are taken as mementos of the six-day ordeal. Some of them will be used to coach students in the kind of reading, thinking, and writing the next test will involve. I am reminded here of the Zanzibar effect: When French sailors landed at Zanzibar, they set their watches by the town's clock, while the inhabitants set their clocks by the arrival of the sailors. So while the test and the rubric are devised to test student ability to write and think, the students are being trained to think and write as the test and rubric demand.

Both reductionism and reflexivity corrupt course integrity. If the course bows to the test, the broader demands of a discipline and of education are violated. To concentrate on a certain set of works to be read in a certain way and selected without regard to subtle continuities of time, place, and discipline drains the full meaning and glory of a liberal education.

Then there is the rubric. While the test question makes certain assumptions about the nature of writing, the rubric used to evaluate the student's writing specifies as quantitatively as possible what the characteristics of that writing will be.

No doubt there is wisdom in the rubric. No one hoping for a positive response to a letter of application would write in stream of consciousness; nor would army field communicators use Cicero as a model. Yet some principles pervade all effective writing whether embodied in telic, pentad, or rubric. Given the realities of writing quality on the high school and college levels, the AP rubric shines like a knight of deliverance. After all, shouldn't a reader/writer be cognizant of the central conflict of a work, the effect and implications of the conflict, supporting details, the relation of the specific to the general? Shouldn't a reader/writer be expected to be precise and clear? Of course. Then why not teach the rubric? The answer is that most of us do. But we teach it as part of a larger pattern of possibilities. The rubric concentrates on one model of writing behavior—a mechanical model that measures writing in terms of generalization and support, cause and effect, factual data and pattern. Certainly, these are all worthy characteristics of good writing. The trouble, however, is that the rubric leaves little room for stylistic syntactic patterns, sentence sophistication, diction, metaphorical dimensions, turn of phrase, experimentation, and generalizations that pass into insight. Of course, they may be covered by the rubric's term "good writing," but AP readers have been known to resist the temptation to honor these elements of style unless they are already sheltered by the obvious criteria of the rubric. After all, readers are also being judged. And it is much easier and safer to defend the terms of the rubric than to whisper a long defense of style in a hall of colleagues.

The result is reductionism applied to writing, for the impression is left among students and teachers that other forms of writing are either undesirable or inferior. Focusing on the rubric and test can hurt the most creative among students or those who may have the greatest potential for development, while it rewards those who can most quickly conform to mechanical and formal restrictions. Conformity to the mechanical can also be seen in the experience of some readers at the reading. After the third day of reading, the reader becomes more mechanical, scanning the paper for the right signals, holding to them tenaciously as if only chaos lies beyond the rubric. Woe to readers who allow another model to slip into their judgments because what can follow is a form of angst—indecision, apprehension, rereadings of the paper, a breakdown in rhythm. They may put the paper aside until the comfortable tyranny of the rubric and its rhythms have been re-established.

This experience of readers should be a warning to teachers who find that they are bowing to pressure and teaching to the test, for to teach only the rubric is to submit to a view and practice of writing that exclude possibilities of language that rim the perimeter of the rubric. It is at this point, in the teaching of the test, that a student's education is compromised. So if it comes to a choice between the integrity of courses and the demands of the test, the teacher's choice should be clear. Yet, this is a dilemma that need not occur.

What Is to Be Done?

The question is not how to prepare students for the test while preserving the integrity of courses, but how to improve the education of students. To prepare students for the test will inevitably subvert the integrity of the course, for while the presence of the test remains a certainty, integrity easily assumes a variety of masks. This subversion is evident in those courses based solely on the test and in teachers who have become mere coaches for Advanced Placement. Such misuse of the test may herald initial success in the number of students passing the test, but it can doom students to educational deficiencies that will plague them long after the celebration of that success. What is needed is that schools must improve their AP courses. If quality is raised, if courses have intellectual substance and rigor, the harmful potential of the test would be eliminated. If the AP course is a true college-level course and students are taught well, then students should still be able to perform well on any AP test.

Schools can begin to look more seriously at literature courses. Are the works being chosen by the faculty with honest conviction about what constitutes a college education in our complex civilization? Are they chosen with the intent of enlarging a student's vision? Are they chosen to stimulate modes of thinking not familiar to the student? Are they chosen to present the past not in slavish reverence but as a dynamic living presence? Or are they chosen with both eyes on the test?

Rather than courses based on theme and genre (the first can be reductive and the second unnecessarily narrow in a high school curriculum), why not a course concentrating on a few major periods of the past, each exemplified by a major literary work and by a variety of shorter pieces? Such a course would assure a prolonged and significant immersion in a period so that students can develop a sense of a cultural construct different from their own. It would treat *Oedipus Rex*, for example, not in modern dress, but in relation to triglyph and column, mathematical proportions and armed wisdom, sun and cave. Through this kind of fidelity to the past, the works would become more than modes of modern sensibility, and paradoxically, they would become more relevant to our times. Such a course would eliminate a repetitious and mechanical approach to plot, conflict, characterization, and theme too often found in courses with a linear arrangement of works, and would encourage the view that each work creates its own critical invitation and aura. It also would allow greater concentration on the major work, enriching it with overlays of the culture that produced it.

Critical Thinking and the College Course in English

Above all, critical thinking must be central to all AP courses. How often have we heard teachers say, "The trouble is, they can't think"? Of course they can't think if they aren't trained for the levels of abstraction that we require of them. Of course they cannot think if we present writing or literature in terms of dead categories and in a vacuum, as if we were trying to enable students to walk a tightrope by teaching them the laws of equilibrium. True college-level courses deal with such topics as modes of inquiry, problem-solving, reaching consensus, the world as text, fiction and reality as constructs. With writing as central, such courses fuse symbol and articulation, cognition and material, and once more give rationality hegemony over the nonrational impulses of our times. After all, college courses, in literature or in writing, are also courses in critical thinking.

That thinking and writing are related has been well argued by others. We may not be sure as to what thinking really is, but we are aware of some of the skills and processes involved in it. We know, too, that it isn't enough for students to be aware of the importance of thinking and thought; they must understand the process that gets them to their ends. Not only do they need a grounding in the basics of critical thinking, but also thorough training in the rhetorical and cognitive strategies of definition, classification, comparison, contrast, analogy, and generalization. These are processes that need to be fostered as students develop cognitively.

A critical thinking approach would demonstrate to students that metaphor can control thinking, that language can shape thought and perception. They could then enter the realm of magic that has always been ascribed to language and literature. But they cannot reclaim these magical properties of language unless they free themselves from the view that language is a passive, malleable instrument of last resort in human affairs. Or that it is simply a means of empirical and reportorial communication. It will have to be seen as an abstract, transcending construct that reveals not only what is not obvious to common sense but also what may lie beneath the level of conscious threshold. It will have to be treated as an active instrument that shapes, modifies, influences, and creates reality.

But we can never transmit these views unless we are convinced that the teaching of writing is more than calculating and tabulating errors and giving a grade in relation to the amount of red ink on a theme. So long as individuals have not been reduced to mechanical beings, they cannot be taught writing effectively by mechanical means, for writing is not a matter of right and wrong but of nuance and shaping, of critical thinking made manifest.

Although critical thinking approaches bring students into greater awareness of linguistic possibilities, their need to *see* critically must be emphasized. Critical awareness is fundamental to good writing and interpretation. After all, unseen details cannot be arranged in larger patterns of meaning. To this end then, AP courses should be broadened to include other arts. The exposure of students to other arts would open new ways to apprehend and interpret reality. Their grammar would enlarge and give resonance to the grammar of literature and help raise students' level of articulation. At the same time, the sister arts would delineate more clearly the purposes, possibilities, and limitations of literary works. How often have teachers been told by students, often defending poor performance in literature, that they are a visual generation—that film is their medium. When I was told this during a film course, I ran the first ten minutes of Bergman's *Wild Strawberries* and then asked the class to point out details they had seen. The responses were dismal—the visual generation was not able to perceive significant details in a film even after repeated reruns. This defect has deep roots, for no matter what they confronted—a novel, a film, the world—the students were unable to see because they had been trained by the culture and the schools to be passive. Lacking the skill to see actively and critically, they had no basis for feeling or thinking. What was left then was sensation—the passive disease of our time.

Most importantly, teaching students to think and write critically gives them a method of approaching *all* works, literary or nonliterary; teaching to the test only enables students to pass it. This process reminds me of the saying "Give a man a fish and you feed him for one day; teach him to fish and you feed him for a lifetime." AP teachers need to prepare students for a lifetime, not for just one AP test.

The Need For Self-Criticism

We should always be aware that institutions develop dynamic lives of their own. As they grow, they become labyrinthine and then remote, mysterious, ritualized, and rigid. A priesthood, a language, even an architecture may develop. Finally, institutions become sacred. Created to serve, they soon threaten the individuals they were meant to benefit, often with the support of such individuals. What is needed in a democratic society, then, is a continuing desacralization of its institutions through scrutiny, rational discourse, responsiveness, openness, and change. Teachers have this responsibility as well as the responsibility to scrutinize their own purposes and attitudes so that institutions that begin as benefactors remain benefactors. But sadly, teachers who teach for the test may be incapable of such self-examination.

The present system, especially when the focus is on teaching for the test, habituates students not to rational and critical thinking but to the logic of conformity. Belief becomes the highest virtue, and assent to the values of the tribe the highest good. But we cannot passively train students to become active citizens. We cannot honor and revive language by subverting its potential, and we cannot resurrect education if we are too willing to submit to the idol of a test. Schools stimulated by AP and college-level courses centered on critical thinking and writing can more than resist the submissive tendencies that threaten us. They can develop students who can use language to give form to life and world, who can independently and critically navigate between the meretricious and the enduring, and who, finally, have the skills and attitudes to deal with the broader tests of a complex society.

Such an achievement would eliminate any concern we may have about the threat of a test or an institution. In fact, it may even help us glimpse at least the dream of early nineteenth-century thinkers who felt that freedom in education would lead to the emancipation of the people from ignorance and make them self-reliant, ready for any test.

Work Cited

"AP Teachers Say Program Raises Educational Standards in Schools." *College Board News* 14.2 (1985–86): 7.

PART III

Alternative Advanced
Placement Programs

10

Implementing a Collaborative High School/University English Program

MARILYN S. STERNGLASS
City University of New York

THOMAS VANDER VEN
Indiana University—South Bend

The authors describe the Advance College Project (ACP), an alternative to College Board's AP program. ACP allows high school students to earn college credit based on their performance in a university course taught in their high school. The program enables the school system to bypass the enormous bureaucracy of College Board and institute its own quality controls.

At a time when collaborative programs between high schools and colleges are burgeoning, administrators and teachers now have several choices available when they make decisions about what will best serve the needs of their students. When selecting programs that will challenge their advanced students, they will want to weigh carefully the advantages of each option and think about the implications for students, instructors, and the school system. One such alternative, the Advance College Project (ACP), initiated at the Bloomington campus of Indiana University in 1982, is a cooperative program between Indiana University and high schools in Indiana.

The Advance College Project began by offering courses in English composition, mathematics, and chemistry, and later added courses in psychology and literature. High school teachers are trained to teach the college courses, and their students enroll as special students in the university. Unlike comparable Advanced Placement programs, the Advance College Project permits students to use the same course materials offered in college courses and also permits students to be evaluated by their instructors on their work over the entire semester, rather than by their performance on a single examination prepared and judged by individuals distant from the students' instructional experiences. In the English Composition course, a pretest/post-test writing sample is collected to ensure comparability with the university on-campus students' performance, but this is only one of the written tests used by the high school English instructors to grade their students.

Through the ACP, high school content-area teachers come to the university each summer for a week-long, intensive seminar that prepares them to teach a freshman-level college course to their high school students. The students earn dual high school/college credit. ACP is based on a similar program begun in 1973 at Syracuse University, but it differs in many curricular, administrative, and evaluative details. Central to the implementation of the program are such issues as the type of preparation to be given to the high school teachers in the summer, the adaptation of the college course to a five-day-a-week classroom, the amount of flexibility teachers have in adapting the campus curriculum to their classrooms, the attitudes and skills of the high school students in comparison with their college counterparts, the role of site visits to the high schools, and the type of evaluation program necessary to justify Indiana University transcripts for completed college work that would be recognized and accepted by colleges and universities to which the students wished to transfer credit. As we discuss later in this chapter, although Indiana University has been scrupulous in its efforts to demonstrate comparability between on-campus offerings and high school-conducted classes, the proliferation of these types of programs within the state, including some with less rigorous standards, has seriously compromised the acceptance of college transcripts for all such programs.

With well-established Advanced Placement programs, in Indiana or anywhere in the country, a question arises as to why high schools should prefer the Advance College Project. From an administrative point of view, there is much closer contact between the schools and the university. The schools can select discipline areas, recommend teachers, and maintain ongoing contact with the university administrators and faculty who visit their schools. Because of our roles in the English program [Marilyn Sternglass, director of the English composition component for the first four years; Tom

Vander Ven, site director in South Bend since 1983 and director of the English composition program in 1984–85], we are able to describe in detail the implementation and development of the English Composition component. It has been clear from the beginning that the program's most attractive incentive for high schools is its genuine collaborative nature. Although the university initiated the project, the input of the participating schools and, particularly, the teachers was seriously integrated in the program as it was tested and developed.

It is readily apparent that the Advance College Project shares a common goal with the ETS Advanced Placement program: to accelerate the movement into college of capable high school seniors, thereby enhancing their educational opportunity. What is less apparent is the quite different character of its educational politics. The great promise of Indiana University's ACP, as well as its possible undoing, lies in its present relationship to the established structure of education, a relationship that is essentially subversive. It is a constructive subversion, in that its method of acceleration is leading to a real fusion of secondary and higher education. It trains select high school teachers and grants them the credentials to teach college-credit courses as part of their normal daily teaching load. It automatically accepts the grades that they assign and furnishes the students with transcripts bearing Indiana University's name.

In terms of the politics of institutional power, the placement of the University's Advance College Project inside high school walls constitutes a substantial surrender of control by both sides. On one side, the university grants the power to teach and grade to a faculty member it has in no real sense hired; it allows the course to function miles from campus, out of range of close formal evaluation; it allows its daily business to be interrupted by intercom announcements about pep assemblies. On the other side, each high school grants to the university the power to train its participating teachers in a particular pedagogy and to select textbooks; it even allows the university to send professorial evaluators to observe classroom teaching.

The Training Seminar

Each year, the new participating schools select one primary teacher and one back-up teacher to attend a week-long summer training seminar for those who will teach the course. Teachers are required to have a master's degree and five years' teaching experience. Their credentials are reviewed by the director of the academic program. Although the seminar is not viewed as an additional screening device, it does permit an additional evaluation of the teachers' suitability for the program.

The plan was to select one of the syllabi currently being used on the Bloomington campus of Indiana University and use it as the basis for instruction in the freshman composition course as it would be offered in the high schools. The reading/writing approach (described at the end of this chapter) was selected and used for the first four years of the program, the syllabus in the high schools being modified as it was modified on campus over that time period. The philosophy underlying the reading/writing approach was to engage students in prereading activities that would relate their background knowledge and experience to the topics introduced by writers in their texts and to encourage the use of the processes of analysis and synthesis in formulating responses to writing tasks. A current book for teachers, *Facts, Artifacts, and Counterfacts* by David Bartholomae and Anthony Petrosky, provides both a theoretical justification for this transactional approach to reading and writing and descriptions of curricular approaches to such instruction. Instructors in the high schools, like their university counterparts, were encouraged to use supplementary readers and bring in individual readings of their choice. They were urged, though, to concentrate on teaching the processes of analysis and synthesis, the central focus of the on-campus course.

Because the composition course itself was based on current theoretical understandings of reading and writing processes, in the summer seminar the teachers were first given an opportunity to familiarize themselves with some current theoretical work, such as Lee Odell's work on composing processes and evaluative criteria and Carolyn Burke's work on transactional models of reading. The next few days were spent reading the textbook and trying out some of the reading and writing activities the students would undertake. Next, evaluative criteria for the writing assignments were discussed. The group read and responded to papers written by on-campus students in response to textbook assignments, and they developed a consensus for evaluative criteria. The group also discussed means of evaluating the entire program. Finally, each teacher developed an individual syllabus to use in his or her classroom.

Normally, descriptions of such training seminars suggest that everything runs smoothly, and there are no serious issues or problems between the university faculty and the teacher-participants. We don't wish to overstate the problems, but it is important to acknowledge that it takes real effort to establish a collaborative environment, especially between groups where hierarchical relationships have been the longstanding tradition. One issue that came up in the first year of the seminars has already been briefly alluded to: Were the teachers going to be judged by the university faculty after their credentials had been initially approved? Although this was not the university's intention, and no teacher was ever prevented from teaching the composition course, the possibility existed that some teachers could be reevaluated and denied permission to continue their participation in the program.

One teacher in that first year received notice before the seminar began that his credentials looked somewhat weak and his role in the seminar would be monitored closely. Another back-up teacher was so resistant to the process method of pedagogy presented in the seminar that ACP coordinators might have been reluctant to allow him to teach in the program had he been assigned the course in his school. The teachers' sensitivity to the possibility of being evaluated arose when they were asked to share with each other and the university faculty some of their written responses to the textbook tasks. The teachers not only felt uncomfortable sharing with others whom they didn't know well (giving them considerable empathy with their students when this issue was later discussed), but they also felt that they might be judged by the faculty. When these issues were aired and defused, everyone felt more comfortable. This discussion also made us more sensitive to these feelings and allowed us to anticipate and discuss them with teachers in the seminar in subsequent years before serious tensions arose. We feel that over the years the relationships between the teachers and the university participants have proven to be satisfying to both. A typical comment from one of the teachers summarizes the collaborative nature of the relationship that evolved: "Working with the IU faculty continues to be one of the most satisfying aspects of teaching in the ACP. The exchange of ideas has proven to be stimulating, an important impetus to refining classroom strategies" (Gudaitis, *ACP Final Evaluation* 30–31).

As a follow-up to the seminar, three meetings are scheduled on the university campus during the academic year. During the fall semester, the teachers return twice to share their perceptions of the course and to offer constructive suggestions to each other and the university faculty and administrators. From such meetings have come suggestions for improved registration procedures and plans for ACP teachers to recruit students by visiting junior English classes prior to the students' selecting courses for their senior year. After the first year, teachers from all prior years were invited to the spring semester meeting so that a community of high school teachers from across the state began to interact with each other in an area of common interest: the teaching of writing. From these spring meetings came substantive recommendations that were incorporated into the program, particularly suggestions about how the program evaluation should be designed and carried out.

Adaptation of the Course

The college freshman course had to be adapted to the high school setting in two significant ways. First, the college course was designed for two or three rather than five class meetings each week. For the high school teachers, this meant breaking down assignments and class activities into smaller chunks than had been designed for the college curriculum. In practice, this didn't present any difficulties, as the course was designed to encourage much small-group work in class in response to the reading and writing tasks, and the general process approach lent itself easily to scheduling adaptations.

Second, unlike the college setting (and AP classes), there were schools and classrooms where not all the students were enrolled for college credit. This came about for several reasons: in some schools, the school adopted the college course as its regular senior course and then gave students the option of enrolling for college credit; in other schools, particularly smaller ones where only one or two senior English courses were offered, students were allowed to participate in the ACP course (in order to fill the classroom to a level that justified such a section) even if they didn't wish to enroll for college credit. There were few reports that these mixed classes disrupted the quality of the program. Most students in these classes, whether enrolled for college credit or not, were pleased to have the opportunity to practice college-level work.

Although the university administrators encouraged the high schools to set up separate sections for the college composition course, they recognized that this was not always feasible. For example, in 1982–83, in eight of the eleven schools, the sections were composed totally of ACP students. But of the seven schools added in the 1983–84 academic year, four had college composition enrollments of fewer than ten students, while the other three had enrollments ranging from 19 to 29 (Gudaitis, *ACP Course Enrollment* 9–10). Thus, establishing separate college-enrolled sections was an economic as well as educational issue, with principals being concerned that all teachers in the school or discipline area carry equitable loads. With each subsequent year in a high school, though, the proportion of students enrolled for college credit increased so that establishing mixed classes in new schools was usually regarded as an investment in the future of the program.

Teacher Flexibility

The on-campus syllabus and textbooks served as the focal points of the course, but individual variation in materials and tasks was welcomed. Since the kinds of schools where the program was being implemented varied, individual teachers adjusted the syllabus to meet the needs of their students. For example, teachers in suburban high schools, where large percentages of their students went on to higher education, demanded more rigorous research papers from their students than did teachers in some of the smaller high schools. One of the interesting findings of the research on students in the ACP program was that their SAT verbal scores were higher than those of the IU-Bloomington students (Gudaitis, *ACP Final Evaluation* 10). This may be accounted for, in part, by the fact that more confident students chose to enroll for college credit, even though many of their noncredit classmates also anticipated entering college.

In addition, since the participating teachers were often the most enterprising and energetic ones in their schools, it wasn't surprising that many of them had developed particular activities that they had used successfully with their students in the past. They frequently incorporated or modified these to become consistent with the goals of the composition course, and they were encouraged to do so. Every time a teacher could make the course his or her own, that teacher felt more strongly identified with the course and more committed to its success.

Attitudes and Skills of High School Students

To be accepted into the program, students had to meet the minimum entrance criteria for IU-Bloomington (IUB) students. The majority of both IUB and ACP students had high academic credentials. The latter as a group scored slightly higher than IUB students in both verbal and math aptitudes on the SAT tests. They also placed higher in high school class rankings, with 65 percent of the ACP students in the top 20 percent of their class compared to 52 percent of the IUB students (Gudaitis *ACP Final Evaluation* 9).

On a questionnaire completed after they had taken the course, the students registered their satisfaction, with 76.1 percent reporting that they were "very glad," 20.3 percent "somewhat glad," 1.9 percent "a little sorry" and 0.6 percent "sorry" (Gudaitis, *ACP Final Evaluation* 14). This strong vote of confidence in the course was reinforced by their individual comments on the questionnaire. Students who were "very glad" that they took the course noted improvement in organizing their papers, in accepting criticism, in writing a variety of types of papers, and in their own confidence in their writing skills. Students who were "somewhat glad" noted the course's difficulty and their own wish that they had studied more (Gudaitis, 14–19).

One major advantage for students taking the ACP course rather than AP English is that they are given opportunities to improve their work over an entire semester and are evaluated by their performance in the course itself rather than on a single examination designed and evaluated elsewhere and insensitive to the work students have done all semester. (See Sylvia Holladay's chapter on the issue of evaluation instruments and sensitivity to instructional objectives.) It makes a great deal of sense to have the evaluation instruments designed locally to examine what has actually been stressed in the design and implementation of the course. Furthermore, there is no question as to whether the students are receiving an experience equivalent to the college course experience, inasmuch as they are taking the same course the college students take.

Evaluating the ACP Program

One of the hallmarks of the ACP program developed at Indiana University has been its commitment to an extensive evaluation program. Aware that it would have to justify awarding college credit and determined to maintain the integrity of the IU transcript, ACP organizers set up an extensive evaluation apparatus as soon as the program was initiated. In addition to substantial administrative support within the Office of Summer Sessions, the director of the program, Dr. Leslie Coyne, hired an administrator and evaluator to work exclusively with the program. The evaluator, Janice Lave Gudaitis, immediately designed questionnaires for participating teachers to respond to when they entered the program, after they completed the seminar, and at the end of each semester during which they taught a course in the program. She also designed questionnaires for the students to fill out after they had completed a course and after they had completed a semester of college work.

In a questionnaire students filled out after completing the English composition course, the students responded in the following way:

1. I am now looking forward to attending college.
   81.1 percent agreed;   3.3 percent disagreed;   15.6 percent were not sure.
2. I have now gained new skills that will be useful in college.
   82.7 percent agreed;   5.3 percent disagreed;   12 percent were not sure.
3. I now feel uncertain of my ability to do college work.
   9.2 percent agreed;   78.6 percent disagreed;   12.2 percent were not sure.
4. I discovered that I will have to work/study harder in college than I did in high school.
   67.7 percent agreed;   14.7 percent disagreed;   17.6 percent were not sure.
5. I needed to spend more time studying.
   56.4 percent agreed;   29.1 percent disagreed;   14.6 percent were not sure.
6. My study habits and time-management skills have improved.
   60.5 percent agreed;   14.8 percent disagreed;   24.7 percent were not sure.
7. I feel my high school should continue to offer college courses.
   97 percent agreed;   1 percent disagreed;   2 percent were not sure.
8. I would recommend this ACP course (English Composition) to other high school students.
   96 percent agreed;   2 percent disagreed;   2 percent were not sure.
                                    (Gudaitas, *ACP Final Evaluation* 17–21)

Responses to the last two questions evidence overwhelming approval of the ACP composition course, while responses to the first few questions demonstrate the students' conviction that they were experiencing a real college course over the entire semester. They had been learning not only substantive content and process in their course, but also about themselves as potential and present college students.

The design of the evaluation instrument for the English course was left to the university English faculty to ensure comparability between the university and the high school experience. Because there had been extensive pretesting and post-testing in the freshman composition program at Indiana

University, we decided to develop similar writing tasks for the ACP students and compare their performance with that of on-campus students enrolled in the same course and who would write on the same topics. Initially, the students were given the same writing task both at the beginning and end of the semester. The papers were coded and mixed with papers written on the same topic by IUB students enrolled in freshman composition classes. The raters, graduate student instructors of freshman composition, were trained in holistic rating procedures through the university's Bureau of Evaluation Studies and Testing (which also carried out the statistical analyses). The raters could not determine from the coding whether any paper was an IUB or ACP paper or a pre- or post-test paper. Each paper was read by three raters. The ratings, subjected to rating-reliability tests, were always reliable at a .90 figure or higher.

During the first two years, there was considerable dissatisfaction expressed by ACP teachers because there had been misunderstandings about how the pre- and post-test papers would be incorporated within the course and because the topics for the tests did not seem sufficiently challenging and interesting to the students. As a result, the first year's results were analyzed quantitatively (with ACP students and on-campus students performing statistically similarly at both pre- and post-test points) and qualitatively during the second year. In the second year, James Anderson, a graduate composition student, evaluated the IUB and ACP papers using the criteria of Andrew Wilkinson's scale (linguistic, cognitive, affective, and moral dimensions). Students had been given identical topics in pre- and post-test writings. Anderson found that the students both on-campus and in the ACP program had written about a subject on the pretest that they felt very strongly about, and thus their writing was generally more effective in their pretest writing.

In subsequent years, the writing tasks were modified so that half the students wrote on one task at the beginning of the term and the other half wrote on an alternate task. The students then reversed tasks at the end of the semester. Topic awareness, a problem when the same topic was used for pre- and post-writing, was never raised as an issue by the teachers when the new format was utilized. The teachers agreed that the pretest papers could be used instructionally in the course and that the post-test paper should be graded and counted as one of the final papers in the course, an attempt to counter senioritis and motivate students to take the post-test assignment seriously. All of these modifications were made at the recommendation of the participating teachers, particularly as they met during the annual spring meetings and reviewed all aspects of the course.

Site Visits

The ACP site visitor entering the high school looms with authority to praise or condemn but probably feels just as uncomfortable about classroom visitations as the teacher does. The visitor must know that, in the role of superior from a higher institutional level, he or she can never be wholly welcome. Certainly, the site visitor's arrival is authorized; the professor has a standing invitation. Moreover, the site visitor had been a coequal participant with the teacher in the summer training seminar at Bloomington. There, they had considered the merits of process teaching, the philosophy of letter grades on papers, and the endless war on plagiarism. The site visit awakens memories in both of an intensive week in June on a hot campus, full of rare good talk about the teaching of writing.

Collegial chumming aside, the site visitor serves as a liaison for practical matters. While the ACP office publishes extensive instructions on all aspects of program implementation, there are always questions. Does Ball State University accept ACP credit? Can a student currently taking an ACP class for high school credit only now apply for retroactive admission to ACP? What if a parent objects to the readings in the text?

The site visitor comes also as a consultant on syllabus and classroom management. Questions arise during site visits on the structure of the course. Do five organized, teacher-dominated meetings a week vitiate the opportunity for students to work independently and maturely, as they must learn to do in college? Should Tuesdays and Thursdays be scheduled for students to work individually and in small peer review groups? (One school system forbids this practice; teachers should teach.)

Observing a class session on research paper documentation, one site visitor was asked by the teacher about variant citation methods. There and elsewhere, he discovered that teachers of five oversized English classes, with three preparations, hall duty, and dance chaperoning do not eagerly surrender the scholastic familiarity of *ibid.* and *op. cit.* for the strangeness of cryptic in-text citations without so much as a "pp."

Naturally, the site visitor must evaluate as well as consult. In a visit of a few hours, he or she must determine whether a classroom and its teacher truly bring Indiana University, its curriculum, and its academic standards to these high schoolers in the Northern Valley of the state. Is progress through the syllabus on schedule? Do students appear to understand the hour's activities in the context of course objectives? Do they demonstrate the cognition and communication skills of college students? Do they perceive their teacher and themselves as members of a college classroom?

After observing these classes, the site visitor files a form report with the ACP office, noting any problem areas that need attention. Over two years of visits to seven teachers in six schools, the English site visitor has found no serious deficiencies. This isn't surprising since the high schools nominate experienced writing teachers, and the university provides extensive training for them. ACP knows its personnel. Teachers are urged to remain in the program only if they find their own methods and goals compatible with the ACP pedagogy. For the most part, then, the site visitor's evaluation is an act of confirmation.

In his own practice—and it isn't atypical—IUB site visitor Tom Vander

Ven strives to subordinate the evaluation component of his visits to a quiet subtext. Although evaluation is implicit in the process of visitation, he strives through tone and statement to subvert his image as judge and to confirm the image of the teacher as college instructor and colleague. He notes that he says "strive" because the cultural stereotype of the English professor from the higher institution as an abstracted, polysyllabic, and unforgiving protector and critic of the language stands between him and the students. More than once, the teacher has said, *sotto voce*, "They're awfully quiet. I think they're a little afraid of you."

Worrying whether the class will go well, a teacher can find it hard to remember that ACP faculty are as much members of a teaching team as perhaps they will ever be. Colleagues with adjoining campus offices often say less to each other about the methods and goals of teaching English than does the ACP team of teachers and site visitors.

Directors of ACP, university faculty, and high school administrators and teachers play as a team. From the initial presentation of ACP to prospective schools to the seminars and site visitations, ACP administrators and university faculty have, in our experience, displayed neither the hard-sell tone of empire builders nor the condescension of reformers. They have consistently and effectively sought the fusion of the university and the high school at cooperative points on the educational continuum.

In the Advance College Project, this sharing of ideas and techniques continues at the high school sites. For example, Gordon Schermer of Penn High School reported that his students had some uncertainty about paper evaluation criteria and what constituted actual university writing standards. In fact, they wondered whether they were really doing college level work. In an open exchange before his class, Gordon and Tom compared their evaluations of sample student work. The students learned that, while the instructors differed in some details and in critical emphases, they agreed essentially on the strengths and limitations of the samples.

This last experience dramatizes, most of all, that the site visitor's main role is to validate the high school classroom as a university site. When Tom talks to students about the Advance College Project and about their course work, he tries to make references to the summer seminars in Bloomington where the teacher, other ACP teachers, and university faculty together study the text and develop the syllabus. Clearly, the students' self-image as part-time college students includes the image of their teacher as college teacher. They also are pleased to hear that the project's extensive comparative evaluation of ACP and university-campus writing samples has shown no significant difference in performance levels.

The Status of the Program

ACP teachers themselves do more to confirm the course's status than merely maintain sound academic standards. Naomi Kent and Gloria Murphy of South Bend Riley High School insist that their students go to the IU-South Bend campus bookstore to buy their texts. Paulette Cwidak's students at South Bend Adams, in the tribal spirit, have worn red IU sweatshirts with "ACP" on the back. A photograph of Eleanor Bell of Elkhart Memorial, together with a site visitor and an ACP student, appeared in the *Elkhart Truth*. School systems want their constituency to know that they have brought the university to the high school.

And yet the insistent promotion of the Advance College Project as an experience in higher education fundamentally opposes the highest purpose of the project—the fusion of the university and the high school at cooperative points on the educational continuum. The greater the promotion of ACP as a college program, the greater its image of separation from its own high school site. Tom learned at one high school that the promotion of ACP composition among junior-year prospects is hampered by a lack of informed support among English faculty. They don't understand ACP; in fact, at its inception they had not been informed of the opportunity to teach in the project because the school wanted to avoid the disruptive effects of competition. Secrecy and jealousy from within may yet raise serious threats to the longevity of the Advance College Project.

External Threats to the Project

Far more dangerous than the internal threats to the project's survival, however, is the threat of its being discredited from without. At the root of this threat lies both economic competition for enrollments among colleges and universities and a healthy suspicion of the legitimacy of extramural credit programs. So long as there are schools hungry for students and tuition dollars, projects such as ACP must work overtime at quality control and public relations. So long as there are mail-order divinity degrees, the fear that all such programs are scams will endure. So long as a real or perceived gap remains between the quality of secondary and higher education, the validity of college credit earned in high school classrooms will be suspect.

Currently in Indiana, the acceptance of ACP credit by other schools is ebbing. Purdue University, originally willing to transfer ACP credit, has reversed its policy. At this writing, Purdue's mathematics department will again accept ACP math credit, but ACP English credit remains under negotiation. Ball State University once accepted ACP credit, but its admissions officers have recently informed one high school guidance office that ACP credits will no longer transfer. And an association of Indiana small colleges is now deliberating a policy of not accepting ACP credits. Because at least one college in Indiana has sold college credit for high school courses based solely on an evaluation of the course description, and because some competing programs have made little effort to establish a uniform curriculum and procedures for the control of standards, the directors of Indiana University's Advance College Project have become firefighters, trying to put out blazes of rejection around the state. The project's hectic defensive stance on several fronts is frustrating since from the beginning the project's developers have been totally committed to uniformity and quality throughout all of the field schools.

Despite the established excellence of the Advance College Project, it remains vulnerable to a variety of pressures, some healthy and warranted, others counterproductive to the goals of this program, which are to create alternatives that accelerate and deepen our students' educations, while making better use of existing institutional systems. ACP enables qualified students to earn legitimate college-level credit early, within the familiar social environment of their high schools. It is a worthy alternative to AP programs, especially in environments like those created by Indiana University-Bloomington where the evaluation component has been such an integral part of program planning, ensuring the integrity of the quality of the experiences for students, teachers, administrators, and communities where such programs are so highly valued.

APPENDIX
THE READING/WRITING COURSE PLAN

TEXTS:

Reading, Writing and Reasoning by Marilyn Sternglass (Macmillan, 1983)

The Little, Brown Reader, 3rd ed., edited by Stubbs & Barnet

The Little English Handbook, edited by Corbett (Optional)

Both reading and writing are active struggles to create meaning. In the academic environment, the two processes invariably go together. This five-unit course plan is set up to make students conscious of this connection and to provide them with basic strategies that will help them in their college writing.

Current research indicates that reading and writing are transactional processes. Transactions occur between the writer and the text; the knowledge that people bring to the text determines the meaning that they will construct from it. Moreover, reading and writing work in tandem; reading, whether it is of their own text or someone else's, enables writers to refine and reformulate their ideas. Those interested in finding out more about research in this area should refer to the bibliography at the end of the course plan.

The texts for this course were chosen with this conception of reading and writing in mind. The basic text is Marilyn Sternglass's *Reading, Writing and Reasoning* (RWR), which contains a sequence of assignments built around prewriting, reading, and writing. Sternglass's text provides a basic framework for reading/writing assignments; within this framework we have provided students with alternate selections from *The Little, Brown Reader*. We believe that giving students a choice of reading assignments is crucial to the success of this course, for it allows them a greater opportunity to bring their own interests and knowledge to bear upon the writing process.

This course plan describes the general sequence for the first four units of the course. Unit I covers the first four chapters of *Reading, Writing and Reasoning;* Unit II covers Chapter 5; Unit III is Chapter 8; and Unit IV is Chapter 9. We suggest that teachers incorporate the material in Chapters 6 and 8 on revising and paragraphing where it's most useful. Our model syllabus calls for revising to be included in Unit I with the first major paper, and for interspersing material from Chapter 8 with the appropriate writing assignments. Since the research assignments in *Reading, Writing and Reasoning* allow students to choose their own topics, we suggest that for Unit V on the research paper, instructors refer to the general principles outlined in Chapters 10 and 11 of the Sternglass text. The research section of *The Little English Handbook* provides a useful supplement.

UNIT I

The first unit introduces students to the concept of reading and writing as transactive processes, and to several reading/writing strategies based upon that concept. These strategies, variations of which will be used throughout the semester, include predicting, previewing, summarizing, and synthesis-building. In this unit, students will be expected to read four or five selections, write two short papers, and take part in class and small-group discussions.

From the start, students need to be made aware of how much they already know about language and the world and how such prior knowledge can be used to construct meaning from even the most unpromising texts. We suggest, then, that most of the first two class meetings be used for introspection on the reading/writing process. CLOZE tests (short passages with key words or phrases blacked out) and similar exercises are especially useful in getting students to re-examine their notions of reading and writing.

With the ice broken, students should be asked to read a full-length essay, employing the predicting and previewing strategies outlined in Chapter 1 of *Reading, Writing and Reasoning.* Teachers have the option here of using the assignment laid out in Chapters 1 and 3 of *RWR,* or of using an equivalent assignment based on essays in *The Little, Brown Reader.* In the *RWR* version, students read a selection from *Return to Laughter,* a novel about an anthropologist's experiences in an African village, and then write a short paper comparing the anthropologist's experience to a similar one of their own. In the *Little, Brown* version, students read and discuss "The Patterns of Eating" (91–95) and "The Playground" (318–19), and then write a short paper comparing a social custom from their lives to one of those described in the readings. Both versions of the assignment involve students in creating a synthesis of textual and personal knowledge.

After completing the first paper, the class should read and discuss Chapter 2 of *RWR,* which gives a brief introduction to the principles of deductive and inductive reasoning. At most, only one class period should be spent on this chapter, the idea being not to teach inductive and deductive reasoning but simply to define the terms. Thus, as students engage in these kinds of reasoning during the semester, they will have a word for what they are doing.

Chapter 4 of *RWR* introduces the types and uses of summary writing and then models the summary process, using Thurber's essay "What a Lovely Generalization!" Teachers may use this lesson as it stands or substitute an equivalent lesson based on "TV Can't Educate" in *Little, Brown* (216–19). Having modeled summarizing, teachers should have students practice it in class using some of the "Short Views" in *Little, Brown*, with special attention to the "analytical summary" as defined in *RWR*. Students should now be asked to read one of three long essays and to write an analytical summary of it. They may choose from among "Are All Generalizations False?" (in *RWR*), "Fear of Food," or "Animal Liberation" (in *Little, Brown*). The analytical summary ends Unit I.

UNIT II

This section on analysis and synthesis includes six different reading assignments—four prose, two poetry—from which to draw material. The theme that unites them is family background and familial experiences based, for the most part, on Thomas Wolfe's lament that "You can't go home again." Each reading is written in the first person, and carries with it dawning self-realizations about the author's relations to his family and his feelings about his past and future. The selections from *Reading, Writing and Reasoning* are "On Becoming a Chicano" by Richard Rodriguez, and "A Diary of a Winner" by Liv Ullmann. The Rodriguez essay discusses the author's relationships with his family and culture and how they affected his feelings toward himself and his career. Similarly, the Ullmann excerpt describes the demands of her career and how it has affected her personal life and her relationship with her daughter. The prereading exercises prepare students to think about their own background by focusing on ethnic background and career choices. The exercises that precede the Ullmann selection might have to be modified to better orient students toward the theme of family relationships, but the post-reading exercises serve the purpose, as does the end of the chapter under "Building Synthesis." In fact, this section can be applied to synthesize whichever readings the student chooses.

The other readings, taken from *The Little, Brown Reader*, comprise two prose and two poetry selections. "The Girls' Room" by Laura Cunningham looks back on the author's experiences of sharing her bedroom and youth with her senile grandmother; "My Papa's Waltz" by Theodore Roethke is a son's bittersweet remembrance of his father; "On Going Home" by Joan Didion discusses how going home to visit often jars with one's present lifestyle; "The Lake Isle of Innisfree" by William Butler Yeats describes the author's memory of home. The range of these selections should elicit some sort of response from every reader. Moveover, their variety allows this section of the syllabus to provide something to suit the tastes of both student and instructor. While *Little, Brown* has no prereading exercises, the *RWR* exercises in Chapter 5 can be adapted, and while it also does not have postreading exercises *per se*, some of the questions that follow each reading can be rephrased to stimulate synthesis and topic-building.

UNIT III

Unit III focuses on students' ability to construct generalizations from their reading and personal experiences to develop inductive reasoning skills from these seemingly disparate activities. Therefore, students must be able to analyze not only the concepts of the reading material but their own personal histories as well. Such connections between reading and writing are necessary if writing is to be an important part of the students' lives. The ability to effectively use generalizations enables students to hone their inductive skills. The purpose of this unit is for students to analyze and synthesize material to learn to formulate a tentative thesis sentence and supporting evidence for their first draft.

Students are asked to perform pre- and postreading exercises (*RWR*, Chapter 8) that enable them to predict and evaluate their responses to the readings while incorporating their experiences into the overall project. Students create generalizations based upon all of the information they have collected from the exercises. Finally, students pull together all of this information so they can form topic relationships. They are guided by their notes to develop a prospective thesis supported by the evidence they have selected as pertinent to their topic. They then design a model to focus attention on specific aspects of the larger issue to be investigated, and to indicate the direction and development the paper will take. The model is only a guide, and the tentative structural design may necessitate alteration if the student feels a need to modify it.

The next step is to write a first draft that serves to explain the topic to the student. The draft is re-worked until the student is satisfied with the topic and the evidence needed to support it. We suggest four class sessions for this unit.

For the sake of variety, students may choose from two sets of essays: interviews from Studs Terkel's *Working* and Bertrand Russell's "Work" in *RWR*. The second set of readings comes from *The Little, Brown Reader:* Judy Syfers's "Why I Want a Wife," Virginia Woolf's "Professions for Women," and John R. Coleman's "Blue-Collar Journal." All of these essays focus on the choice of a career, an obsession with most of our first-year students, which becomes a fully developed theme during the second half of the course. Yet, each essay has a different emphasis and may raise issues that are of great importance to most of the student population. Discussion should greatly increase at this point in the course since the issues raised are controversial and may serve as a way to motivate interest. Since this unit prepares students for the argumentative paper, we feel this is a good point for students to become familiar with analyzing material to develop skills in constructing and analyzing an argument. The analytical skills developed in this unit integrate reading, writing, and personal experience, and aid the student in discovering the strength that lies in writing.

UNIT IV

This unit provides students with the opportunity to practice reading and analyzing argumentative essays and then to construct such an essay themselves, based on the readings they have analyzed. This analysis occurs on two levels, both equally important: close examination of the general organization of arguments, with particular attention to the use of counter-arguments and rebuttals; and discussion of the types of appeals—to reason, emotion, and personality—commonly found in arguments. Students are often unaware of the need to present all sides of an issue explicitly or of the need to refute opponents' arguments. Often, they feel as if all they need to do is present how they feel—the truth, as they see it—and their audience will be convinced. Since this is not the case for most of the persuasive writing students will have to do in college, the aim of this unit is to make them conscious of the nature of argument and to provide them with a variety of argumentative strategies to use in their own writing.

Chapter 9 of *RWR* contains three basic activities: a prereading class discussion on the general issues dealt with in the essays, a detailed analysis of the structure and logic of the essays themselves, and the writing of an argumentative essay on a topic connected to the readings. We suggest the following schedule: one class period devoted to the prereading discussion, two on the analysis of the essays, and two in preparing the students to write their own essays. This timetable can, of course, be modified to meet the demands of your class. If the students prove adept at analyzing the essays, you may prefer to spend only one class session on this, and have them work on their own papers over three sessions. You may plan two or three of these sessions as workshops for students to develop their arguments, or you may turn the last session into an editing session. Again, your choices will reflect your students' needs.

Your students may choose to work with one of two pairs of essays: "Where College Fails Us" by Caroline Bird and "Does College Really Matter Any More?" (both provided in *RWR*), or the following two essays from *The Little, Brown Reader:* Neil Postman's "Order in the Classroom" and John Holt's "The Right to Control One's Learning." All of these es-says deal with educational issues, a theme that allows students to draw on their own experiences in constructing their arguments, but each set has a different emphasis. The class will be divided into two groups—one work-ing with each set of essays—for many of the discussion sessions. You will want to take advantage of this division; since each half of the class will not be working closely with the essays the other half will be writing about, the members of each group should be able to provide very useful responses to the arguments of the other group, whether these are presented orally or in writing.

A Selected Bibliography for ACP Teachers

Emig, Janet. "Writing as a Mode of Learning." *College Composition and Communication* 28 (1977), 122–28.
Flower, Linda. "Writer-based Prose: A Cognitive Basis for Problems in Writing." *College English* 41 (1979), 19–37.
Goodman, Kenneth. "Reading: A Psycholinguistic Guessing Game." *Journal of the Reading Specialist* 6 (1967), 126–35.
Kennedy, Mary Lynch. "Reading and Writing: Interrelated Skills of Literacy on the College Level." *Reading World* 20 (1980), 131–41.
Smith, Frank. *Understanding Reading.* New York: Holt, 1978.
Sternglass, Marilyn. "A Theoretical Basis for Integrating Instruction in Reading, Writing and Reasoning." *The Writer's Mind in Writing as a Mode of Thinking.* Ed. Janice Hays, Phyllis Roth, Jon Ramsey, and Robert Foulke. Urbana: NCTE, 1983.

Works Cited

Bartholomae, David, and Anthony Petrosky. *Facts, Artifacts and Counterfacts: Theory and Method for a Reading and Writing Course.* Portsmouth, NH: Boynton/ Cook, 1986.
Gudaitis, Janice Lave. *Advance College Project: Course Enrollment Trends and Factors, 1982–85.* Unpublished report. Bloomington, IN: Indiana U, 1985.
———. *Advance College Project: Final Evaluation Report, 1984–85 School Year.* Unpublished report. Bloomington, IN: Indiana U, 1986.
Wilkinson, Andrew, et al. *Assessing Language Development.* Oxford: Oxford UP, 1980.

11

Project Advance
An Alternative to AP

BETTE GAINES
Syracuse University

ROSANNA GRASSI
Syracuse University

In 1973, Syracuse University created a historic alternative to the Advanced Placement program: Project Advance. The authors describe this program and contrast it with AP.

Syracuse University's Project Advance (SUPA) provides high school students an alternative to Advanced Placement. Like Advanced Placement, Project Advance offers students an opportunity to earn college credit before they graduate from high school. But unlike the AP model, which prepares students to take a placement exam, the Project Advance model allows students to enroll in and attend college courses that meet in their high schools. Syracuse University ensures that instruction, content, and evaluation in these courses are demonstrably equivalent to that provided in the same course on the college campus.

Why an Alternative to Advanced Placement?

After several decades of successful operation, Advanced Placement needs neither an explanation nor a champion here; its strong points are argued elsewhere in this collection. Why then should anyone desire an alternative to AP? The public school superintendents and high school principals who first approached Syracuse University in 1972 were seeking a challenging program for their strongest students, even though several of the schools were already offering AP courses. In fact, most schools that currently offer SUPA also continue to offer AP. However, many school administrators believe that AP exam results inaccurately represent the ability and achievement of some students; they feel, too, that test anxiety tends to weaken some students' performance on the exam. And they are concerned particularly about problems in motivation and achievement in some large AP classes, as evidenced by the relatively few students electing to take the exam.

Given only the AP exam by which to evaluate students' college-level achievement, some students who are academically ready for more advanced courses in college but who do not perform well on the exam are required to repeat work that they have already studied in high school AP classes. The exam measures readiness for further study in a general way, but SUPA solves the problem faced by students whose classroom performance is not accurately reflected by a single examination. The model provides broad evidence of students' work in an actual college course where it may be compared with work done by several thousand coursemates. In other words, many public school administrators are firm in their conviction that, for some students, participation in a college course offers a more appropriate college experience and a stronger preparation for advanced college study than does the AP model.

Definition and Description of SUPA

The Project Advance program, begun in 1973 by Syracuse University and six cooperating high schools, now annually enrolls approximately 3,600 students in some 80 schools in regular college courses. Most of the schools are in central or eastern New York, with a few scattered throughout New England, New Jersey, and Michigan. Through Project Advance, students may take one or more freshman-level courses in their own schools during the regular school day. Project Advance students in English are drawn, typically, from the upper 15 percent of the high school senior class. They have generally maintained "B" averages in earlier high school English classes, and they must be willing to devote extra time to keep abreast of rigorous reading and writing requirements.

In effect, Project Advance takes the university to schools where college courses are taught by qualified high school faculty. In some academic areas, the teachers' preparation must include highly specific coursework. To be considered for training to teach any of the university courses, a teacher must have successful teaching experience and a master's degree or its equivalent—the same credentials required for campus instructors who teach the same courses. Prospective SUPA instructors are first recommended by their high school administrators. After the university reviews their credentials, qualified candidates are trained for appointment as Syracuse University adjunct instructors in strict accordance with university standards.

University faculty serve as liaison between the sponsoring academic department and the high schools. They also teach summer training workshops and plan semiannual seminars that are held while the course is offered. These required workshops familiarize future adjunct instructors with course content, structure, and goals, as well as with the kinds of skills that students will need to learn. These instructors discuss suggested goals and teaching strategies, and they practice using course materials and responding to and evaluating student work. Evaluation standards are clarified by examining and discussing typical student essays. The grading workshop, similar to those used to train AP graders, is begun at the summer workshop and continued in refresher sessions at the semiannual seminars.

At the end of the summer workshop, each instructor writes a proposal for implementing the university course in his or her high school. The proposal describes how the college course will fit into the school's program and objectives. The university faculty member responsible for the supervision of the high school sections reads the proposal and suggests modifications that will ensure the integrity of the course. (Final approval for the course is given by the appropriate academic department.) Training continues each semester with a required faculty enrichment seminar that allows high school and college faculties to interact, share ideas, and discuss curriculum and evaluation.

In addition to the workshop and seminars, university faculty maintain contact with the schools through site visits. Selected instructors who teach the same courses on campus visit each class at least once a semester. These collegial visitors, working under the direction of the faculty colleague who bears responsibility for the program, review students' work and discuss problems and achievements with instructors and students. In all, approximately 20 campus faculty from 8 academic areas carry out training, supervision, and visits to the approximately 80 schools offering one or more university courses in the SUPA program.

The high school must be prepared to accommodate the SUPA course. For example, enrollment in the SUPA English sections is limited to 20 students, so that each student may receive individual attention. A place for conferences with students is important, as is a class load that will allow the instructor sufficient time to prepare for the course, as well as to respond to student writing. The high school assumes the cost of training the instructor and allows the instructor time to attend workshops and enrichment seminars.

The high school administration and staff must also accept responsibility for advising and screening students.

The Project Advance staff provides logistical support for this academic team. An evaluator and two graduate assistants (doctoral candidates in instructional development, design, and evaluation) conduct periodic studies responding to questions important to faculty, students, the cooperating institutions, and the hundreds of institutions to which students transfer. The questions address such concerns as student achievement, the ability of SUPA grades to predict later college performance, the comparability of on-campus and off-campus students and their achievement, and the transferability of earned credit. The evaluators also conduct student surveys that provide helpful information for SUPA instructors and the visitors from the campus. The evaluation staff additionally offers its assistance to teachers seeking to conduct classroom research. A clerk works with the university registrar to maintain records for the approximately 3,600–4,000 students who annually take coursework through SUPA. Reports and correspondence are handled by four word-processing specialists who share responsibilities for bookkeeping, communication, and travel arrangements for the site visits. An office manager coordinates the clerical positions.

The SUPA staff is headed by a director and three associates, one of whom is the evaluator mentioned above. The expense of the program is borne by the participating high schools and the students who enroll in the courses for college credit. Teacher training costs, textbooks, and incidental costs are paid by the schools. Students pay a modest tuition ($36 per credit hour is the tuition for the 1986–87 academic year). Courses that include a two-semester sequence are paid for in full in the fall, one-semester courses at the beginning of the semester of study. The university houses the SUPA office and handles academic records just as it does for other part-time students. The program is largely self-supporting because its budget is raised through tuition. Although participating students are excellent candidates for admission, the university regards the program as a service; it has never been used to recruit students.

The Freshman Composition Course

Freshman English, the required six-credit freshman composition sequence for Syracuse University students, was the first course offered through SUPA and remains the most popular of the eight courses presently available. The course comprises fairly traditional components of freshman composition and literature. Unlike AP English, in which students earn up to six college credits based exclusively on examination scores, SUPA students can earn up to six credits based on the number of modules they complete successfully. There are six one-credit units in the sequence: general essays, fiction, poetry, a choice of two mini-courses, and a research paper.

This variable-credit structure allows the instructor to hold students in the initial unit of the course until they demonstrate sufficient control of their writing to move on to other units. This includes being able to limit a topic to a thesis manageable for a 500-word essay, achieve a clear sense of audience and purpose, organize a coherent defense for the thesis, integrate appropriate support for assertions that form that defense, and exhibit a clear sense of organization. Although expectations for in-class essays are modest, students' revisions are expected to show a genuine reconsideration of the topic in the light of a taped critique from the instructor and, in many instances, peer review, and conferencing. The students move into the later units when the instructor, applying college standards, judges that they are able to write the sort of effective essays that college courses typically require.

This initial unit requires both impromptu writing and careful revision. Some students' essays show very early that they can already write well enough to satisfy the requirements of this initial unit: mastery of fundamental composing skills and writing conventions. These students move quickly; generally, after two or three essays and at least one major revision project, they are awarded a "pass" and begin the first of two units focused on a literary genre: fiction or poetry. Others remain longer in this early unit without academic penalty. They are allowed additional time to learn these composition skills. The average SUPA student spends about six weeks in the initial writing unit. Students are judged ready for the subsequent "literary" units when they show competence in impromptu writing and the practice of careful, thoughtful revision.

All students study fiction and poetry, and these modules may be taken in either order, depending on when a student finishes the argumentative essay unit. Each short fiction or poetry unit requires five weeks. In each of these one-credit units, students write at least two out-of-class papers that demonstrate their understanding of the works. They are taught to look closely at such literary elements as characterization, imagery, and structure, and to write clear and interesting discussions of the texts. Thus, the goals of the SUPA sections and AP classes preparing students for the Literature and Composition exam are similar in their emphasis on literary analysis and judgment. The Project Advance student, however, builds a day-to-day record of achievement, expressed for the record in unit grades ranging from "A" to "F." Each unit grade appears separately on the transcript.

The remaining units of the course consist of two mini-courses and a one-credit independent research paper. Students select mini-courses that reflect their interests. These are designed by instructors and approved by the university's English curriculum committee. The mini-courses may be thematically unified, or they may focus on a genre, mode, or author. In each of them, however, the emphasis is on writing, with the assignments determined by the content and goals of the unit. SUPA schools attempt to offer as wide a choice of topics for the mini-courses as possible, depending, of course, on the number of instructors involved. At least two papers are required for any single unit of credit in these modules.

The independent research paper is a one-credit unit that students must complete to earn six credits. Students are encouraged to pursue a narrowly focused question—either literary or nonliterary. The paper is at least 2,000 words and involves scholarly research leading to a major assertion that the writer must support and defend fully. For some students and teachers, the research paper provides greater satisfaction than any other part of the course. Students report that this is an enjoyable and challenging part of their experience. Many students open up areas of inquiry that extend the teacher's knowledge as well as their own. In any case, students have the opportunity to learn research strategies that they can draw upon later.

The goals of the university English course and those of the AP program are similar: to encourage close reading, independence of thought, and clarity of expression. In the SUPA classes, however, the students accumulate individual portfolios of the writing done in the course. These portfolios are available for review by the colleges to which students go after graduation. The files remain in the schools for one year after completion of the course, should students wish to present them for such review.

Research and Evaluation

SUPA students engage in the same sort of reading and writing that typical AP students do. Their success in the SUPA program varies, just as grades on the AP exam vary. They earn grades that reflect these differences, not through a score earned in a single sitting but through the daily effort typically required in college studies. That all students don't earn "A's" is no more surprising than that all students don't earn 5's on the AP exam.

Like AP, Syracuse University's Project Advance can describe its students and predict subsequent college performance. Students who earn "C" or better can be expected to do at least as well in advanced, related coursework. Both programs document high correlations between their predictions of performance and actual student grades. Two follow-up studies in 1980 and 1982 by the SUPA evaluation staff (Mercurio; Mercurio et al.) have surveyed students four years after high school graduation to gather information about their actual academic performance in college. (Most do not matriculate at Syracuse University.) Both studies found that, although most students earn grades of "C" in the university freshman English course taken through SUPA, approximately 30 percent go on to earn higher grades in subsequent English courses on college campuses. None of the students surveyed earned lower grades in advanced English courses than they had earned in the freshman course as SUPA students. Furthermore, Mercurio's studies show that the record of success in their degree programs is more than twice the national average (98 percent as compared to 47 percent nationally). Most remain for their baccalaureate years in the institutions where they begin their matriculation. Their college grade point averages typically place them in the top 20 percent of their classes.

The SUPA evaluators also annually survey a sample (approximately one-third) of the students who were enrolled in SUPA sections of the various courses to learn what their experience was regarding credit transfer and/or exemption from similar courses and how well their SUPA experience prepared them for advanced coursework. The surveys allow students to comment freely. Their comments regarding the SUPA experience are sent to their high schools without identifying the individual student. (SUPA staff members believe, perhaps naively, that guaranteed anonymity encourages candor.) More than 90 percent of the students say they would recommend the course to other high school seniors. Typically, they refer to the SUPA experience in the English course as "rigorous" and the "most valuable" course they have taken; many claim that the course was more challenging than advanced courses taken in the colleges and universities they attend (Kelly and Chapman; Chapman and Kelly).

The research clearly shows that the SUPA design for early college study offers a true college experience in the high school. SUPA students' writing is comparable in quality and content to that of their campus peers (Lambert and Gaines; Kelly et al.). Also, a study of the relationships among teaching behaviors, social characteristics of the class, and student achievement shows in both campus and SUPA sections a clear relationship between achievement and classroom management that affects individual performance (Gaines). No significant differences relate to the location in which the class is taught.

Conclusion

Given the choice of SUPA, an AP-designated course, or the AP examination, quite possibly a bright, motivated, and verbally skilled student would elect simply to take the exam. A special AP course in preparation for the exam may not be necessary for some students. The freedom that teachers have in planning the AP preparatory course may be more appealing to some teachers than the modest structure of the SUPA course. The decision to offer SUPA or AP, however, should be based upon a careful assessment of the needs of the particular group of students, faculty, and public involved. Ideally, choices should be offered to allow for options within the high school.

SUPA appeals to those for whom a single course must serve a broad audience: the very best students, who will pass quickly through the early units, and the highly motivated students, who will see the course through and have an opportunity to show their academic strength. The strength of the Project Advance model for English lies in its well structured course taught by carefully selected and trained faculty. Close cooperation and communication between the participating faculties regarding course development and standards are noteworthy characteristics of the model—a model that has been adapted by other institutions across the United States. (See, for example, the chapter in this text by Sternglass and Vander Ven.) Although less than half the age of AP, the Project Advance model is an alternative well worth considering for able, motivated students.

Postscript

The course structure we have just described has recently changed with the creation of a new writing program on the Syracuse University campus. The program emphasizes that writing is a cross-curricular responsibility in the University. During the fairly rapid changes that have taken place, the Project Advance sections have modified the structure described earlier as the first semester program gradually shifts the focus away from literature, placing it among the many forms of written expression with which students will become familiar during their four-year writing sequence.

The variable-credit structure has been modified, in the transitional sections of ENG 101, and during the 1988–89 academic year the new first-semester course, WRT 105, a single three-credit unit, is being piloted in four schools and in parallel campus sections. The model used in these sections, with any modifications that their experience dictates, will replace ENG 101 throughout the SUPA program in the fall semester of 1989. WRT 105, Studio I, heavily emphasizes prewriting and revision in interactive classrooms where students participate in critiquing one another's work. Their development is further encouraged by a grading system that allows students to try new approaches, different from the safe forms that may have served them in the past. Not all papers are graded, although all receive "readerly" comments from other students or the teacher or both. These comments *guide* the revisions, but writers are encouraged to weigh, not blindly follow, the readers' advice. The portfolio approach encourages students to rework pieces that they find interesting, and writers are encouraged to take increasing responsibility for choices made in revising.

Students use journals to explore their thinking, free-writing on topics under discussion in preparation for further discussion, debate, or writing. First drafts of most papers are written in class on topics announced before the writing day. All essays are persuasive or argumentative, but the sources of evidence change from personal to public to literary, a developmental progression added to the course. The form, too, may change from essay to essay as students experiment with different patterns of persuasion.

One of the points of fragility in cooperative programs of this kind lies in the extent to which they accommodate changes in leadership, content, or structure that occur on the college campus. Some of the changes being explored in the pilot WRT 105 course have already been introduced during the 1987–88 academic year in the traditional ENG 101 classes. This transitional period during which changes are made gradually will help to preserve the course's integrity as a college course while introducing change in an orderly way.

Early indications show that better writing accompanies these changed emphases and strategies. Formal studies of the new structure are underway. The shape and the name have changed, but there is every reason to believe that WRT 105 will also be a valid alternative to AP English for the able, college-bound student.

Works Cited

Chapman, David, and Edward Kelly. *Classroom Behavior Survey: Administration and Interpretation.* Syracuse, NY: Syracuse U, 1984.

Gaines, Betty. *An Investigation of the Relationship between Instruction and Learning to Write about Poetry in Freshman English Classes.* Diss. Syracuse U, Ann Arbor: UMI, 1984. 84–10712.

Kelly, Edward, and David Chapman. *Classroom Behavior Survey.* Syracuse, NY: Syracuse U, 1978.

Kelly, Edward, et al. "English Pilot Program Evaluation." Unpublished Research Report. Syracuse, NY: Syracuse U, Center for Instructional Development, 1978.

Lambert, Leo, and Betty Gaines. "Assessing the Comparability of a College Freshman English Course Taught on Campus and in High Schools." Unpublished Research Report. Syracuse, NY: Syracuse U, 1985.

Mercurio, Joseph. "College Courses in the High School: A Follow-Up Study." *College and University* 56 (1980): 83–91.

Mercurio, Joseph, et al. "College Courses in the High School: A Four-Year Follow-Up of the Syracuse University Class of 1977." *College and University* 58 (1982): 5–18.

Publications Available from the College Board

The following is a list of publications available from the College Board. For information about prices and ordering procedures, contact: Advanced Placement Program; CN6670; Princeton, NJ 08541–6670.

GENERAL INFORMATION

A Guide to the Advanced Placement Program (201140)
Bulletin for Students, Advanced Placement Program (200978)
Information for Coordinators, Advanced Placement Examinations (200974)
1986 Sophomore Standing through the Advanced Placement Program (218213)
Some Questions and Answers about the Advanced Placement Program (258821)
What College Students Say about Advanced Placement, by Patricia Lund Casserly (297902)
Complete List of the Readers of the 1986 Advanced Placement Examinations (200981)
Using the PSAT/NMSQT to Help Identify Advanced Placement Students (273678)
Comparing the Performance of College Students and AP Candidates on AP Examinations (273623)
Table of Candidate Grade Distributions (252400)
Advanced Placement Program—What It Means to Students (297904)
School Administrator's Guide to the Advanced Placement Program (208909)
Complete set of 14 course descriptions (201485)
Advanced Placement Explorer (IBM PC/XT) (002520)
Advanced Placement Explorer (Apple IIe, II + (64k), IIc) (002512)

AP ENGLISH

1987 AP Course Description in English (201475)
Set of free-response questions used in recent years (254956)
Teacher's Guide to AP Courses in English Language and Composition (208962)
Teacher's Guide to AP Courses in English Literature and Composition (208956)
Grading the AP Examination in English Language and Composition (235492)
Grading the AP Examination in English Literature and Composition (235494)
Multiple-Choice Testing in Literature-AP English (273715)
The Entire 1982 AP English Language and Composition Examination and Key (468220)

The above examination only (packets of 10) (254893)
The Entire 1982 AP English Literature and Composition Examination and Key
(468219)
The above examination only (packets of 10) (254892)

APPENDIX B

1988 Language and Composition Essay Topics

ENGLISH LANGUAGE AND COMPOSITION
SECTION II
Total time—2 hours

Question 1

(Suggested time–40 minutes.
This question counts one-third of the total essay section score.)

Read the following passage carefully. Then write an essay evaluating De Tocqueville's assertions about democracy and aristocracy and his conclusion that democracy "throws [man] back forever upon himself alone."

Among aristocratic nations, as families remain for centuries in the same condition, often on the same spot, all generations become, as it were, contemporaneous. A man almost always knows his forefathers and respects them; he thinks he already sees his remote descendants and he loves them. He willingly imposes duties on himself towards the former and the latter, and he will frequently sacrifice his personal gratifications to those who went before and to those who will come after him. Aristocratic institutions, moreover, have the effect of closely binding every man to several of his fellow citizens. As the classes of an aristocratic people are strongly marked and permanent, each of them is regarded by its own members as a sort of lesser country, more tangible and more cherished than the country at large. As in aristocratic communities all the citizens occupy fixed positions, one above another, the result is that each of them always sees a man above himself whose patronage is necessary to him, and below himself another man whose co-operation he may claim. Men living in aristocratic ages are therefore almost always closely attached to something placed out of their own sphere, and they are often disposed to forget themselves. It is true that in these ages the notion of human fellowship is faint and that men seldom think of sacrificing themselves for mankind; but they often sacrifice themselves for other

183

men. In democratic times, on the contrary, when the duties of each individual to the race are much more clear, devoted service to any one man becomes more rare; the bond of human affection is extended, but it is relaxed.

Among democratic nations new families are constantly springing up, others are constantly falling away, and all that remain change their condition; the woof of time is every instant broken and the track of generations effaced. Those who went before are soon forgotten; of those who will come after, no one has any idea; the interest of man is confined to those in close propinquity to himself. As each class gradually approaches others and mingles with them, its members become undifferentiated and lose their class identity for each other. Aristocracy had made a chain of all the members of the community, from the peasant to the king; democracy breaks that chain and severs every link of it.

As social conditions become more equal, the number of persons increases who, although they are neither rich nor powerful enough to exercise any great influence over their fellows, have nevertheless acquired or retained sufficient education and fortune to satisfy their own wants. They owe nothing to any man, they expect nothing from any man; they acquire the habit of always considering themselves as standing alone, and they are apt to imagine that their whole destiny is in their own hands.

Thus not only does democracy make every man forget his ancestors, but it hides his descendants and separates his contemporaries from him; it throws him back forever upon himself alone and threatens in the end to confine him entirely within the solitude of his own heart.

—Alexis De Tocqueville,
Democracy in America (1835, 1840)

Question 2

(Suggested time—40 minutes.
This question counts one-third of the total essay section score.)

Read the following passage in which Frederick Douglass recounts his emotions on escaping slavery and arriving in New York in 1838. Then write an essay in which you analyze the language—especially the figures of speech and syntax—Douglass uses to convey his states of mind.

The wretchedness of slavery, and the blessedness of freedom, were perpetually before me. It was life and death with me. But I remained firm, and according to my solution, on the third day of September, 1838, I left my chains, and succeeded in reaching New York without the slightest interruption of any kind. How I did so— what means I adopted,—what direction I travelled, and by what mode of conveyance,—I must leave unexplained, for the reasons before mentioned.

I have been frequently asked how I felt when I found myself in a free State. I have never been able to answer the question with any satisfaction to myself. It was a moment of the highest excitement I ever experienced. I suppose I felt as one may imagine the unarmed mariner to feel when he is rescued by a friendly man-of-war from the pursuit of a pirate. In writing to a dear friend, immediately after my arrival at New York, I said I felt like one who had escaped a den of hungry lions. This state of mind, however, very soon subsided; and I was again seized with a feeling of great insecurity and loneliness. I was yet liable to be taken back, and subjected to all the tortures of slavery. This in itself was enough to damp the ardor of my enthusiasm. But the loneliness overcame me. There I was in the midst of thousands, and yet a perfect stranger; without home and without friends, in the midst of thousands of my own brethren—children of a common Father, and yet I dared not to unfold to any one of them my sad condition. I was afraid to speak to any one for fear of speaking to the wrong one, and thereby falling into the hands of money-loving kidnappers, whose business it was to lie in wait for the panting fugitive, as the ferocious beasts of the forest lie in wait for their prey. The motto which I adopted when I started from slavery was this—"Trust no man!" I saw in every white man an enemy, and in almost every colored man cause for distrust. It was a most painful situation; and, to understand it, one must needs experience it, or imagine himself in similar circumstances. Let him be a fugitive slave in a strange land—a land given up to be the hunting-ground for slave-holders—whose inhabitants are legalized kidnappers— where he is every moment subjected to the terrible liability of being seized upon by his fellow-men, as the hideous crocodile seizes upon his prey!—I say, let him place himself in my situation—without home or friends—without money or credit— wanting shelter, and no one to give it—wanting bread, and no money to buy it,— and at the same time let him feel that he is pursued by merciless men-hunters, and in total darkness as to what to do, where to go, or where to stay,—perfectly helpless both as to the means of defense and means of escape,—in the midst of plenty, yet suffering the terrible gnawings of hunger,—in the midst of houses, yet having no home,—among fellow-men, yet feeling as if in the midst of wild beasts, whose greediness to swallow up the trembling and half-famished fugitive is only equalled by that with which the monsters of the deep swallow up the helpless fish which they subsist,—I say, let him be placed in this most trying situation,—the situation in which I was placed,—then and not till then, will he fully appreciate the hardships of, and know how to sympathize with, the toil-worn and whip-scarred fugitive slave.

—Frederick Douglass

Question 3
(Suggested time—40 minutes.
This question counts one-third of the total essay section score.)

Imagine that you have been asked to contribute to a magazine or newspaper an article about a specific place. Write such an article, describing a place that you know well and that might be of interest or significance to your readers. Besides defining that interest or significance, your article should use its descriptive detail to make clear your attitude toward the place you describe.

1988 Literature and Composition Essay Topics

ENGLISH LITERATURE AND
COMPOSITION
SECTION II
Total time—2 hours

Question 1

(Suggested time—40 minutes. This question counts
one-third of the total essay section score.)

Read the following two poems very carefully, noting that the second includes
an allusion to the first. Then write a well-organized essay in which you discuss their
similarities and differences. In your essay, be sure to consider both theme and style.

I

Bright Star

Bright star! would I were steadfast as thou art—
Not in lone splendor hung aloft the night,
And watching, with eternal lids apart,
Line   Like nature's patient, sleepless Eremite*
(5)   The moving waters at their priest-like task
Of pure ablution round earth's human shores,
Or gazing on the new soft-fallen mask
Of snow upon the mountains and the moors—
No—yet still steadfast, still unchangeable,
(10)   Pillowed upon my fair love's ripening breast,
To feel for ever its soft fall and swell,
Awake for ever in a sweet unrest,

Still, still to hear her tender-taken breath,
And so live ever—or else swoon to death.

—John Keats

*hermit

II

Choose Something Like a Star

O Star (the fairest one in sight),
We grant your loftiness the right
To some obscurity of cloud—
Line   It will not do to say of night,
(5)   Since dark is what brings out your light.
Some mystery becomes the proud.
But to be wholly taciturn
In your reserve is not allowed.
Say something to us we can learn
(10)   By heart and when alone repeat.
Say something! And it says, 'I burn.'
But say with what degree of heat.
Talk Fahrenheit, talk Centigrade.
Use Language we can comprehend.
(15)   Tell us what elements you blend.
It gives us strangely little aid,
But does tell something in the end.
And steadfast as Keats' Eremite,
Not even stooping from its sphere,
(20)   It asks a little of us here.
It asks of us a certain height,
So when at times the mob is swayed
To carry praise or blame too far,
We may choose something like a star
To stay our minds on and be staid.

—Robert Frost

Question 2

(Suggested time—40 minutes. This question counts one-third of the total essay
section score.)

Below is a complete short story. Read it carefully. Then write a well-organized
essay in which you analyze the blend of humor, pathos, and the grotesque in the
story.

Reunion

The last time I saw my father was in Grand Central
Station. I was going from my grandmother's in the

Adirondacks to a cottage on the Cape that my mother
had rented, and I wrote my father that I would be in
New York between trains for an hour and a half, and
asked if we could have lunch together. His secretary
wrote to say that he would meet me at the information
booth at noon, and at twelve o'clock sharp I saw him
coming through the crowd. He was a stranger to me—
my mother divorced him three years ago and I hadn't
been with him since—but as soon as I saw him I felt
that he was my father, my flesh and blood, my future
and my doom. I knew that when I was grown I would
be something like him; I would have to plan my
campaigns within his limitations. He was a big, good-
looking man, and I was terribly happy to see him
again. He struck me on the back and shook my hand.
"Hi, Charlie," he said. "Hi, boy. I'd like to take you up
to my club, but it's in the Sixties, and if you have to
catch an early train I guess we'd better get something to
eat around here." He put his arm around me, and I
smelled my father the way my mother sniffs a rose. It
was a rich compound of whiskey, after-shave lotion,
shoe polish, woolens, and the rankness of a mature
male. I hoped that someone would see us together. I
wished that we could be photographed. I wanted some
record of our having been together.

　　We went out of the station and up a side street to a
restaurant. It was still early, and the place was empty.
The bartender was quarreling with a delivery boy, and
there was one very old waiter in a red coat down by the
kitchen door. We sat down, and my father hailed the
waiter in a loud voice. "*Kellner!*" he shouted. "*Garçon!
Cameriere! You!*" His boisterousness in the empty
restaurant seemed out of place. "Could we have a little
service here!" he shouted. "Chop-chop." Then he
clapped his hands. This caught the waiter's attention,
and he shuffled over to our table. "Were you clapping
your hands at me?" he asked. "Calm down, calm
down, *sommelier*," my father said. "If it isn't too much
to ask of you—if it wouldn't be too much above and
beyond the call of duty, we would like a couple of
Beefeater Gibsons."

　　"I don't like to be clapped at," the waiter said.

　　"I should have brought my whistle," my father said.
"I have a whistle that is audible only to the ears of old
waiters. Now, take out your little pad and your little
pencil and see if you can get this straight: two
Beefeater Gibsons. Repeat after me: two Beefeater
Gibsons."

　　"I think you'd better go somewhere else," the waiter
said quietly.

　　"That," said my father, "is one of the most brilliant
suggestions I have ever heard. Come on, Charlie, let's
get the hell out of here."

　　I followed my father out of that restaurant into

another. He was not so boisterous this time. Our drinks
came, and he cross-questioned me about the baseball
season. He then struck the edge of his empty glass with
(60)   his knife and began shouting again. "*Garçon! Kellner!
Cameriere! You!* Could we trouble you to bring us two
more of the same."
      "How old is the boy?" the waiter asked.
      "That," my father said, "is none of your
(65)   Goddamned business."
      "I'm sorry sir," the waiter said, "but I won't serve
the boy another drink."
      "Well, I have some news for you," my father said.
"I have some very interesting news for you. This
(70)   doesn't happen to be the only restaurant in New York.
They've opened another on the corner. Come on,
Charlie."
      He paid the bill, and I followed him out of that
restaurant into another. Here the waiters wore pink
(75)   jackets like hunting coats, and there was a lot of horse
tack on the walls. We sat down, and my father began
to shout again. "Master of the hounds! Tallyhoo and
all that sort of thing. We'd like a little something in the
way of a stirrup cup. Namely, two Bibson Geefeaters."
(80)   "Two Bibson Geefeaters?" the waiter asked, smiling.
      "You know damned well what I want," my father
said angrily. "I want two Beefeater Gibsons, and make
it snappy. Things have changed in jolly old England. So
my friend the duke tells me. Let's see what England can
(85)   produce in the way of a cocktail."
      "This isn't England," the waiter said.
      "Don't argue with me," my father said. "Just do as
you're told."
      "I just thought you might like to know where you
(90)   are," the waiter said.
      "If there is one thing I cannot tolerate," my father
said, "it is an impudent domestic. Come on, Charlie."
      The fourth place we went to was Italian. "*Buon
giorno,*" my father said. "*Per favore, possiamo avere
(95)   due cocktail americani, forti, forti. Molto gin, poco
vermut.*"
      "I don't understand Italian," the waiter said.
      "Oh, come off it," my father said. "You understand
Italian, and you know damned well you do, *Vogliamo
(100) due cocktail americani. Subito.*"
      The waiter left us and spoke with the captain, who
came over to our table and said, "I'm sorry, sir, but
this table is reserved."
      "All right," my father said. "Get us another table"
(105)   "All the tables are reserved," the captain said.
      "I get it," my father said. "You don't desire our
patronage. Is that it? Well, the hell with you. *Vada
all'inferno.* Let's go, Charlie."
      "I have to get my train," I said.
(110)   "I'm sorry, sonny," my father said. "I'm terribly

sorry." He put his arm around me and pressed me
against him. "I'll walk you back to the station. If there
had only been time to go up to my club."

"That's all right, Daddy," I said.

(115)   "I'll get you a paper," he said. "I'll get you a paper
to read on the train."

Then he went up to a newsstand and said, "Kind sir,
will you be good enough to favor me with one of your
God-damned, no-good, ten-cent afternoon papers?"

(120)   The clerk turned away from him and stared at a
magazine cover. "Is it asking too much for you to sell
me one of your disgusting specimens of yellow jour-
nalism?"

"I have to go, Daddy," I said. "It's late."

(125)   "Now, just wait a second, sonny," he said. "Just
wait a second. I want to get a rise out of this chap."

"Goodbye, Daddy," I said, and I went down the
stairs and got my train, and that was the last time I saw
my father.

Question 3

(Suggested time—40 minutes. This question counts one-third of the total essay
section score.

Choose a distinguished novel or play in which some of the most significant
events are mental or psychological; for example, awakenings, discoveries, changes
in consciousness. In a well-organized essay, describe how the author manages to
give these internal events the sense of excitement, suspense, and climax usually
associated with external action. Do not merely summarize the plot.

You may choose one of the works listed below or another of comparable quality
that is appropriate to the question.

Baldwin, *Go Tell It on the Mountain*
Sophocles, *Oedipus Rex*
Shakespeare, *Hamlet; Othello; King Lear*
Ibsen, *A Doll's House*
James, *The Portrait of a Lady*
Joyce, *A Portrait of the Artist as a Young Man*
Forster, *A Passage to India*
Brontë, *Jane Eyre*
Ellison, *Invisible Man*
Austen, *Pride and Prejudice*
Hawthorne, *The Scarlet Letter*
Fitzgerald, *The Great Gatsby*
Dostoevsky, *Crime and Punishment*
Dickens, *Great Expectations*
Miller, *Death of a Salesman*
Albee, *Who's Afraid of Virginia Woolf?*
Morrison, *Song of Solomon*
Woolf, *To the Lighthouse*
Hurston, *Their Eyes Were Watching God*
Chopin, *The Awakening*

APPENDIX D

Rubrics for the 1987 Literature and Composition Essay Topics

Literature Question 1

General Directions This scoring guide will be useful for most of the essays you read, but for cases in which it seems inadequate, consult your Table Leader. The score you assign should reflect your judgment of the quality of the essay as a whole. Reward the writers for what they do well. The score for a particularly well-written essay may be raised by one point from the score otherwise appropriate. In no case may a poorly written essay be scored higher than 4. Essays with no response or essays unrelated to the question should not be scored but given to your Table Leader.

9–8 These well-written essays accurately describe Eliot's own views on some of the social aspects of leisure in the past and in her own time. They point specifically to some of the devices Eliot uses to characterize the old and new leisure, such as personification, contrast, connotative diction, and irony. Writers of these essays demonstrate stylistic maturity by an effective command of sentence structure, diction, and organization. The writing need not be without flaws, but it reveals the writer's ability to choose from and control a wide range of the elements of effective writing.

7–6 These essays also accurately describe Eliot's views on the old and new leisure, but they do so with less accuracy and clarity than do the essays in the top range. Their discussion of the devices Eliot uses to present her views will be less thorough and less specific. These essays are well written in an appropriate style, but with less maturity than the top papers. Some lapses in diction or syntax may appear, but the writing demonstrates sufficient control over the elements of composition to present the writer's ideas clearly.

Because the editors were unable to obtain permission from Educational Testing Service to reprint the 1988 Rubrics, the 1987 Rubrics are used as a sample in this Appendix.

5 These essays discuss Eliot's views and the elements of the passage that convey them, but they do so imprecisely or less effectively than essays in the 7–6 range. The discussion of the devices Eliot uses to convey those views will be less specific. They are adequately written, but may demonstrate inconsistent control over the elements of composition. Organization is evident, but it may not be fully realized or particularly effective.

4–3 These essays discuss Eliot's views but do so either inaccurately or without the support of specific or convincing evidence. They might fail to discuss both the old and the new leisure, or they might confuse Eliot's time with our own. The discussion of Eliot's devices may be vague or concentrate on only one feature. They may limit their discussion to mere paraphrase. The writing is sufficient to convey the writer's ideas, but it suggests weak control over diction, syntax, or organization. These essays may reveal some flaws in grammar or consistent spelling errors.

2–1 These essays either ignore Eliot's views or misrepresent them in some significant way; or they may make some accurate observations about the passage, but supply little or no evidence for their assertions. They generally omit discussion of Eliot's devices. Essays in this range are poorly written on several counts or unacceptably brief. The writing reveals consistent weaknesses in grammar or another of the basic elements of composition.

SCORING GUIDELINES 1987

Literature Question 2

General Directions This scoring guide will be useful for most of the essays you read, but for cases in which it seems inadequate, consult your Table Leader. The score you assign should reflect your judgment of the quality of the essay as a whole. Reward the writers for what they do well. The score for a particularly well-written essay may be raised by one point from the score otherwise appropriate. In no case may a poorly written essay be scored higher than 4. Essays with no response or essays unrelated to the question should not be scored but given to your Table Leader.

9–8 These well-written essays accurately identify the treatment of social or political issues in an appropriately chosen work. They also analyze with apt and specific references to the text the techniques used by the author to advocate changes in the attitudes or traditions presented. Writers of these essays demonstrate stylistic maturity by an effective command of sentence structure, diction, and organization. The writing need not be without flaws, but it reveals the writer's ability to choose from and control a wide range of the elements of effective writing.

7–6 These essays discuss the treatment of changes in social or political attitudes in the work, but they do so in a less accurate or convincing way. They deal directly with the techniques the author uses, but they do so with less precision than is the case in the top essays. They are well-written in an appropriate style, but with less maturity than the top papers. Some lapses in diction or syntax may appear, but the writing demonstrates sufficient control over the elements of composition to present the writer's ideas clearly. Statements are supported by relevant evidence, but with less specificity or effectiveness than in essays in the 9–8 range.

5 These essays deal with social or political issues, but in a more general way, and they may deal only minimally with the techniques the author uses to present those issues. They are adequately written, but may demonstrate inconsistent control over the elements of composition. Organization is evident, but it may not be fully realized or particularly effective. Supporting evidence may be somewhat vague or unpersuasive.

4–3 These essays discuss some social or political issues, but they do so either inaccurately or without dealing specifically with the way they are presented. They might have chosen an inappropriate work for the purposes of the question, or their presentation is largely plot-summary. The writing is sufficient to convey the writer's ideas, but it suggests weak control over diction, syntax, or organization. These essays may contain consistent spelling errors or some flaws in grammar.

2–1 These essays either fail to present a clear description of social or political issues, or they completely avoid discussing the techniques the author uses to present them. They attempt to respond to the question and may make some reasonable observations about the work, but they supply little or no evidence for their assertions. Essays in this range are unacceptably brief or poorly written on several counts. The writing reveals consistent weaknesses in grammar or another of the basic elements of composition.

SCORING GUIDELINES 1987

Literature Question 3

General Directions This scoring guide will be useful for most of the essays you read, but for cases in which it seems inadequate, consult your Table Leader. The score you assign should reflect your judgment of the quality of the essay as a whole. Reward the writers for what they do well. The score for a particularly well-written essay may be raised by one point from the score otherwise appropriate. In no case may a poorly written essay be scored higher than 4. Essays with no response or essays unrelated to the question should not be scored but given to your Table Leader.

9–8 These well-written essays contain an accurate and perceptive analysis of the presentation of the sow. They reveal the writer's clear understanding of the poem, and they deal effectively with the various ways the sow is portrayed. They demonstrate that the writer recognizes the difference between the neighbor's and the narrator's perceptions, and they distinguish among the romanticized and realistic images. They include appropriate examples of the significant elements of the poem, such as diction and allusions. They also demonstrate stylistic maturity by an effective command of sentence structure, diction, and organization. The writing need not be without flaws, but it reveals the writer's ability to choose from and control a wide range of the elements of effective writing.

7–6 These essays also reveal an understanding of the poem and the various ways in which the sow is presented, but compared to the best essays, the discussion of the sow may be less precise or the treatment of the devices may be less convincing. They successfully distinguish between the romanticized and realistic images, though they may not be as explicit or detailed as the top papers. These essays are well-written in an appropriate style, but with less maturity than the top papers. Some lapses in diction or syntax may appear, but the writing demonstrates sufficient control over the elements of composition to present the writer's ideas clearly. Statements are supported by relevant evidence, but with less specificity or effectiveness than in essays in the 9–8 range.

5 These essays address both the presentation of the sow and the language of the poem, but they may make somewhat superficial or inaccurate generalizations about the sow, or their treatment of the poetic devices may be somewhat vague. They are adequately written, but may demonstrate inconsistent control over the elements of composition. Organization is evident, but it may not be fully realized or particularly effective.

4–3 These essays address the poem and the directions, but they discuss the presentation of the sow inaccurately or unclearly. They may misinterpret significant parts of the poem or blur its meaning; for example, by suggesting that the narrator views the pig as ordinary or disgusting. They also seem weak in their treatment of the poetic devices. The writing is sufficient to convey the writer's ideas, but it suggests weak control over diction, syntax, or organization. These essays may contain consistent spelling errors or some flaws in grammar.

2–1 These essays reveal some fundamental misunderstanding of the poem or concentrate on an irrelevant or far-fetched interpretation of the sow. They attempt to respond to the question and may make some accurate observations about the poem, but they supply little or no evidence for their assertions. Essays in this range are unacceptably brief or poorly written on several counts. The writing reveals consistent weaknesses in grammar or another of the basic elements of composition.

Selected Bibliography

Aarons, Victoria. "The AP Dilemma: Formula or Process?" *Journal of Teaching Writing* 6.1 (1987): 127–32.

Abraham, A. A. "The Disadvantaged and Acceleration: Coping with the Barriers." *College Board Review* 110 (1978): 10–13.

"Advanced Placement Continues to Be Popular." *Phi Delta Kappan* 66 (1985): 381–82.

Alpern, Mildred, and Pierre-Henri Laurent. "Teachers Trading Places: Models and Vision." *College Board Review* 135 (1985): 22–30.

Alvino, James J., and Jerome Wieler. "How Standardized Testing Fails to Identify the Gifted and What Teachers Can Do About It." *Phi Delta Kappan* 61 (1979): 106–09.

American Association for Gifted Children. *Reaching Out: Advocacy for the Gifted and Talented.* New York: Teachers College P, 1980.

"AP Teachers Say Program Raises Educational Standards in Schools." *College Board News* 14.2 (1985–86): 7.

Arbolino, Jack N. "What's Wrong with the Advanced Placement Program?" *Education Digest* May 1961: 19–21.

Benbow, Camilla P., and Julian Stanley. "Constructing Educational Bridges between High School and College." *Gifted Child Quarterly* 27 (1983): 111–13.

Bradgon, Henry W. "Advanced Placement: Rising Tide with Breakers Ahead." *College Board Review* 42 (1960): 18–20.

Burnham, Paul S., and Benjamin A. Hewitt. "Advanced Placement Scores: Their Predictive Validity." *Educational and Psychological Measurement* 31 (1971): 939–45.

———. "The Rock Stands, Mr. Noyes." *College Board Review* 83 (1972): 25–29.

Carine, Edwin T. "Credit-by-Examination Games." *Journal of National Association of College Admissions Counselors* 21.1 (1976): 24–25.

Chamberlain, Philip C., Richard C. Pugh, and James Schellhammer. "Does Advanced Placement Continue throughout the Undergraduate Years?" *College and University* 53 (1978): 195–200.

Chapman, David, et al. *Project Advance Evaluation.* Syracuse, NY: Syracuse U, 1976. ERIC ED 129135.

Clendening, Corinne, and Ruth Ann Davies. *Challenging the Gifted: Curriculum Enrichment and Acceleration Models.* New York: Bowker, 1983.

Coleman, Laurence J. *Schooling the Gifted.* Menlo Park, CA: Addison-Wesley, 1985.

Copley, Frank O. *The American High School and the Talented Student.* Ann Arbor: U of Michigan P, 1961.

Cornog, William H. "The Advanced Placement Program: Reflections on Its Origins." *College Board Review* 115 (1980): 14–17.

Cox, June. "Advanced Placement: An Exemplary Honors Model." *G/C/T* 26 (1983): 47–51.

Daly, William T., ed. *College-School Collaboration: Appraising the Major Approaches.* San Francisco: Jossey-Bass, 1985.

Davis, Gary A., and Sylvia B. Rimine. *Education of the Gifted and Talented.* Englewood Cliffs, NJ: Prentice, 1985.

Davis, James E., and Hazel K. Davis, eds. *Collaboration between College English Departments and Secondary Schools.* Urbana: NCTE, 1988.

Diamond, Robert M., and Robert Holloway. *Project Advance: An Alternative Approach to High School-College Articulation.* Syracuse, NY: Syracuse U, 1975. ERIC ED 105660.

Dillon, D. H. "The Advanced Placement Factor." *Journal of College Admissions* 113 (1982): 14–18.

Estrin, Herman A. "Articulation of High School and College English: A Program in Action." *English Journal* 55 (1966): 211–13.

Feldhusen, John. "University Services for Highly Gifted Youth." *College Board Review* 129 (1983): 18–22.

———, ed. *Toward Excellence in Gifted Education.* Denver: Love, 1985.

Fenton, Edwin. "Honors Programs in the Secondary Schools." *The Superior Student in American Higher Education.* Ed. Joseph W. Cohen. New York: McGraw, 1966. 219–52.

Ferrin, Richard I., and Warren W. Willinsham. *Practices of Southern Institutions in Recognizing College-Level Achievement.* New York: College Entrance Examination Board, 1970.

Fincher, C. "Standardized Tests, Group Differences, and Public Policy." *College Board Review* 103 (1977): 19–31.

Frederiksen, Mildred. "Honors Enrichment in the Eleventh Grade." *English Journal* 50 (1961): 620–23.

Friedrich, Gerhard. "Advanced Placement: Some Concerns and Principles." *College Board Review* 78 (1970): 20–21.

———. "A Selective Annotated Bibliography for Teachers of Advanced Placement and Honors English." *California English Journal* 5.1 (1969): 78–84.

Gaines, Bette, and Franklin P. Wilbur. "Early Instruction in the High School: Syracuse's Project Advance." *New Directions for Teaching and Learning* 24 (1985): 27–36.

Galambos, Eva C. "School-College Cooperation for Teaching Gifted Students." *Regional Spotlight* 14.3 (1982): 3–10.

Gerich, J. J., and K. W. Lund. "How Can Advanced Placement Programs Benefit Qualified Students? What are the Implications for the Secondary School Curriculum?" *NASSP Bulletin* 44 (1960): 215–16.

Gold, Suzanne. "Sixty Years of Programming for the Gifted in Cleveland." *Phi Delta Kappan* 65 (1984): 497–99.

Grommon, Alfred H. "The Advanced Placement Program's Implications for the Preparation of Teachers of English." *College English* 21 (1960): 373–78.

Hanson, Harlan P. "Reflections on Thirty Years of AP." *College Board Review* 135 (1985): 10+.

——. "Twenty-five Years of the Advanced Placement Program: Encouraging Able Students." *College Board Review* 115 (1980): 8–12.

Harrison, Charles H. "Options for Excellence: The San Antonio Experience." *College Board Review* 130 (1984): 30–35.

Hart, John A., and Ann L. Hayes. *Analysis, Evaluation, and Revision of Existing Materials for an Advanced Placement English Course.* Pittsburgh: Carnegie Institute of Technology, 1967.

Hart, John A., Ann L. Hayes, and Arthur Erbe. *New Model for an Advanced Placement English Course.* Pittsburgh: Berger, 1985.

Hochman, William R. "Advanced Placement: Can It Change with the Times?" *College Board Review* 77 (1970): 16–19.

Horne, Don L., and Paul J. Dupuy. "In Favor of Acceleration for Gifted Students." *Personnel and Guidance Journal* 60 (1981): 103–6.

Howard, Theresa D. "Cooperative Education from High School through College: A New Approach." *Journal of Cooperative Education* 23 (1986): 37–42.

Johnson, Sharon. "Bridging the Gap between High School and College." *Delta Kappa Gamma Bulletin* 52 (1986): 35–36.

Jones, J. Quentin. "Advanced Placement—Taking a Hard Look." *NASSP Bulletin* 59 (1975): 64–69.

Kaloger, James H. *Characteristics of Grosse Pointe High School Students in Advanced Placement Programs.* Diss. U of Michigan, 1970. Ann Arbor: UMI, 1971. 71–15193.

Keller, Charles R. "AP: Reflections of the First Director." *College Board Review* 116 (1980): 22–23.

Kelly, Gary F. "Entering College Early: It's Time to Make the Experiments Work." *Journal of College Admissions* 108 (1985): 29–31.

Lake, Sara. *Gifted Education: A Special Interest Resource Guide in Education.* Phoenix: Oryx, 1981.

Lee, Jack D. "Advanced Placement in the Total School Program." *California English Journal* 3 (1967): 30–35.

LeMay, M. "Academic Achievement of Students Who Received AP Credit." *College and University* 60 (1985): 155–59.

Lockerbie, D. Bruce. "Following Through on Advanced Placement." *College Board Review* 75 (1970): 25–26.

Losak, John, and Tien-teh Lin. "A Comparison of Academic Success: College Credit via General Examinations or Course Enrollment." *Journal of Educational Research* 67 (1973): 127–30.

Lundy, Ruthe. "AP in PA: Advanced Program in Palo Alto." *Gifted Child Quarterly* 23 (1979): 526–31.

Lynch, James J. "An Alternative for the College-Bound Senior: CEEB-AP or College Courses?" Paper presented at the Annual Conference of the Association for Supervision and Curriculum Development (March 1980). ERIC ED 187287.

——. "Practices Involving CEEB Advanced Placement and Transfer of College Credit Earned in High School." *Keystone Schoolmaster* 21.1 (1980). ERIC ED 181797.

Maeroff, Gene I. *School and College: Partnerships in Education.* Princeton: Princeton UP, 1983.

Marland, Sidney P., Jr. "Advanced Placement: An Above-Average Opportunity." *NASSP Bulletin* 59 (1975): 33–41.

McGrew, Jean B. "Early Identification of High Performers." Paper presented at the 68th Annual Meeting of the American Education Research Association. New Orleans, Apr. 1984. ERIC ED 244997.

Menacker, Julius. "Subject Articulation between High School and College." *Clearing House* 44 (1969): 220–23.

Mercurio, Joseph. "College Courses in the High School: A Follow-Up Study." *College and University* 56 (1980): 83–91.

Mercurio, Joseph, and Leo Lambert. "Making Decisions: College Credits Earned in High School." *Journal for College Admissions* 111 (1986): 28–32.

Mercurio, Joseph, Susan Schwartz, and Roger Oesterle. "College Courses in High School: A Four Year Follow-up of the Syracuse University Project Advance Class of 1977." *College and University* 58 (1982): 5–18.

Mercurio, Joseph, et al. "College Credit Earned in High School: Comparing Student Performance in Project Advance and Advanced Placement." *College and University* 59 (1983): 74–86.

Mickelson, Douglas J., and Frederick E. Sperry. "A Model for Improving the Preparation of High School Students." *Journal of College Admissions* 112 (1986): 3–9.

Middleton, Doris Marie. *A Study of Advanced Placement English in the Memphis City School System.* Diss. U of Mississippi, 1975. Ann Arbor: UMI, 1976. 76–00461.

Modu, Christopher C., and Eric Wimmers. "Validity of the Advanced Placement English Language and Composition Examination." *College English* 43 (1981): 609–20. [Discussion, 44 (September 1982), 532–45: Comment and response, James Vopat, Eric Wimmers, Henry A. Wicke, Jr., Robert Tucker.]

Morgan, Harry J., Carolyn G. Tennant, and Milton J. Gold. *Elementary and Secondary Level Programs for the Gifted and Talented.* New York: Teachers College P, Columbia U, 1980.

Mulhern, John D., and Robert C. Morris. "Some Guideposts for Educating the Gifted." *Education* 105 (1985): 274–78.

Nairn, Allan. *The Reign of ETS: The Corporation that Makes Up Minds.* The Ralph Nader Report on the Educational Testing Service. Washington, DC: Nairn, 1980.

NEA Reporter 19.1 (1980): A special issue on "The Testing Rip-off."

Neil, Daniel. "College: A Transitional Viewpoint." *Roeper Review* 7 (1985): 235–37.

New York State. Education Dept. *The Advanced Placement Program: English. A Course Description for Schools in New York State.* Albany: Bureau of Secondary Curriculum Development, 1967.

Nolan, James, and Rita Lyons. *Bibliographic Guide for Advanced Placement: English.* Albany: New York State Education Dept., 1965. ERIC ED 033129.

"Number of Students in AP Program Nearly Triples in Past Decade." *Phi Delta Kappan* 66 (1985): 588.

Olson, Gary A. "The Advanced Placement Language and Composition Course." *Journal of Teaching Writing* 3.1 (1984): 37–44.

Owen, David. *None of the Above: Behind the Myth of Scholastic Aptitude.* Boston: Houghton, 1985.

Paschal, Elizabeth. *Encouraging the Excellent.* New York: The Carnegie Fund for the Advancement of Education, 1960.

Pelton, Claire L. "Quality and Quantity in the Advanced Placement English Program." *English Journal* 54 (1965): 502–03.

Phelps, M. Overton, and Claire C. Swann. "Credit Prior to Enrollment—Computer Reporting of Exemptions and Advanced Placement Credit." *College and University* 50 (1975): 276–79.

Radcliffe, Shirley A., and Winslow R. Hatch. *Advanced Standing.* Washington: Office of Education, 1961.

Renzulli, Joseph S. "What Makes Giftedness: Re-Examining a Definition." *Phi Delta Kappan* 60 (1978): 180–84.

Rice, Joseph P. *The Gifted.* 2nd ed. Springfield, IL: Charles C. Thomas, 1985.

Richardson, Mary W. *Educational Usefulness of the AP English Course in New York State.* Diss. U of Sarasota, 1978. ERIC ED 163037.

Rogers, Robert W. "Articulating High School and College Teaching of English." *English Journal* 54 (1965): 370+.

Sauer, Edwin H. "Programs for the Academically Talented in English: What Are the Gains?" *English Journal* 49 (1960): 10–15.

Sawyer, Robert N. "The Early Identification and Education of Brilliant Students: The Duke Model." *College Board Review* 135 (1985): 12+.

Schwartz, Susan M., and Franklin P. Wilbur. "Predicting College Achievement Using Performance in College-Level Courses." Paper presented at the Annual Meeting of the Eastern Educational Research Association. Philadelphia, Mar. 1981. ERIC ED 207414.

Shaw, Jane S. "Speeded-Up, Souped-Up and Skip-a-Year Programs Get Kids into— and out of—College Sooner." *Nation's Schools and Colleges* 1.2 (1974): 35–42.

Silberman, Arlene. "The Tests That Cheat Our Children." *Reader's Digest* July 1977: 127–30.

Slotnick, Henry, et al. *Project Advance Evaluation Series A: 1973–74.* Syracuse, NY: Syracuse U, 1975. ERIC ED 105661.

Smart, John M., and Charles Evans. "State Policymakers and Time-Shortened Degree Programs." *Journal of Higher Education* 48 (1977): 202–15.

Smith, Eugene H. "English Composition in the Advanced Placement Program." *English Journal* 54 (1965): 495–501.

———. "Fragile Coalition: University and High School." *Clearing House* 55 (1981): 113–18.

Smith, Paul. "Language, Literature, and Advanced Placement." *Journal of Education* 162.2 (1980): 114–25.

———. "The Tests and the Discipline." *ADE Bulletin* 57 (1978): 26–29.

Solomon, Robert J. "Giving Credit Where It's Due." *Educational Record* 51 (1970): 301–04.

Stanley, Julian C. "Identifying and Nurturing the Intellectually Gifted." *Phi Delta Kappan* 57 (1976): 234–37.

Sternberg, Robert J. *Beyond I.Q.: A Triarchic Theory of Intelligence.* New York: Cambridge UP, 1985.

Stonebraker, David. "Turgenev and a Hint of Rain: Impressions of an AP Summer Institute." *College Board Review* 135 (1985): 18+.

Stratopoulos, Irene Chachas. *The Advanced Placement English Program in Salt Lake and Granite School Districts.* Diss. U of Utah, 1969. Ann Arbor: UMI, 1970. 70–01686.

Tincher, Wilbur A., and Richard E. Brogdon. "Attitudes toward Teaching of High Aptitude High School Seniors." *Education* 107 (1986): 35–40.

Traubitz, Nancy, and Cheryl Pfetsch. *Exploring the Third World: Two Interdisciplinary Units for Advanced Placement English.* Silver Spring, MD: N.p., 1985. ERIC ED 278008.

Tully, G. Emerson, and Philippe Olivier. "Credit-by-Examination as Seen by Secondary School Teachers and Coordinators of Accountability in Florida." *Florida Journal of Educational Research* 18 (1976): 1.

Tursman, Cindy. "Challenging Gifted Students." *School Administrator* 40.1 (1983): 9–12.

Tuttle, Frederick B., Jr., and Laurence A. Becker. *Characteristics and Identification of Gifted and Talented Students.* Washington: National Education Association, 1980.

———. *Program Design and Development for Gifted and Talented Students.* Washington: National Education Association, 1983.

Vaccaro, John. "College Admissions and the Transition to Postsecondary Education." Testimony to the National Commission on Excellence in Education. Public Hearing, Chicago, June 1982.

Vopat, James B. "Going APE: Reading the Advanced Placement Examination in English Composition and Literature." *College English* 43 (1981): 284–92.

White, Darrell K. "AP Advanced Placement Year in Utah." *College Board Review* 93 (1974): 7–9.

Wilbur, Franklin P., and David W. Chapman. *College Courses in the High School.* Reston, VA: National Association of Secondary School Principals, 1978.

————. "The Transferability of College Credit Earned during High School." *College and University* 52 (1977): 280–87.

Wilcox, Edward T. "Advanced Placement at Harvard." *College Board Review* 41 (1960): 17–20.

Winer, Robert D. "Students Intern in High School: New AP Opportunities." *College Board Review* 115 (1980): 12–13.

Wonnberger, Carl G. "A Report on a Report: Preparation in English for College-Bound Students." *English Journal* 50 (1961): 321–26.

"Workshop Reports of the Annual Conference on College Composition and Communication." *College Composition and Communication* 17 (1966): 175–200.

Zak, Paula M., Camilla P. Benbow, and Julian C. Stanley. "AP Exams: The Way to Go!" *Roeper Review* 6 (1983): 100–01.

Notes on the Contributors

Evelyn Ashton-Jones is Assistant Professor of English at the University of Idaho, where she teaches graduate and undergraduate courses in composition and rhetoric. She serves as Associate Editor of the *Journal of Advanced Composition*, has published articles in such journals as *Writing Program Administration* and *Writing Center Journal*, and is currently completing an advanced composition reader (forthcoming from Random House) as well as a study that examines the social dynamics of collaborative learning groups.

Gretchen Flesher coordinates the college-wide writing committee and teaches writing in the English Department at Gustavus Adolphus College in St. Peter, Minnesota.

David Foster is Professor of English at Drake University, where he has served as Director of Graduate Programs in English and as Director of Composition. Author of the influential *A Primer for Writing Teachers* (Boynton/Cook) and over 15 articles in major journals, Foster has served as a consultant to the Educational Testing Service for several years.

Bette Gaines is Project Advance Associate Director for Teacher Training and Supervision at Syracuse University. Formerly a high school English teacher, she has taught both Advanced Placement and Project Advance English classes. Her publications, workshops, and presentations focus on teaching and curriculum development in English education.

Rosanna Grassi is Assistant Dean for Academic Affairs in the School of Public Communications and formerly Assistant Director of Freshman English at Syracuse University. She coauthored *Composition and Literature: A Rhetoric for Critical Writing* (Prentice) and is a consultant for Project Advance.

Jan Guffin is Chair of the English Department and Coordinator of the International Baccalaureate Program at North Central High School in Indianapolis, Indiana. He received his Ph.D. in English education from Duke University and has chaired several College Board committees, including the AP English Test Development Committee (1980–82) and the AP English Advisory Committee (1982–84).

Sylvia A. Holladay is Professor of English and Assistant Chair at St. Petersburg Junior College, where she teaches and evaluates all levels of college writing and reading—developmental, freshman, honors, advanced, and technical. Since 1979, she has been a member of the Florida College-Level Academic Skills Project (CLASP), the faculty advisory group for the statewide sophomore-exit competency test, and since 1984 has chaired the CLASP Communications Task Force. Currently, she is a member of the CCCC Committee on Assessment and works with various colleges and secondary schools as a consultant in composition and assessment.

John Iorio is Professor of English at the University of South Florida. He has published extensively in literary journals and has been an Advanced Placement reader for many years. A collection of his short stories has recently been published by Juniper Press.

Diane Y. Kanzler has been teaching secondary English for 19 years. In 1983, she instituted the Advanced Placement English program at Southeast High School in Bradenton, Florida, where, in 1988, she was named Teacher of the Year. For the last three years, she has served as a reader for the essay section of the AP English examinations, and as a reader for the National Teachers Examination.

Elizabeth Metzger is Associate Professor and Director of Freshman English at the University of South Florida, where she teaches undergraduate and graduate courses in composition. For several years she has trained English teachers in the Hillsborough County secondary schools to teach writing as a process. She has presented papers at CCCC and NCTE conventions on the writing processes of high school and college students.

Gary A. Olson is Associate Professor of English at the University of South Florida, where he teaches graduate rhetoric and technical writing. He is author or co-author of six writing texts and numerous articles. Olson is Editor of the *Journal of Advanced Composition* and of the National Council of Teachers of English (NCTE) publication *Writing Centers: Theory and Administration*. For several years he served as a consultant for the College Board and conducted seminars throughout the South on the Advanced Placement English Program.

R. W. Reising is Professor of Communicative Arts and American Indian Studies at Pembroke State University. He has earned degrees from Michigan State, the University of Connecticut, and Duke University, where he completed a doctorate in English education. He has worked for over two decades with high school teachers in graduate courses and workshops treating Advanced Placement English. His publications include essays and book chapters on AP English.

Karen Spear is Professor of English and Associate Dean of the University of South Florida at St. Petersburg. She has published articles on writing and cognitive development in *College Composition and Communication, Writing Program Administration, Liberal Education*, and other journals and NCTE collections. She edited *New Directions for Teaching and Learning: Rejuvenating Introductory Courses* and wrote *Sharing Writing*, a book on the use of peer response groups in writing classes, published by Boynton/Cook.

Marilyn S. Sternglass is Professor of English at City College of the City University of New York, where she is Director of the M.A. Program in Language and Literacy. She has published extensively on language and reading/writing relationships and is author of *Reading, Writing and Reasoning* and *The Presence of Thought: Introspective Accounts of Reading and Writing*.

Benjamin J. Stewart teaches Advanced Placement English at Pine Forest Senior High School in Cumberland County, North Carolina, where he also serves as Instructional Specialist for Remediation in Language Arts/English. He earned a B.S. and M.Ed. in English education from Campbell University. During 1987–88 he served as President of the North Carolina English Teachers Association. With R. W. Reising, he authored the chapter on "Grading and Evaluation" in *Composition and Rhetoric: A Bibliographic Resource.*

Thomas Vander Ven is Professor of English at Indiana University—South Bend, Director of First Year English, and a playwright. He has been very active in the Advance College Project. In 1987 he wrote a play on the constitutional convention for the bicentennial.

James B. Vopat is Professor of English at Carroll College and Director of the Milwaukee Area Writing Project. In addition to articles on the teaching and evaluation of writing, he is co-author of *What Makes Writing Good.* His service as a reader for the Advanced Placement English Examinations in 1978, 1979, and 1980 led him to publish essays on AP in *College English, CLAC,* and *The Washington Monthly.* Vopat has made numerous conference presentations concerning Advanced Placement English, including speeches at NCTE, CCCC, and the Wyoming Conference on Freshman and Sophomore Composition.